## *THE LONSDALE LIBRARY*

HORSEMANSHIP  Maj-Gen Geoffrey Brooke

TROUT FISHING  Eric Taverner

FINE ANGLING FOR COARSE FISH  Eric Parker, etc

HOUNDS AND DOGS  A Croxton Smith, etc

BIG GAME SHOOTING IN AFRICA  Major H. C. Maydon, H.R.H. the Duke of Gloucester, etc

THE LONSDALE KEEPERS' BOOK  Eric Parker and well-known gamekeepers

WILDFOWLING  T. Bland, John Inge, etc

STEEPLECHASING  Lord Willoughby, de Broke, etc

SEATROUT FISHING  Jock Scott, etc

*THE LONSDALE LIBRARY*
*founded by*
THE RIGHT HON. THE 6TH EARL OF LONSDALE
KG, GCVO, DL

# SALMON FISHING

*Editor*
Major Peter Verney

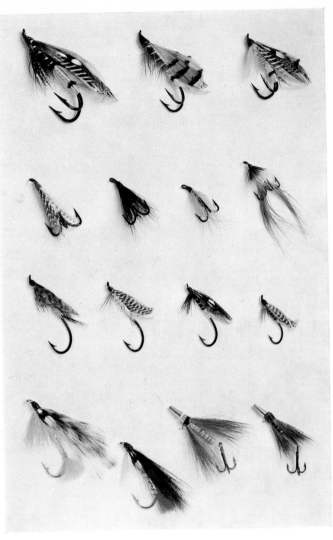

*Top Row:*
DOUBLE-HOOKED FULL DRESSED: Jock Scot; Durham Ranger; Green Highlander

*Second Row:*
ESMOND DRURY TREBLES: Silver Doctor; Stoatstail; Torrish; Shrimp Fly

*Third Row:*
LOW-WATER: March Brown; Silver Blue; Jeannie; Blue Charm

*Fourth Row:*
2 AYLOTT SALMON FLIES (Carters): TUBE FLIES: Torrish, Blue Charm

*THE LONSDALE LIBRARY*

# SALMON FISHING

ERIC TAVERNER
AND
JOCK SCOTT

with contributions by S. DRUMMOND SEDGWICK,
DR D. H. MILLS, A. H. E. WOOD, G. M. L. LA BRANCHE,
W. J. M. MENZIES and DR R. R. TAYLOR, Q.C.

LONDON
SEELEY, SERVICE & CO
1972

First published in Great Britain 1931
by Seeley, Service & Co
196 Shaftesbury Avenue, London, WC2H 8JL
First published in this revised edition, 1972

Printed in Great Britain by
Clarke, Doble & Brendon Ltd
Plymouth

# INTRODUCTION
## by
### THE 7TH EARL OF LONSDALE

I AM indeed honoured to have been asked by the publishers of the Lonsdale Library, to which my great-uncle originally lent his name, to write an introduction for the new volumes in a series which, in its time, was the classic work of reference for sportsmen throughout the world.

I think it is worthwhile quoting a paragraph from his foreword to the old series; words which are as true today as they were then.

"It is now a long time since a Library of volumes on Sport and Games was first put before the public. During these many years great changes have taken place, in men and in methods; how numerous and how great those changes have been, it needs no more than a glance at the text and illustrations of the older existing volumes to discover. The traditions, the customs, the guiding principles of the great sports and games doubtless remain; but as the years go on new discoveries are made, new developments follow, new methods are found to be successful. In the process of time these demand notice and explanation."

I am certain that the new volumes in the Lonsdale Library which incorporate so much of the developments and discoveries in relation to sport and recreation of the last few decades will achieve great popularity, especially as more and more people come to enjoy the increasing facilities which are being provided so extensively nowadays and which are accessible to the public at large in a way they never have been before.

T HE original edition of this work was written in 1931 and, although subsequently reprinted from time to time, it remained basically unaltered. In the intervening years, however, salmon fishing has developed enormously; tackle and equipment has changed along with the methods of using it and some rivers lovingly referred to by Eric Taverner no longer, alas, even hold salmon.

Nevertheless, despite these changes, much of Eric Taverner's writing remains as valid today as it ever was, and as far as possible I have left the author's text as in the original volume. I hope that the revision which was, however, frequently necessary will enhance the stature of this book to the fisherman today.

I have to express my thanks to the contributors to this edition. To Dr. Derek Mills for his chapter on the life history of the salmon. To Dr. R. R. Taylor for revising the legal section. To W. J. M. Menzies for his most interesting chapter on salmon scales and to the Inspector of Salmon Fisheries for Scotland, S. Drummond Sedgwick, for his appreciation of the author of this book, and his work.

My thanks are also due to the Publishers, and especially to the Director most concerned, Alastair Service, who has given me much help and encouragement in a very difficult task. I must also acknowledge the assistance accorded by Messrs Hardy of Alnwick in the production of this book and express my thanks to those who have allowed me to reproduce copyright photographs.

JOCK SCOTT

9

# CONTENTS

| | | |
|---|---|---|
| 1 | THE LIFE HISTORY OF THE SALMON | 19 |
| 2 | TACKLE AND EQUIPMENT I | 36 |
| 3 | TACKLE AND EQUIPMENT II | 52 |
| 4 | FISHING | 62 |
| 5 | SALMON HOOKS | 71 |
| 6 | CASTING A SALMON FLY | 73 |
| 7 | WATERMANSHIP | 91 |
| 8 | SUNK-FLY FISHING | 118 |
| 9 | FLOATING-LINE FISHING | 131 |
| 10 | DRY-FLY FISHING | 162 |
| 11 | OTHER METHODS OF FLY-FISHING FOR SALMON | 170 |
| 12 | SALMON-FLIES | 175 |
| 13 | SPINNING FOR SALMON | 186 |
| 14 | PRAWN, SHRIMP AND WORM | 204 |
| 15 | HOOKING, PLAYING AND LANDING | 222 |
| 16 | SALMON SCALES | 239 |
| 17 | LITERATURE | 258 |
| 18 | THE LAW AND SALMON FISHING | 264 |
| | *Appendix*: SALMON-FISHING WATERS OF THE WORLD | 271 |
| | *Index* | 273 |

# LIST OF PLATES

Standard Salmon Flies                                    *Frontispiece*

BETWEEN PAGES 24–25

1    Salmon leaping, River Feugh *(Thompson Picture Service)*
2    The difference between a spawned and a maiden fish
       *(J. A. Hutton)*
3    Male and Female Salmon *(J. A. Hutton)*
4    Fresh Salmon and Kelt *(Arthur Oglesby)*
5    Sea lice on a fresh fish *(Arthur Oglesby)*
6    The early stages of U.D.N. *(Arthur Oglesby)*
7    The later stages of U.D.N. *(Arthur Oglesby)*

BETWEEN PAGES 104–105

8    Difficult wading *(L. S. Paterson)*
9    A 34lb fish from the River Avon *(John Tarlton)*
10 & 11  Spey casting *(Dr Alastair Perry)*
12   The River Tweed in February *(R. Clapperton)*
13   The River Garry in August *(G. L. Carlisle)*

                                                    *Facing page*
14   The Yorkshire Esk at Glaisdale *(Arthur Oglesby)*     128
15   The River Dee at Dinnet *(Arthur Oglesby)*            128
16   The River Spey at Ballycarney *(Pix Photos)*          129
17   The River Slaney at Ballycarney *(Pix Photos)*        129
18   The River Namsen, Norway *(Arthur Oglesby)*           144
19   Loch Naver, North Sutherland *(L. S. Paterson)*       144
20   Worming on the River Lune near Tebay
       *(T. Parker)*                                       145
21   The River Spey near Grantown *(Arthur Oglesby)*       145
22   Coracles on the River Dee at Llangollen *(Topical
       Press Agency)*                                      176
23   The Clay Pool on the River Awe *(Arthur Oglesby)*     176
24   Tailing a Salmon on the River Dee
       *(Arthur Oglesby)*                                  177

*Facing page*

| | | |
|---|---|---|
| 25 | Nearing the gaff *(A. D. S. Macpherson)* | 177 |
| 26 | Gaffed! On the River Vosso, Norway *(Arthur Oglesby)* | 192 |
| 27 | Conversation Piece *(Arthur Oglesby)* | 193 |
| 28 | The Traditional Ghillie *(Central Press Photos Ltd)* | 193 |
| 29 | The Salmon Pass, Llangollen Weir *(C. V. Hancock)* | 224 |
| 30 | The Salmon Ladder, Loch Faskally *(L. S. Paterson)* | 224 |
| 31 | Catching Grilse in an upstream trap *(Central Press Photos Ltd)* | 225 |
| 32 | Otter Falls on the Alaskan Highway *(Canadian Government Travel Bureau)* | 240 |
| 33 | The River Hrutafiardara, Iceland | 240 |
| 34 | Smolt Scale | 241 |
| 35 | Grilse Scale | 241 |
| 36 | Hatchery Smolt Scale | 241 |
| 37 | Grilse Scale | 241 |

BETWEEN PAGES 248–249

| | |
|---|---|
| 38 | Very Large Spring Fish Scale |
| 39 | Small Summer Fish Scale |
| 40 | Previously Spawned Fish Scale |
| 41 | Previously Spawned Fish Scale |
| 42 | Previously Spawned Fish Scale |
| 43 | Small Spring Fish Scale |
| 44 | A Malformed Scale *(34–44 W. J. M. Menzies)* |

# TEXT ILLUSTRATIONS

| | | | |
|---|---|---|---|
| 1 | Young Trout and Salmon | *page* | 24 |
| 2 | Distinguishing Sea Trout from Salmon | | 25 |
| 3 | A Joint with Spring-loops | | 39 |
| 4 | Types of Rod Ring | | 40 |
| 5 | A Salmon Fly-Fishing Reel | | 45 |
| 6 | Types of Fly Line | | 47 |
| 7 | A Salmon Gaff | | 52 |
| 8 | A Tailer set for Use | | 53 |
| 9 | Two Kinds of Priest | | 54 |
| 10 | Rush-Packing a Salmon | | 56 |
| 11 & 12 | Two Fundamental Knots: The Thumb and Figure-of-Eight | | 62 |
| 13 | The Double Fisherman's Knot | | 62 |
| 14 & 15 | The Right-hand half and the completed Double Blood Knot | | 63 |
| 16 | A Dropper Attachment | | 64 |
| 17 | The Turle Knot | | 64 |
| 18–20 | The Single Cairnton | | 65 |
| 21 | The Double Cairnton | | 65 |
| 22 | The Two-Circle Turle Knot | | 65 |
| 23 & 24 | Chaytor's Reef Knot Jamb | | 66 |
| 25 | The Half Blood Knot | | 66 |
| 26 & 27 | Joining Wire to a Swivel Ring | | 67 |
| 28 | The Blood Bight Knot | | 67 |
| 29–31 | The Whip Finish | | 68 |
| 32 | The Whip Finish in the Middle of the Rod | | 68 |
| 33 & 34 | The Loop Finish | | 69 |
| 35–37 | The Needle or Nail Knot | | 69 |
| 38–41 | The Double-Handed Overhead Cast | | 75 |
| 42–45 | The Single-Handed Overhead Cast | | 81, 82 |
| 46–49 | The Switch Cast | | 84 |
| 50–54 | The Single Spey Cast | | 86, 87 |
| 55–62 | The Double Spey Cast | | 88, 89 |

| 63 | *Wading* | *page* 109 |
| 64–66 | *Recovering a Fly from a Tree* | 112, 113, 114 |
| 67–68 | *The Otter* | 115, 116 |
| 69–77 | *Greased Line Tactics* | 137–153 |
| 78 | *Effects of a surface floating line* | 158 |
| 79 | *Fishing small and large flies* | 159 |
| 80 | *Casting angle on varied water* | 160 |
| 81 | *Line Flotation* | 160 |
| 82 | *Dry Fly versus Wet Fly* | 168 |
| 83 | *Salmon Hook Sizes* | 181 |
| 84 | *The Silex Reel* | 188 |
| 85 | *The Ambassadeur 6000* | 189 |
| 86 | *The Abumatic 280* | 191 |
| 87 | *Types of lead* | 193 |
| 88 | *A Devon Minnow* | 194 |
| 89 | *A Wooden Minnow* | 195 |
| 90–92 | *Spoons* | 196 |
| 93 | *A Dead Bait Mount* | 198 |
| 94 & 95 | *Prawn Mounts* | 206 |
| 96 | *The Leaded Prawn* | 208 |
| 97 | *Prawn Tactics* | 210 |
| 98 | *The Mounted Shrimp* | 214 |
| 99–103 | *Worm-Tackles* | 217 |
| 104 | *The Worm Tackle weighted above the worm* | 219 |
| 105 | *Rod Power* | 226 |
| 106 | *Side Strain* | 231 |
| 107 | *Turning a Fish* | 232 |
| 108 | *The proper way to tail a fish* | 237 |

# FOREWORD

BY S. DRUMMOND SEDGWICK

*Inspector of Salmon Fisheries for Scotland*

T HIS brief foreword is by someone who knew Eric Taverner, now all too many years ago, when we were both living in Devonshire. I remember, as a comparatively young man, being invited to have luncheon with him in his bungalow which stood high on a wooded bank above the Taw. The windows of his study looked over a natural garden, at that time grown about with birch trees coming into leaf and beneath them primroses, wood anemones and a few early bluebells. The garden was full of birds.

Eric Tavener was firstly a naturalist and his delight was in observing all the aspects of the country which are met with by the water path. Fishing was a pleasure but not an end in itself. The approach of the naturalist is illustrated in his own prologue to the first edition of this book. He refers there to "man the angler, man the poacher and man the polluter of rivers". This latter aspect of human activity is all too evident about us today and it would have disgusted Taverner to see the apathy with which we accept the poisoning of our own terrestrial environment as well as our rivers and seas.

In those earlier days simple issues of the water such as essential purity and quantity were all that concerned those who sought to preserve our heritage of salmon. Otherwise it was only necessary to see to it that the adult fish had free access to their spawning grounds and that their progeny could in due course descend safely to the sea. Now much has changed and we are faced with complicated international issues which have arisen from the discovery of the ways of salmon in saltwater. Failure to reach useful international agreement means that they can be caught with impunity, in any quantity, on the high seas, without recognition of the rights and conservation policies of the country from whose parent rivers the fish are derived.

In face of all that has happened in recent years which might have had the effect of reducing our catches of salmon and grilse, it may seem strange to reflect that in Scotland the average catches in the years 1960 to 1970 have greatly exceeded average catches made in the years 1950 to 60. This does not mean that high-seas fishing for salmon in the North Atlantic has not affected our stocks of these fish, but it indicates that the policies for conservation and management of salmon fisheries, which have been adopted in the British Isles since before the First World War, are now paying off so handsomely that so far we have been able to absorb the drain on our stock made outside home waters. How long this can go on is a debatable point : we may indeed have the answer to this debate before another edition of this book can be published. My hope is that a further edition will in fact be called for by the continued presence of Atlantic salmon in our British rivers and that my successor in writing a foreword will be able to record the continued progress and improvement of our salmon fisheries and the general preservation of our resources.

## CHAPTER ONE

# THE LIFE HISTORY OF THE SALMON

## BY DEREK MILLS, M. SC., Ph. D.

*Introduction*

A SALMON depends on two environments for the successful fulfilment of its life history : (1) a freshwater environment in which the reproductive and nursery phase of its life cycle occur and (2) a marine environment for its main feeding phase, during which it grows very fast.

The salmon enters the rivers at all times of the year; if it has spent two, three or four years at sea before returning to freshwater, it is known as a *"salmon"*, but if the fish has only spent a little over a year at sea before returning it is termed a *"grilse"*. Quite often there is little difference in the size of these fish, but their age can be determined by examining their scales (see Chapter 16), in which are laid down rings in a seasonal pattern.

On approaching freshwater the salmon stops feeding and will not feed again until its return to salt water as a spent fish or *kelt*, which may be a year or more later. Once in freshwater the salmon will work its way upstream at varying speeds depending on the time of year, water temperature and strength of the current.

*Spawning* or egg laying starts in the late autumn. The eggs are deposited by the female in hollows cut in silt-free gravel and then the male adds his milk or sperm. The female finally covers the eggs with several inches of gravel and the mounds so formed are called *redds*. Some fish will lay their eggs in November, but those which have entered the river late in the season may not deposit theirs until even January or February. After spawning most of the males die but a relatively small proportion of the females return to spawn a second time.

*Return to the river*

Probably one of the most intriguing aspects of the salmon's life history is its homing instinct. Many theories have been put forward to explain the way in which salmon find their way back to their parent river. Some believe temperature determines the choice of tributary. Others consider that current, temperature or quality of water and the amount and direction of light are all important factors influencing migration. Probably the theory which has most acceptance is one derived from the work of Hasler and Wisby (1951 and 1954) which demonstrated the importance of stream odours in the orientation of fish.

The time of entry of the main runs of fish varies from river to river. Some rivers such as the Tweed, Tay, Findhorn, Spey and Inverness-shire Garry have early runs of spring fish while others, such as those on the west coast of Scotland, may have very few spring fish and the first large runs of fish only start to enter the rivers in June and July as grilse and summer fish. Again there are rivers such as the Tweed and Annan which have a large run of autumn fish which may continue well into December. And, as for instance, on the Rivers Taw and Torridge in Devonshire there is a run of winter fish known as "greenbacks".

A host of factors are said to be responsible for the entry of salmon into rivers and their subsequent upstream migration. Hayes (1953) found that fish move out of tidal waters into fresh water at dusk and came to the conclusion that light change might be the operating factor. He also had evidence that fairly strong onshore winds approaching 20 m.p.h. induce salmon to concentrate in the river estuary and eventually ascend. Hayes also showed that large natural freshets can initiate a major run of fish into the river provided that wind and tide are favourable. Water temperature too is of great importance to fish movement in the spring, and until it reaches 42° F. there is little upstream movement of fish over obstacles.

Upstream migration is also associated with thyroid activity as the salmon becomes sexually mature and Fontaine (1951) has suggested that the alternating periods of activity and torpor which characterize the behaviour of ascending salmon may be due to variations in the activity of the thyroid gland.

In 1962 a study of behaviour of salmon at natural obstacles

was made by Stuart. He found that the stimulus for a salmon to leap was closely related to the presence of a standing wave, or hydraulic jump, and the location of the standing wave distant to the obstacle influenced the success of the leap. Thus in shallow fall pools and pools below sloping weirs the standing wave becomes located too far downstream for the fish to strike the crest of the fall on the upward arc of its trajectory. If the fish strikes the falling water on the downward arc it is immediately swept downstream. This has been a valuable contribution toward the design of fish passes.

After entering freshwater the salmon changes in appearance, and in particular some of the bones in the skull and the main bones in the jaw increase in size. This is particularly noticeable in the male which develops a hooked lower jaw or *kype*. These bones require a large amount of material, particularly calcium, and, as the salmon does not feed during the time it is in freshwater, the material has to come from other parts of the body. Some of this calcium is taken from the scales and there is therefore considerable scale erosion and, in the male, the scales become deeply embedded in the spongy "skin".

As has been mentioned earlier, particular rivers may be characterized by the time of year when salmon enter them and by the proportions among them of grilse and salmon. These facts have been commonly interpreted as meaning that there are more or less distinct races in the various rivers, characterized by such behaviour and also by certain body proportions. This conception has been generally accepted and in the past a great deal of work was done in describing the characteristics of salmon of individual rivers from the results of a study of their scales. As White and Huntsman (1938) stated "Even for one river the salmon may come in from the sea at quite different seasons and these 'runs' may differ quite considerably in character, such as size and body proportions. The theory has been extended to fit these facts by the supposition that there are more or less distinct early-running and late-running races in the one river."

Recently the Salmon Research Trust of Ireland has undertaken the rearing of fish of known ancestry and their subsequent tagging, release and recapture. In these experiments fish derived from spring fish parents have returned as spring fish and those derived from grilse parents have returned as grilse. However, it was found that spring fish do not *invariably* breed spring fish nor do grilse *invariably* breed grilse, although the majority of smolts derived from grilse have returned as grilse. There was also a tendency for smolts of spring fish to return as grilse. A similar situation has been observed in hatchery-reared smolts in Scotland and Sweden where many fish, but by no means all, tend to return as grilse irrespective of their parentage.

Studies have now been started to investigate the existence of distinct salmon races by the analysis of the haemoglobins in the blood by means of microelectrophoresis. Wilkins (1967) was one of the early pioneers to observe differences in the pattern of the haemoglobin electropherograms of Scottish and Swedish salmon. However, these could not be attributed to a difference in geographical origin or genetic variation.

Koch, Bergström and Evans (1964), however, did find that with an increase in the size of the salmon a developmental pattern is observed in each group of haemoglobins and a final pattern is reached in the sexually mature fish. Wilkins (1968) then suggested that geographic races may yet be determined by the rate of development of this final pattern.

After spawning both male and female fish are known as kelts, and it is clear that the death rate after spawning is high, especially among male fish. The second spawning salmon are recruited from the more vigorous individuals which manage to recover their strength before being subjected to a hostile environment. The proportion of previously spawned fish in the rivers of various countries is very similar on average and is in the region of 3 to 6 per cent. However, there are some short course rivers, such as those in the west of Scotland and parts of eastern Canada where the proportion of previously spawned fish may be as high as 34 per cent. Balding (1934) considered that the cause of the high mortality in salmon after spawning is a severe reduction in body weight.

Some adult fish, generally females, may not spawn due to either some physical abnormality or the absence of one of the opposite sex. These fish are known as baggots or rawners and return to the sea with eggs or milt unshed.

There are a number of physical characteristics which are supposed to distinguish a previous spawner from a virgin fish. Probably the most reliable are (1) previous spawners invariably have gill maggots on their gills on entering freshwater (2) the scales of previous spawners bear a spawning mark and, less reliable, (3) previous spawners generally have many more spots, especially on the back and gill covers.

## The juvenile phase

The eggs deposited in the redds may be under six to twelve inches of gravel and the time required for their hatching ranges from 70 to 120 days depending on water temperature. On hatching—which usually occurs in late March or early April—the fish, which is about an inch long, is called an *alevin* and possesses a large yolk sac attached to its underside.

This yolk sac is absorbed after four or five weeks and the young fish emerge as *fry*, and during the first few weeks there is a high mortality due to starvation, predation and competition for space. The fish remain in the fry stage for about a year, at the end of which time they are known as *parr* and can be recognized by the dark blotches or "parr marks" along each side of the body.

The characteristics by which the salmon parr can be distinguished from the trout are the relative length of the maxilla or upper jaw bone and the number of scales in an oblique series from the posterior edge of the adipose fin, downwards and forwards to the lateral line. In the salmon the distal point of the maxilla extends only fractionally behind the mid-point of the eye.

Young salmon are strongly territorial and tend to remain in their positions in the stream for long periods. In streams with large stones there are more but smaller territories available for young salmon owing to them being out of sight of each other, while in streams with only a few stones on a substratum of gravel territories are necessarily large due to the antagonistic behaviour of neighbouring fish.

In a study of the food, growth and population structure of young salmon and trout in two Scottish Highland streams, Egglishaw (1967) found that the variation in the kind and amount of food found in the stomachs of salmon and trout is very large. A great deal of this variation, and the apparent selection of food by some fish, can probably be attributed to the distribution or behaviour of certain bottom-living organisms and the type of

FIG 1
*Top* : YOUNG TROUT
*Middle* : SALMON PARR
*Bottom* : SALMON SMOLT

This shows clearly the difference between the tails of parr and
of young trout; and also how the mouth of the latter extends
further back in relation to the eye. Finger-markings are no sure
test, as they are frequently present in young trout as well.

habitat in which they are feeding. Salmon parr from pools in the
River Almond, in Perthshire, for instance, contained significantly
more emerging chironomidae and terrestrial organisms than
salmon from the riffles. Both Egglishaw (1967) and Mills (1964)
found that trout tend to eat more terrestrial organisms than

1   A 20lb. Salmon leaping upstream above the Bridge of Feugh

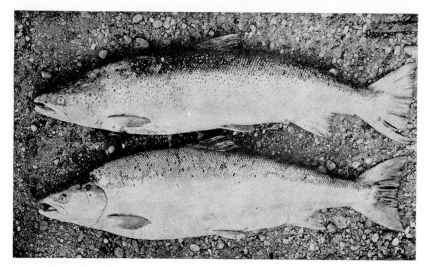

2 The difference in body-marking between a salmon that has spawned and is on its way up-river for the second time and (*below*) a maiden fish. In the former there are many spots on the gill-covers and in the region *below* the median line

3 The distinctive difference between the male (*below*) and female salmon

4    The difference between a fresh salmon and a kelt (*above*)

5    Sea lice on a fresh fish

6   The early stages of U.D.N.

7   The later stages of U.D.N.

salmon parr. A varying proportion of male parr attain sexual maturity before leaving the river and Jones (1959) concluded that the presence of ripe male parr on the spawning grounds was to insure fertilization of the eggs in case of lack of fertilization by the adult male.

The length of time the parr spend in the river before going to sea as smolts varies with geographical location. In the Hampshire Avon for instance 90 per cent of the parr became smolts at the start of their second year of life, while in northern Scandinavia parr stay in the rivers for seven or eight years before becoming smolts. Elson (1957) showed that, as a general rule, parr which have reached 10 cm. by the end of one growing season are likely to become *smolts* at the next season of smolt descent. In the spring during transformation of the parr to the smolt stage the fish turn silver due to a subcutaneous deposit of guanin being laid down thus concealing the parr markings. The pectoral and caudal fins also turn black.

In addition to the associated changes in appearance, smolt development consists of a growing susceptibility to migration-producing stimuli. A number of attempts have been made to correlate the onset of smolt migration with various environmental

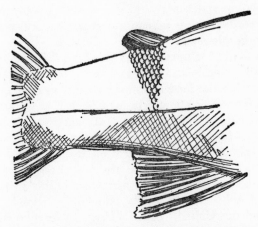

FIG 2   TO DISTINGUISH SALMON FROM SEATROUT
In a salmon the number of scales from the forward edge of the adipose fin to the lateral will usually be found to be eleven. In a seatrout there are normally fourteen.

factors such as rainfall, radiation and water temperature. Thus
it has been found that during the early part of the smolt migration
in April and early May smolts move mainly during the hours
of darkness but later on in late May and early June they move
during the middle part of the day.

*Life in the sea*

Once the smolts have entered the sea little is generally known
of their movements. Smolts from northern Swedish rivers have
been caught in the Gulf of Bothnia and have been recorded taking
insects blown off the land; other tagged smolts released in these
northern Swedish rivers have later been recaptured as adults in
the southern Baltic. So here the picture of the salmon's migrations
is fairly complete. But for smolts entering the North Sea and
Atlantic from the rivers of the British Isles, Canada and Norway
the picture is rather different. However, with the advent of the
Greenland fishery much more is now known about the sea life
of the salmon than was previously. Nevertheless, the general
picture of the salmon's sea life can only be gradually pieced
together from isolated records. Many of these records have been
collected as a result of the examination of the stomachs of other
fish. This is a particularly useful area of information as it indicates
the sources of mortality at sea. It is interesting to note that among
the fish recorded eating salmon are skate, halibut, pollack, cod
and the porbeagle shark.

The sea food of salmon consists chiefly of fish such as herring,
capelin and sandeels and certain large zooplankton organisms.
During research the food of salmon caught in drift nets off the
east Scottish coast was found to include marine worms, herring,
sprats, sandeels and whiting, whereas salmon caught in the Greenland area had been feeding mainly on capelin.

Since a salmon fishery developed off the west coast of Greenland in 1957 knowledge of the sea migrations of salmon has
increased enormously due to the recapture in this area of tagged
smolts and kelts from Canada, England, Ireland, Scotland,
Sweden and the United States (Maine). In recent years salmon
have also been caught off the Faeroes, the Lofoten Islands and
the north Norwegian coast.

There is a deal of information on the coastal movements of
adult salmon which have been caught and tagged offshore. The

value of these tagging operations has been to provide data on the coastal movements of adult salmon, the general direction of these movements and the rate of migration.

## Predation

Some mention has already been made of predation in the sea. The most important known marine predator of salmon is the grey seal, which does considerable damage to fish, to nets and to fishing effort. It has been estimated that the average annual monetary loss to the salmon industry on the Scottish east coast is about £67,000 and as a result grey seals are shot near the salmon nets along the Scottish coast and an annual cull of pups is made on some of the seal's breeding grounds. Since the coastal nets have been made of stronger synthetic fibres, however, the damage has lessened considerably as the seals cannot reach the trapped salmon as easily and they cannot hole the nets.

In freshwater, both pike and trout can also be serious predators of young salmon and Mills (1964) estimated that no less than 10 per cent of the smolt run on the River Bran, Ross-shire, was eaten by pike. And a large number of birds and mammals have been recorded eating salmon, including the otter and mink, the cormorant, black-headed gull, goosander and red-breasted merganser.

Since 1962 the Canadian Wildlife Service and the Fisheries Research Board of Canada have been carrying out a joint study on the Margaree River, in Nova Scotia, to test the efficacy of merganser control for improving local fisheries, but little improvement has so far been noticed in angling catches.

## Parasites

The most well-known parasite of salmon is the sea louse *Lepeophtheirus salmonis*. It only lives for a short time in freshwater and its presence on salmon in a river is therefore a good indication that the salmon is only recently in from the sea. The female sea lice, which often have long egg sacs or "streamers" are the most conspicuous. At times salmon may be so heavily infested with sea lice that their body colours are obscured and the death of a number of salmon has been attributed to the areas of abrasion caused by the lice.

The most well-known freshwater parasite of salmon is the gill maggot *Salmincola salmonea*. The free-swimming larvae of this parasitic copepod attach themselves to the gills of a salmon while it is in the estuary. On becoming attached to the gills the larvae moult twice and become either a mature male or a first-stage female, both of them can move about on the gills. After mating the male dies, but the female develops an attachment organ and can no longer move about. About six months after mating eggs are produced. The female moults and the eggs are extruded; two further sets of eggs may be extruded by the female before the salmon returns to the sea. If the kelt returns to the sea before these later generations of eggs have been extruded reproduction is inhibited in the sea and will not be resumed until the fish returns to freshwater. Then the parasite lays its eggs and drops off the gills.

The fish leech *Piscicola geometra* is parasitic on salmon as well as other fish, and leeches have been found on salmon taken from the Tweed at Kelso. Most of these fish were kelts and about 50 per cent were infected. Although leeches were found on all parts of the fish they occurred mainly around the dorsal and pectoral fins, the flanks and the wrist of the tail.

One of the largest of the internal parasites of the salmon is the tapeworm *Eubothrium crassum* which, in its adult stage, may measure between 12 and 60 cm. in length and occurs in the pyloric caecae around the stomach.

## Disease

The salmon is subject to a number of diseases, some of which can be responsible for very high mortalities. The more serious diseases include furunculosis, Dee disease, kidney disease, vibriosis and ulcerative dermal necrosis (U.D.N.).

*Furunculosis* is caused by the bacterium *Aeromonas salmonicida*. Salmon suffering from this disease show a number of external symptoms ranging from congestion of the fins, haemorrhage at the vent and furuncles. At times the only external symptoms may be congestion of the fins and at other times there may be no external symptoms at all. At other times, when fish are dying from the disease, they may swim at the surface in a disorientated manner, going round and round in circles. This disease has been recognized for over 55 years as a cause of death, especially when the rivers are low and the water temperature rises to 55° F. A high incidence of furunculosis has also been reported in kelts which, it has been found, are less likely to develop external symptoms than unspent fish. Smith (1962) noticed that male kelts seem to be more susceptible to furunculosis than unspent males. As some of the kelts which die are suffering from furunculosis and as the bacteria are viable for long periods the dead kelts could well be a source of infection for clean fish entering the river during the winter.

*Dee disease* is so-called because it was first described in salmon from the Aberdeenshire Dee in 1930. Fish suffering from this disease may show congestion of the fins, haemorrhage at the vent and sometimes haemorrhagic spots on the muscle. These symptoms are, however, found in other fish diseases so they are of little value in the diagnosis of Dee disease. Internally the salmon shows very characteristic lesions, the most prevalent one being petechial haemorrhage of the muscle lining the peritoneum. The next organ most often affected is the kidney which, instead of its normal uniform reddish-brown colour, develops greyish-brown areas and, if the disease is more advanced, these areas develop an almost cyst-like appearance. The spleen is also affected and develops creamish-white lesions.

The causative organism of *Vibriosis* is the common marine bacterium *Vibrio anguillarum*. The symptoms of the disease are haemorrhagic spots on the body, particularly the belly, and internal organs show signs of degeneration. Because it is a marine bacterium salmon in salt and brackish waters are often affected, but it also occurs on salmon in most rivers. Frequently infected fish showing signs of vibriosis are believed to be suffering from furunculosis and for this reason a bacteriological examination is necessary before the disease can be correctly diagnosed.

*Ulcerative dermal necrosis* (U.D.N.) was first observed in epidemic proportions in a number of rivers in S.W. Ireland during 1964–65. During 1966 the disease spread to the Lancashire, Cumberland and Solway river systems and by the end of 1967 it had spread to all east coast rivers from the Tweed to the Nairn (with the exception of the Forth and Tay) and, on the west coast, from the Solway Firth to the River Ayr. In 1968 cases too appeared in the Forth, Tay, Ness and Conon river systems.

The first signs of the disease are the appearance of small bleached areas of the skin on the head and back. As the disease progresses areas of a bluish-grey, slimy growth develop over these bleached areas, making the fish very conspicuous in the water. These slimy masses can be pulled away, revealing inflammation or shallow ulceration of the underlying skin. The head may be so badly affected that it seems largely covered by raw, reddish areas which then become infected with the fungus. The fungus spreads and, in the most advanced stages of the disease, the head and tail regions of the fish may be largely covered with fungus. Certain actions such as aquaplaning and jumping with an agitated flapping movement have been described as characteristic of infected fish.

Roberts (1969) considers that the microscopical appearance of the early lesions suggests that a virus is responsible but that it is only the harbinger of the initial skin damage which allows both loss of body proteins and attack of unprotected tissue by fungi. Roberts, Shearer and Elson (1969) then found no definite evidence to suggest a primary virus aetiology, but concluded that the lesions ressembled those produced in the virus symptom of cattle known as mucosal disease, where secondary infection is again a common occurrence.

In 1968 Elson assessed the future position of U.D.N. very optimistically when he said: "During the last decades of the nineteenth century a disease characterized by clinical symptoms similar to those of U.D.N. occurred in many Scottish rivers. This took some time to die out, e.g. the River Tweed was seriously affected over the fifteen-year period from 1879 to 1893, and though there are now methods for treating bacterial fish disease which were not available seventy or eighty years ago, these are economically impracticable in an open river system and recovery must still, presumably, depend upon a balance taking place between the host and the pathogen by the process of natural selection. In this context, a certain number of kelts have been observed to show repair tissue, and experiments carried out in Ireland have indicated that the progeny of diseased salmon were apparently healthy and showed no evidence of U.D.N."

### The influence of man

Man influences the stocks of salmon directly by his predation on them by commercial and sport fishing and indirectly by the harmful effects of his industrial and agricultural activities. There is little doubt that salmon rivers have been put in greatest jeopardy by pollution and hydro-electric developments.

Although rivers such as the Clyde, the Tees and the Thames are and will probably remain too polluted to hold salmon; *pollution* is becoming less serious. The Tweed is now cleaner than it was at the end of last century and the Rivers (Prevention of Pollution) Acts of 1951, 1961 and 1965 have been a great help in curbing and reducing pollution—the legislation being enforced by the River Purification Boards in Scotland and the River Authorities in England and Wales. There are, though, some industries which still need "to put their house in order", particularly pulp and tanning. Other industries, such as distilling, have already done much to treat their waste, and distilleries on the Spey now produce a very harmless effluent having converted their by-products into animal feeding stuffs.

One of the most harmful forms of pollution still existing is that from insecticides, fungicides and herbicides. The organo-chlorines, such as DDT and dieldrin, can cause fish mortalities through either accumulating in the fish through the food chain until a lethal level is reached, or through the direct effects of spraying. It was found that spraying of DDT on the forests in the Miramichi watershed in northern New Brunswick had a tremendous impact on the stream populations of young salmon. It has also recently been discovered that small concentrations of DDT can affect the learning ability of young salmon with the probability of frightening repercussions.

Salmon rivers are in many cases a natural source of hydro-electric development. Often the rivers originate in mountainous country with a high rainfall and in their upper reaches are torrential and fast-flowing. The associated installations are dams and power stations, with the water being diverted from the reservoirs through tunnels and aqueducts to power stations hundreds of feet below to produce a powerful head of water to operate the turbines which produce the electricity. So salmon in rivers harnessed for power may be faced with a number of hazards. (1) The dams act as barriers to ascending adults and descending smolts and kelts while (2) the power stations are a potential hazard to the adults which, attracted by their high flow, attempt to swim up the draught tubes—with fatal results—and to the smolts passing downstream through the turbines. (3) Reservoirs may flood spawning and nursery areas. Some of the problems which arose on the Conon River system in Ross-shire after hydro-electric development have been described by Pyefinch and Mills (1963).

Most countries have now, at great cost, successfully overcome these problems in various ways. Scotland, Ireland, Canada and Norway have built fish passes and fish ladders to enable salmon to pass upstream and downstream through the dams, and screened the entrances to the turbines. In cases where spawning areas have been flooded salmon stocks have been supplemented with hatchery-reared young. Salmon stocks in many of the Scottish "hydro" rivers now appear to have successfully "adapted" to the new régime. Although some anglers still complain of the rapidly fluctuating river flows associated with these rivers, others success-fully take advantage of the new conditions. In Sweden many of her northern salmon rivers, where the salmon do not come readily to anglers' lures, have been handed over to the engineer for the production of power; but the stocks of salmon in the Baltic, where most of the commercial fishing is done, have been maintained by the annual production of hundreds of thousands of smolts at large modern hatcheries.

For centuries salmon have been exploited commercially and legislation has existed to attempt to limit over-exploitation. Weekly close-times have given stocks a respite while annual close-seasons have protected salmon during the spawning period. Legis-lation was considered generally satisfactory by both commercial and rod fishermen, with only an occasional moan being emitted by the anglers if they felt estuary sweep nets were taking too many fish during low river flows. However, in recent years two developments have changed the *status quo*. One was the advent of drift netting for salmon off the east Scottish coast in 1960 by inshore sea-fishermen. This resulted in considerable concern for the salmon stocks and as there was some evidence to suggest that drift netting introduced a serious risk of overfishing—in September 1962 it was prohibited by Ministerial Order. The advent of drift netting, however, did highlight the need for a review of the existing laws relating to salmon and trout fisheries in Scotland and an enquiry into the extent to which salmon and trout fishing should be regulated. This requirement was realized by the government and in 1962 the Secretary of State for Scotland appointed the Hunter Committee to undertake such a review. Their findings have been published in two White Papers.

The second and more far-reaching development has been the establishment and rapid expansion of the Greenland salmon fishery. This started as an inshore fishery in 1956 and 1957 with an annual catch of some 2 metric tons, but soon spread to offshore waters and then extended to other areas of the high seas around the Faeroes, the Lofoten Islands and the north Norwegian coast. In 1969 the total inshore and offshore catches off West Greenland had risen to approximately 2,110 metric tons. These high seas fisheries have resulted in a "free for all" without any apparent thought to regulations governing type of gear, size of net mesh or quota to insure an adequate escapement of stock for breeding. However, there is not yet sufficient evidence to indicate any effects they may be having on Scottish or Canadian stocks. Meanwhile discussions at an international level continue, with those countries with salmon rivers urging Denmark, the country mainly engaged in the high seas fishery, to exercise some control. Fortunately fish stocks are very resilient and the possibility of the salmon becoming extinct is most unlikely.

## BIBLIOGRAPHY

*Salmon Hatching and Salmon Migrations.* W. L. Calderwood. 1931.

*The Cause of the High Mortality in the Atlantic Salmon after Spawning* (Trans. Amer. Fish. Soc.). D. L. Balding. 1934.

*Is Local Behaviour in Salmon Heritable?* (J. Fish. Res. Bd. Can. 4). H. C. White and A. G. Huntsman. 1938.

*Discrimination of Stream Odours by Fishes and its Relation to Parent Stream Behaviour* (Amer. Nat.). A. D. Hasler and Wisby. 1951.

*Remarquées sur certain comportements du saumon* (Bull. Français de Pisciculture). M. Fontaine. 1951.

*Artificial Freshets and other Factors Controlling the Ascent and Population of Atlantic Salmon in the La Have River, Nova Scotia* (Bull. Fish. Res. Bd. Can. 99). F. R. Hayes. 1953.

*Odor Perception and Orientation in Fishes* (J. Fish. Res. Bd. Can. 11). A. D. Hasler. 1954.

c

*Irish Salmon and Salmon Fisheries.* A. E. J. Went. 1955.

*A Review of the Literature on the Biology of the Atlantic Salmon (Salmo Salar* Linn.) (Freshwat. Salm. Fish. Res. *9*). K. A. Pyefinch. 1955.

*The Importance of Size in the Change from Parr to Smolt in Atlantic Salmon* (Can. Fish. Cult. *21*). P. F. Elson. 1957.

*The Salmon.* J. W. Jones. 1959.

*The Fecundity of the Atlantic Salmon (Salmo Salar* Linn.) (Freshwat. Salm. Fish. Res. *26*). J. A. Pope, D. H. Mills, and W. M. Shearer. 1961.

*The Goosander and Red-breasted Merganser as Predators of Salmon in Scottish Waters* (Freshwat. Salm. Fish. Res. *29*). D. H. Mills. 1962.

*Furunculosis in Kelts* (Freshwat. Salm. Fish. Res. *27*). I. W. Smith. 1962.

*The Leaping Behaviour of Salmon and Trout at Falls and Obstructions* (Freshwat. Salm. Fish. Res. *28*). T. A. Stuart. 1962.

*Predator-prey Relationship Between Fish-eating Birds and Atlantic Salmon* (Bull. Fish. Res. Bd. Can. *133*). P. F. Elson. 1962.

*Bibliographie du Saumon de L'Atlantique* (Contrib. du Ministre de la Chasse et des Pêcheries, Quebec *88*). J. Bergeron. 1962.

*Territorial Behaviour of Juvenile Atlantic Salmon (Salmo Salar* Linn.) (Behaviour. *19* (1)). M. H. A. Keenleyside and F. T. Yamamoto. 1962.

*Scottish Salmon and Trout Fisheries* (H.M.S.O. Cmnd. *2096*). *Anon.* 1963.

*Observations on the Movements of Atlantic Salmon in the River Conon and the River Meig, Ross-shire* (Freshwat. Salm. Fish. Res. *31*). K. A. Pyefinch and D. H. Mills. 1963.

*The Microelectrophoretic Separation on Starch Gel of the Haemoglobins of Salmo Salar* Linn. (Mededel. Vlaamse. Acad. Kl. Wet. *26* (9)). H. J. A. Koch, E. Bergström and J. C. Evans. 1964.

*The Ecology of the Young Stages of the Atlantic Salmon in the River Bran, Rosss-shire* (Freshwat. Salm. Fish. Res. *32*). D. H. Mills. 1964.

*The Pursuit of Salmon in Ireland* (Proc. Roy. Irish Acad. *63* (c)). A. E. J. Went. 1964.

*Irish Salmon—a Review of Investigations up to 1963* (Sci. Proc. R. Dublin Soc. Ser. A. *1* (15)). A. E. J. Went. 1964.

*Seal Damage to Salmon Fisheries* (Mar. Res. Scot. *2*). B. B. Rae and W. M. Shearer. 1965.

*Scottish Salmon and Trout Fisheries* (H.M.S.O. Cmnd. *269*). Anon. 1965.

*Immunology, Sciology and Blood Group Research in Fishes* (Polymorphismes biochemique des animaux 355–359 of Inst. Natl. Rech. Agronom, Paris). N. P. Wilkins. 1967.

*The Food, Growth and Population Structure of Salmon and Trout in Two Streams in the Scottish Highlands* (Freshwat. Salm. Fish. Res. *28*). H. J. Egglishaw. 1967.

*The Past and Future in Salmon Fisheries* (Assn. of River Authorities Year Book *199*). W. J. M. Menzies. 1967.

*Salmon Disease in Scotland* (Salmon Net. *iv*). K. R. Elson. 1968.

*The Atlantic Salmon, a Vanishing Species*. A. Netboy. 1968.

*Multiple Haemoglobins of the Atlantic Salmon* (J. Fish. Res. Bd. Can. *25* (12)). N. P. Wilkins. 1968.

*The Greenland and Davis Strait Fisheries* (Salm. Trout Mag. *184*). T. B. Fraser. 1968.

*The Survival of Hatchery-reared Salmon Fry in some Scottish Streams* (Freshwat. Salm. Fish. Res. *39*). D. H. Mills. 1969.

*The Pathology of Ulcerative Dermal Necrosis of Scottish Salmon* (J. Path. *97* (3)). R. J. Roberts, W. M. Shearer and K. R. Elson. 1969.

*The Pathology of Salmon Disease* (Salmon Net. v). R. J. Roberts. 1969.

*A Review of the Literature on the Upstream Migration of Adult Salmonids* (J. Fish. Biol. *1*). J. W. Banks. 1969.

*Salmon Conservation in Sweden* (Swedish Salmon Research Institute—Report L.F.I. Medd 2/1969). B. Carlin. 1969.

*Talking Points in Salmonid Research* (Salm. Trout Mag. *185*). D. J. Piggins. 1969.

*Salmon and Trout. A Resource, its Ecology, Conservation and Management*. D. H. Mills. 1971.

## CHAPTER TWO

# TACKLE AND EQUIPMENT I

## Salmon Fly-Rods

THE functions of a rod are threefold: to *cast*, to *play the fish* and to *save the cast* or "leader" as it is called in North America. The forward propulsion of the line through the air requires less effort than lifting it out of the water and, as the neatness with which the line is lifted clear is the making of a good cast, it would be accurate to say that recovery is the first duty of the rod. A flexible rod-point which springs back quickly and without undue vibration will act as a perfect intermediary, a sort of spring-buffer, between the tension on the reel and the pull of the fish. It gives immediately to an increase of strain upon the line, until the resistance of the check of the reel is gradually overcome. Whenever a fish moves a little nearer to the angler, the rod-point returns towards the straight position, so that in theory the tension on the line is never relaxed and the hook cannot disengage. This is the reason why the rod should always be kept up (see p. 226) during the playing of a fish. A rod-point, lowered towards the fish, enables an angler to put far more strain on a fish and is to be employed in the later stages of the fight; but it will then cease to act as a compensator to sudden strains on the cast.

The cardinal virtues in a rod are that kind of lightness which comes from *balance*; a *delicacy* which limits the strain transmitted by a powerful rod to the line and cast, so that the finer grades of cast may not be broken by the sudden snatch at the fly or by the unpredictable strains set up in fighting a strong fish; and also *hooking-power*.

Balance is so vital a quality, that it can be a redeeming feature in an otherwise ill-found rod. The weight of a rod is certainly important, but far less than its distribution or, in other words, its balance. The action of a rod is likewise determined by the distribution of its power and its resilience. Hooking-power is the capacity of the rod-tip to follow faithfully the upward movement of the hand in tightening on a fish with the minimal amount of downward flexion. This characteristic is of less importance in salmon fishing than in fly-fishing for trout and in float-fishing for certain coarse fishes.

## Rod Actions

The speed of a rod depends on two things: how far it bends, and how strong it is. The less a rod bends the quicker is its tip; while, conversely, the further a rod bends the slower is its tip.

Rod actions today are either fast or slow. A fast or stiff rod, when under strain, does not bend so much as a slow or supple one; the action is largely in the top and upper part of the middle joint, the butt being relatively stiff. The tip, therefore, flexes and reflexes with great speed, having only a short distance to travel. The slow rod, on the other hand, bends right down to the handle. Its tip travels a long way at each cast but, although slow, it is very powerful, as it predominantly uses the centre and butt pieces.

The fast rod is ideal for the overhead cast. To execute a long throw overhead high velocity is needed, and it is, of course, more tiring to cast overhead than to switch cast, more force being required. The hardest work involved is lifting the line from the water with a strong pull. In switching, the line is made to lift itself off the water by a downward movement of the rod, which is much easier on the muscles.

The choice of a rod, therefore, depends entirely on the type of fishing to be undertaken, and, therefore, the kind of line to be used. The angler has either to use one style only, or to equip himself with two outfits. Although many so-called "universal" rods are on the market, such a rod with the characteristics of both the slow and the fast rod has yet to be made. As the mechanical requirements of casting are immutable, a dual-purpose rod is at best a compromise, which can never satisfy the perfectionist. I have for years fished big rivers where long casting is essential to cover the fish but the man who fishes smaller rivers can cast sufficient line with any rod he fancies and thus has a far wider choice.

If his river is one on which the pools can be fished by overhead casting he will probably need one of the modern Forward Taper lines which require the use of a fast rod. On the other hand if he is, as I am, a switch caster—and for many years I fished where switching was essential—he will need a slow rod and a Single Taper line. The fast rod will switch, after a fashion, but it will not put out as much line as a slow rod.

The rod action must also be suited to the line in use. Thus we get the following combinations:

*Fast rod*—a Double Taper, Forward Taper, or Level line.

*Slow rod*—a Single Taper line, *i.e.* one increasing steadily in diameter from the tip backwards.

### Salmon-rod Materials

There are commonly four materials from which a salmon-rod is made today. These are: split bamboo-cane, steel, glass-fibre and—still obtainable although becoming increasingly scarce—greenheart. Of these glass-fibre is by far the lightest.

Split-cane rods are made of six triangular strips of bamboo glued together, and can be joined either by metal ferrules or by splices, the latter being preferable if Spey casting is to be employed. It should, however, be emphasized that, if the river demands a great deal of Spey casting, a spliced greenheart will stand up to the work best of all.

Steel rods are made in tubular form, and have the merit of strength and a resistance to accidental blows. But judging by the rods one sees today in action they do not appear to be so popular as rods made of the other three materials.

Glass-fibre rods are gaining in popularity year by year. They too are constructed in the form of tapering tubes joined by ordinary metal or plastic ferrules. These rods are very powerful, exceedingly tough, and will survive accidental blows. They cast just as well as other types and are now made in a variety of actions. They are on the whole cheaper than other types and to my mind the glass-fibre rod will soon predominate. One can also obtain them with spliced joints which transmit a much more pleasant "feel" and action, although a number of people still aver that the "character" of split-cane or more particularly the old greenheart is unrivalled and cannot be emulated.

## Rod Construction

Salmon-rods consist of three pieces, butt, middle and top. They are made up into a whole by means of ferrules, male and female. Heavy and long split-cane rods are united by spiral lockfast joints or stud locking joints; often the shorter are fitted with suction joints, each side of which needs to be made with high precision, in order to achieve a secure fit and prevent an upper piece from being thrown during the action of casting. This method is perfectly satisfactory, and a rod should give years of service provided that the male ferrule is withdrawn with a straight pull—twisting it causes considerable wear.

FIG 3   A JOINT WITH SPRING-LOOPS

In greenheart rods I am more in favour of spliced joints, because the vibrations of the rod proceed from the tip right into the butt, without being partly checked by the harshness of metal ferrules. Further, the main argument which used to count against greenheart rods—that they snap without warning—can no longer be maintained. Provided that the rod is properly cared for.

It is usual to fit split-cane rods with metal ferrules, but these are unsatisfactory if a lot of switch-casting is to be employed, for the torsional strain twists the ferrules around until the rings are out of alignment and this will ultimately throw the rod apart. Nowadays split-cane rods are also made with spliced joints, and this undoubtedly improves the action.

Splices, whether they are fastened with whip-cord, leather thong, adhesive tape or other binding, take less than five minutes to adjust and have a great advantage of solidity over ferrules which, when worn loose, allow the joints to turn. A Tweedside firm of old repute fits all the spliced rods it makes with spring-loops, into which the fine ends of the taper are slipped in readiness for tying down. This ingenious device ensures the joints fitting snugly, even before the insulating tape is applied.

## Rod Rings

There are several types of rod-ring in use today. Intermediate

rings of snake-pattern are fitted to the cheaper rods, but it is
the bridge-ring which is commonly found on all rods of quality,
either in the simple form with an oval transversely-set eye or
open faced (Hardy). Generally, they are all made of German
Silver, or of stainless steel; neither of which will rust nor become
corroded. Butt-rings are normally of the bridge-pattern, large
in size and either of metal throughout or lined with synthetic
agate. Those whipped to the tip are mostly fitted with an agate
lining, set in a deep-rimmed ring and guarded with two lateral
stays, in order to protect from accidental damage. Nevertheless,
the agate is brittle and cracks easily. If this should happen the
dressing will be scratched off the line. And if used with greased
lines there is a tendency for the oval-shaped bridge-ring to collect
grease—and therefore grit—by scraping it from the line as it runs
through. The improved type of bridge-ring and the snake-pattern
are less liable to do this.

If the angler is fishing a river which requires a large amount
of switch casting, and so uses a Single Taper line, he will find
it essential to have the old-fashioned "fall down" or oscillating
rings fitted to his rod. If he uses the Single Taper line without
these rings he will find that, when he tries to make his forward
cast, there will be some slack between the rings: in other words,
the line, being heavier nearer the reel than at the rod tip, tries
to slide down the rod. The oscillating rings, when the rod is
vertical, fall down against the rod and so trap the line.

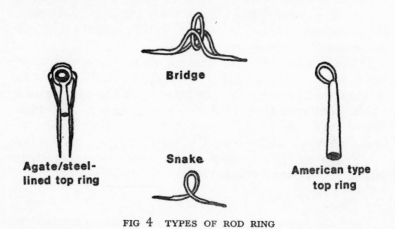

**Bridge**

**Agate/steel-
lined top ring**

**Snake**

**American type
top ring**

FIG 4    TYPES OF ROD RING

*Rod Length*

The size and character of the river to be fished largely governs the choice in length of rod; so does the weather. With many other conditions to be satisfied no angler could be content with a single salmon-rod to serve all occasions. A rod for early season fishing needs to be powerful enough to lift a heavy line from the water and throw it forward again, often against a very strong wind. For this the fisherman will need a good 14–15-footer. My own preference is for a rod of 14-foot or a few inches less. If I had to suggest a second rod for fishing in low water with fine cast and small fly, I should recommend a rod 12-foot long or a little less, but one light enough to be managed occasionally by one hand. This is essential in floating-line fishing, for it is extremely inconvenient with a shorter rod to lift line over and outwards—to "mend" it—when taking out a belly which has been caused by the current. It is hardly possible in salmon fly-fishing to have less than those two rods: 14 or 13¾ foot and 12 to 11½ foot long, each having its special qualities, powers and degrees of delicacy.

The old 18-foot weaver's beams are rarely seen today, if indeed they are now made; but those of a 16-foot length still have their use, heavy though they are, in covering large strong rivers, such as lower Tweed and Tay and some of the great Norwegian rivers, in some of which many heavy salmon are taken every year on long and powerful rods by the method of harling (see p. 172).

If I had to choose a salmon fly-rod to serve all my needs, I should personally select one of thirteen feet. This would be long enough to use in high water and to cast nearly as much line as can be controlled and if it were used with great care, would also be light enough in the hand to prevent too much strain being placed on a fine cast. The longer and more powerful the rod, the greater should be the margin of strength in the cast, or the more delicately should one tighten on and play the fish. If the action of the rod-top is harsh, it is almost impossible to play a fish lightly. The only chance is to keep the rod practically at right angles to the line, vertically or sideways, and play the fish entirely on the top joint.

There are also days when a heavy line is essential, heavy enough to carry against the wind and to sink in flowing water, so that the fly swings at the desired depth. Unless the rod used is fairly powerful, it cannot lift a heavy line nor raise a deeply sunk one without experiencing undue strain. The tendency however is toward lighter and shorter rods and, provided they can handle the line, they are certainly far more comfortable to use and give more pleasure in the playing of a fish.

Wood's chosen length for the three rods he designed for greased-line fishing was 12 feet. He however could wield even the heaviest of them single-handed and with ease, for he was uncommonly strong. Since his day lighter and somewhat shorter rods have been adopted for his method. This calls for a reach rather less than 12 feet and a combination of good balance combined with lightness, a merit which will allow the rod to be used one-handed, in casting and in *lifting over*, by anglers of average physique.

Another factor in the selection of a rod length is that low-water flies are dressed on hooks with such keen points that penetration is effected by the weight of the current alone and little is required of the angler beyond lifting his rod as the fish is felt. But in sunk-fly fishing the hook is a more massive and a blunter affair and a considerable amount of effort is required to make it penetrate a salmon's mouth. This largely dictates the choice of rod in sunk-fly fishing, for a ten-foot trout rod would find difficulty in pulling in a No. 1 hook, although a rod of this size can comfortably deal with fish up to twenty-five pounds or more, provided strong nylon is used. In fact, it is astonishing how well a good ten-foot trout rod stands up to the work. The playing of a salmon may take a little longer, but not very much, because the gentle strain given by a trout rod allows a fish every opportunity of tiring itself out. The most difficult thing is not the playing but the bringing of the quarry to within gaffing distance.

*Choosing a rod*

Here are a few hints on choosing a rod. There should be a feeling of power in the flexions of the rod, especially about the middle; the action should be appreciable right down to the hand; and the point should recover quickly and settle down without quivering. Unless a rod passes these tests, it is not worth giving it the only real test, viz. how it will lift a line from the water.

Balance is a very important matter, because a well-balanced

rod is much easier and less tiring to cast with; and it helps the angler to tighten on a fish at the right moment far more surely than one with small hooking-power.

The quality of a rod depends upon its power to make long-distance casts, accurately and neatly, and also to throw a short straight line: it is not fair to expect a rod to recover from deep under the water the greatest length of line it will cast. A yard or two should be withdrawn by hand before making the next throw, so that the rest can easily be lifted and the slack released at the right moment during the forward cast (see p. 79).

### Care of a Rod

A good rod will stand a great deal of hard work and will last a long time, if it is not asked to attempt tasks beyond its powers and if a little care is taken to keep it in good repair. Below are a few tips culled from bitter experience:

Always, when taking a rod apart, grip the joints by the ferrule. For if you do not, serious damage will be done to the rod and the hold of the ferrules on the bamboo will be slackened. The first sign that all is not well is the opening of a seam, where two sections of bamboo are cemented together. Violent untwisting of refractory ferrules is often the cause of looseness in lockfast joints, so that, after a short period of casting, the male ferrule will be found to have turned, carrying the lock from its proper position. The rings will, accordingly, be out of alignment, and this will in turn hinder the easy running or shooting of the line. Strips of india-rubber tubing give a firm grip on ferrules and should always be used to take the joints apart.

Never grease male ferrules with vaseline. Uncooked mutton fat is the best lubricant I know, but, if the ferrules are rubbed up and down the hair at the back of the neck, they will slip easily into the sockets.

Stoppers to rod-ends are a never-ending source of worry, until one can truthfully say they are lost! One way of keeping them is to sew them into the end of the rod-bag partitions, so that they naturally enter the joint-sockets when the rod is put away; or to sew down to the flap loops of tape, into which they fit tightly.

After the rod has been used it should be dried, put back into its case and hung up by the loop at the lower end. When going

by train or car to a distant river, by all means take the rod in its
bag; but be very careful not to put it inside one that is damp.
Nothing spoils a split-bamboo rod so effectively as dampness on
the one hand and central heating on the other. A better plan
is to place the rod in a tubular container, specially designed for
the purpose and made of aluminium alloy.

This metal tube is designed solely as a protection, when the
hazard of breaking is great, but never for storage in the close
season, during which the rod should be hung in its bag, in contact
with dry air of moderate temperature, or else across a series of
nails protected with leather or flannel, or on wooden pegs. A long,
narrow shelf is the best of all. If the rod is placed leaning against
a wall, the heavier joints may take no harm, but the top-joints are
apt to get warped.

## Reels for Fly-fishing

Any well-made salmon fly-reel of the right size will serve, provided the frame and spool are constructed of gun-metal, or of
aluminium alloy, not of aluminium, as it is too soft and liable
to be bruised by accidental blows. One of a diameter of four
inches or less is the most suitable, because line is recovered more
speedily than with reels of a smaller size. But this advantage of
recovering line on high gear will be lost, if the spool of the reel
has not been properly filled. If the line does not reach within a
quarter of an inch of the bars or distance-pieces across the frame
of the reel, more backing ought to be added. Generally speaking,
a reel, four or three and three-quarter inches in diameter, will fit
a fourteen- or a twelve-foot rod.

It is a pleasure to find a reel accessible for cleaning, oiling and
mechanical adjustments, such as changing the spring or the pawl
of the check. Other excellent features to be looked for are a
revolving surface on the reel or an edge, upon which, by a gentle
pressure of the thumb or forefinger, an additional brake can be
applied to a fish (see below); and also a mechanical means of
adjusting the strength of the regular check. The usual forms of
this check are the friction-drag or the resistance offered by a pawl
to a cog-wheel, fixed on the main axis of the spool; the second
is the sounder method, because most kinds of friction-drag wear
and grow weak and uneven with use. It is a great help in cleaning

and adjusting the moving parts of the reel, if a small screw-driver, a small pair of pliers with a wire-cutter and some paraffin are always ready to hand. The miniature screw-driver with four blades, often supplied with bicycles, is extremely useful and quite strong enough.

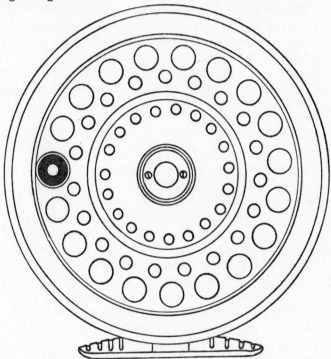

FIG 5 A SALMON FLY REEL—HARDY'S *Marquis*
*Note* : The outer ring acts as a thumb-brake

The original purpose of the check is to prevent the spool from rotating so fast that the line doubles on itself and gets into a snarl; if this should happen and the fish is still running strongly, there is an instant of heavy tension and then the fish is free. The employment of a reel with too strong a check is as bad a practice as using a light check and a cast with a large margin of strength. One will bring disaster through a break; the other does not give the rod-point a chance to play the fish, because the reel gives out line before the rod has had the time to get into the bent position which is the most favourable for playing a fish. It is, in fact, equivalent to playing a fish from the reel without the intervention of the rod.

There are occasions when a fish must be stopped at all costs from running to some part of the river, to which the line cannot reach, or from which it can never be brought to gaff; and also when it is making for a dangerous snag. No ordinary check is of any use in such circumstances and to hold on to the reel-handle is courting disaster. This is where the finger-check mentioned above comes in; and there are few salmon that cannot be stopped in this way. If the tackle gives, there need be no regrets, because you were clearly doomed to lose that fish anyway.

### Care of Reels

Reels should have a periodical overhaul. Every Sunday morning of the season one good friend of mine religiously takes to pieces, cleans and oils the reels he has used during the week! And he breaks or takes apart all joints of the rods in use and thus avoids the possibility of there being a bad jam at the close of the season. When fishing is over for the year, the action of the check should be examined for any wear, the old oil removed by brushing the inside with paraffin, all traces of the paraffin wiped carefully away and fresh oil thinly smeared over the action. Sewing-machine oil and the oil, sold commercially as "Three in One" are the best I have yet discovered for the purpose. After a new reel has been used for a fortnight, it is well to look at the check-action, where the pawl interlocks with the cog-wheel; if either of these shows the slightest sign of wear, one of them is of too soft a temper and the reel should be sent back at once to the makers. River-water in time of spate is full of grit and sand in suspension, which easily find their way into the mechanism of a reel and into the clearance between the frame of the reel and the inner circumference of the spool. This is the natural result of accidentally allowing the reel to be immersed in water. Sand accumulating at these points may easily cause the spool to stick; it will certainly cause a grinding noise and should be cleaned out.

Another way of getting dirt into the reel would hardly be suspected. It is raining very hard; and you take shelter and place your rod with the butt on the bare ground and leaning against a tree. When you use the reel again after the storm, it is long odds that you will hear a noise, like the grinding of grit between the teeth, and will not at first realize it is due to grains in the mud that has been thrown up by the impact of the heavy rain.

## Salmon Fly Lines

Salmon fly lines are today made either of silk or plastic, and each of these materials has special qualities to offer. Up to 1935, or thereabouts, silk was the accepted constituent for all fly or spinning lines. These were dressed with linseed oil and finished with a polished surface. Unfortunately a silk line must be most carefully dried after use or it will rot. Also it tends to go tacky, unless properly looked after. But silk (with a specific gravity of 1·33) had one priceless quality—it could be cast against the wind.

The modern Dacron-centred, plastic-coated fly line is now most generally used by salmon fishermen the world over. They are made in several styles; Sinking lines, floating lines and floating lines with a sinking tip—the sink tip as it is called. They are made in *Double Taper*; *Forward Taper* or *Weight Forward*; *Single Taper* and *Level*. The diagram below describes these various types of line.

This can better be understood if actual measurements of one type of each line is given. In the ordinary *Double Taper line*

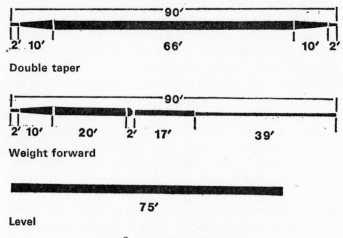

FIG 6   TYPES OF FLY LINE

a thickness of about 0·045 in. gradually increases to 0·06, remains at that thickness for a considerable part of the whole 40 yards and then decreases at the former rate to 0·045. The length of each tapered portion is about 4 yards. In a *Weight Forward line* the fine end, to which the cast will be fastened may be 0·03 in. in diameter. The line then increases very steeply to 0·065, which is maintained for about ten yards, and then for the rest of the 40 yards drops as rapidly to 0·035, that is, just thicker than the fine working end.

These plastic lines have many virtues; they do not go sticky, the floating line really does float without greasing, the sinking line certainly does sink and the sink tip performs its function admirably. The one fault that I have found is that it requires some skill to drive the Double Taper version through a strong wind.

On the other hand the Weight Forward will drive into a wind in excellent style as the entry of the line is quite narrow. With this version, however, cracks are apt to occur in the dressing of the finest part of the line behind the heavy head. This is caused by the modern stainless-steel top rings, which are in effect just steel wire of a comparatively thin gauge, cutting the line dressing when the cast is being made. Nevertheless, with this type of line the rod is made to work fully when only a few yards are through the top ring.

Fly lines for salmon are customarily made in thirty-yard lengths, which is more than enough and allows plenty of backing to be wound on—a matter of some importance. But the junction between cast and line can be a source of weakness. The old-fashioned collar of plaited gut or monofilament nylon helped to maintain the steady taper from line to fly. But this created a weak point in the end of the line, namely, where the top of the whipping ended; and the knuckle thus caused became a potential danger-spot in the line itself. Further, in floating-line fishing the join itself created some disturbance upon the water, in fact fish have been known to rise to the join. Nowadays I always use the nail knot (see p. 69), and this has served me well for many years.

In the 1960s the A.F.T.M. (Association of Fishing Tackle Makers) established a standard form of measuring lines using a number of criteria including the weight of the first thirty foot of line. New rods usually have the A.F.T.M. number of the best line to use engraved near the rod handle—it is as well to use this as an indication, but not to follow it slavishly; for, as in most things in fishing, personal preference is the truest guide. The A.F.T.M. system is as follows:

| AFTM-Class No. | 1 | 2 | 3 | 4 | 5 | 6 | 7 | 8 | 9 | 10 | 11 | 12 |
|---|---|---|---|---|---|---|---|---|---|---|---|---|
| Weight in grammes | 4·0 | 5·3 | 6·6 | 8·0 | 9·3 | 10·6 | 12·3 | 14·0 | 16·0 | 18·6 | 22·0 | 25·3 |

for example: DT (see p. 47) 6F is a Double Taper size 6 Floating line and WF7S is a Weight Forward size 7 Sinking line, etc.

There is one point to watch carefully. The makers state that these lines do not require drying after use. The backing line, however, may not be rot-proof, and a fish could well be lost by the backing breaking. It may also be necessary from time to time to clean these lines of accumulated algae and dirt—soap (not detergent) and water is the best thing to use. And beware, too, of dropping insect repellant on a line or on nylon for that matter. It is guaranteed to rot it.

*Care of a Silk Line*

The quality I look for in a line is suppleness, which is often a matter of individual dressing, as some examples of the same make are much harder than others. The best salmon line I have owned took me a fortnight to break in; the worst was like a spring and had a natural kink in it, so that little bights formed at frequent intervals between the rings and the coils would not lie closely on the reel. I fought this second line for six months, gave it all kinds of dressings (except red deer's fat, Mars oil and vaseline, all of which I have found death to a dressed line) and then I surrendered.

I now expect to have to grease a new silk line a little, but once it is tamed it needs, for sunk-fly fishing, dressing and polishing at the most once a week during the time you are fishing. This attention and the most scrupulous drying after use should find the line in perfect condition at the end of the season, when it should be polished carefully, taken off the reel, spread over a disused bed or hung up in loose coils over laths to prevent the dressing from becoming tacky and covered with newspapers or a dust-sheet. If

D

you go through this simple ritual, there is no reason why a salmon line should not last you for years. If, however, a line has become tacky through use in a hot climate, or from having been left all winter on the reel, you have the choice of sending it to be re-dressed or of buying another; there are no half-measures worth taking in these circumstances. Putting a sticky line into powdered chalk or into whiting I have always found unsuccessful.

## Backing

Backing, called in North America "running line", is a simple means of extending the law that may be given to a fish, beyond the thirty yards allowed by the casting-line, and has therefore to be fairly strong and of small bulk. Fine cable-laid silk lines, any of the silk plaits, known generically as Nottingham lines, and those of flax fulfil these requirements. Linen, that is flax, lines are extraordinarily strong. Backing is sold unprotected by any dressing and should, before use, be treated with one of the preparations now on the market. The quickest and the best way is to put the line and a small quantity of the line-dressing into a small covered tin, warm it, until the preparation is in a liquid state, and shake the tin thoroughly. If the line is then taken out and allowed to dry, it will be found that the grease has gone well inside the texture. Although backing does not often get wet in the river, drops of water and rain work their way through; and it is troublesome, when this has happened, to be compelled to take the whole of the backing off the spool, when the line has to be dried. If the backing is treated in the way just described, it will not rot. Monofilament nylon backing is now increasing in popularity. It is cheap, very strong, and takes up less room on a reel than silk or flax backing. There is a type of nylon, flat in cross-section, which is particularly suitable for this and has the inestimable advantage of not kinking.

At first sight it seems pointless to have more backing on the reel than is ever likely to be used; but, unless the outer end of the casting-line is brought up to a point, where it just clears the reel-bars by a comfortable margin (about one quarter of an inch), the effect of the high-gearing of the reel is lost.

The right length of backing is not always easy to gauge. A good method of doing it is to wind the casting line very gently on to the empty spool, attach the end of the backing and continue until the reel is comfortably full and ample clearance is still left. Cut off the backing and reverse the line; this should give the maximum length of backing consistent with the correct clearance for the dressed line. The safest way of fastening the foreline to the backing is given on page 70. *But always remember to tie the backing securely round the inside of the spool.*

## Casts

The long-used gut cast has now been superseded by mono-filament nylon. This is stronger, lighter, does not need soaking and is more transparent than gut. It is also a great deal cheaper.

For floating line work I use a tapered cast looped on to a collar of single nylon about eighteen inches long. The collar is about one-third the thickness of the fly line and it is attached by means of the needle knot (see page 69). The actual cast is knotless and tapered down to tips varying from 12lb. to 22lb. breaking strain, or 0·35 mm. to 0·5 mm. They are sold in three-yard lengths, and if the angler wishes to fish a three-yard cast it is an easy matter to cut off a sufficient amount from the thick end and to retie the loop. The angler can also add a length of finer gut to the tip to taper his cast. Here I should like to preach a short sermon on the ridiculous habit of keeping old nylon. Some day you will pick up one of these old casts by mistake, hook a twenty-pounder, and the cast will break. *Burn old nylon.*

For high-water fishing, when the river is clearing after a spate, I simply shorten one of these tapered casts. How much to cut off the tip is a matter of experience, but one soon learns to judge the length required.

Nylon is immensely strong for its diameter and provided that the proper knots are used and well-tied it is also reliable. Nylon is also sufficiently invisible not to scare taking fish. I have killed salmon in the lowest of low water with an eight-pound breaking strain tip. This is only 0·010 inch in diameter, or 0·25 mm.

Personally, I have long used nylon casts, and they have been improved year by year. Nowadays the nylon cast meets all my requirements for salmon fishing.

## CHAPTER THREE

# TACKLE AND EQUIPMENT II

## GAFFS, TAILERS AND OTHERS

### Gaffs

THERE are three forms of gaff or cleik commonly used by the waterside. The short gaff-hook made to screw into the ferrule fitted to a wading-staff, to a collapsible handle, or to a long net-handle. Secondly, a long-handled gaff which is needed on some rivers, especially where there are high banks at the water's edge. Under these conditions, the best form of gaff is one with a tapered shank, so that it can be lashed to a corresponding taper on the staff. And, if there is a groove or a shoulder on the taper of the shank to give the lashing a chance of a firm grip, the gaff will neither turn nor draw, when a fish is impaled on it. The point is usually protected by a sleeve of spring-steel, but a cork, fastened round its middle by a piece of cord to the handle and stuck on the point, or a long, narrow sleeve of strong pliant leather that can be slipped up the shank before use, is quite an efficient guard. The third and most handy kind is a collapsible gaff with an extension of thirty or forty inches; this is quite long enough to make it easy for an angler using a fourteen-foot rod, to gaff his own fish.

FIG 7   A SALMON GAFF

The point of every gaff should be very sharp, parallel to the shank, and without that shepherd's crook bend that is sometimes given to it; and the width of the gape should be not less than two and a half inches. Collapsible gaffs, made of ordinary steel, should be dried and oiled after use; they are bound to often get

wet and rust quickly, so that those made of rustless steel are well
worth the additional cost.

*Other Ways to Land a Fish*

On some rivers, and at certain parts of the season in others,
there are times when the use of the gaff is forbidden by the local
River-Board by-laws. Then fish can only be landed by either
beaching, by tailing them with the hand or by using a tailer, or
by netting them (see p. 237 et seq.).

FIG 8    TAILER SET FOR USE

A mechanical tailer is very reliable. It consists of a short handle
fastened to a length of flexible steel rod, which looks like
armoured cable; to the other end of the rod is joined a noose of
fine stranded steel wire ending in a collar that runs along the
rod. The collar is pulled down and the noose is set, so that it
will go easily over a salmon; but, when the handle is raised, it
draws up and grips the fish firmly.

The tailer mentioned above had one fault. If the fish was
tailed in shallow water, the loop could easily hit a rock while
being coaxed over the salmon's tail, and snap tight prematurely.
This has happened to me! The modern tailer now has a trigger
for the forefinger, so that until the loop is well over the fish's tail
it cannot close. Simply place the loop over the tail, press the
trigger, and the fish is yours. It acts splendidly, and like lightning.

Lastly there is the net, which should have at least a depth
of twenty-four inches and be laced to a strong pear-shaped frame.
If a fisherman is by himself, he will find it very difficult to hold
the net with one hand against the force of the stream long enough
to get the salmon into it, head first—which is the only reliable
way. Do not attempt to lift the net with a salmon in it clear of
the water but raise the net frame clear of the surface and drag
it to land.

## The Killer or Priest

The handle of a collapsible gaff is most convenient for killing a salmon, but sometimes it is left at home and the gaff carried is one that is made to be screwed into the end of a wading-staff. One cannot very well beat a salmon with that and a stone is a messy and uncertain way of dispatching it, so that a small, heavy killer or "priest" has been invented for the purpose. Such a killer can be bought at most tackle-dealers.

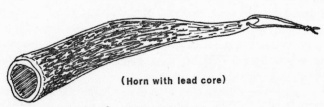

(Horn with lead core)

FIG 9    TWO KINDS OF PRIEST

## Taking a Fish Home

There are several easy methods of carrying a salmon in comfort. If the fish has been killed in a pool above the place to which I have to return, I fasten one end of a piece of cord in the salmon's mouth and keep the other in my hand; the fish is launched and followed downstream as far as my luck holds. But "floating the fish home", as Chaytor who first wrote of this idea calls it, is of little use, where bushes and trees grow right down to the water's edge, and the river-margin is too deep for wading.

For some years past I have therefore carried in my pocket a length of sash or other plaited cord in one end of which I whip or splice an eye, so that a running noose can be made; at the end I put an inch-wide whipping of strong thread. Its total length is, perhaps, a yard, but enough should be allowed to make a noose for the salmon's tail and for the other end to pass through the gills, out at the mouth and there fastened without the fish being too much in a curl when it is lifted up.

The salmon-carrier sold in tackle shops is perhaps more comfortable for the hand. It is a short piece of wood of circular section through the long axis of which passes some whipcord. On one end of the cord is a hook that takes hold of the salmon by the corner of the jaw; the other end is a running noose for the tail.

Another method is to fasten a piece of cord to each end of a stout stick a little longer than the salmon and tie them to its mouth and tail. This has the advantage that the fish arrives home undisfigured by a crease through having being bent up. Two salmon can be carried in this way, but if there is a chance of more than two, it is wise to have some kind of bag.

It is useful to have in your bag some cuts of cheese-cloth of a suitable size to wrap the fish in; this will keep off flies and prevent the inside of the carrier becoming unduly covered with slime from the fish.

*Sending Fish Away*

If a salmon is to be divided and sent in two or more pieces, the difficulty is to pack it so that it shall arrive in good condition and not having leaked on the way. When a salmon is cut into two the entrails are extruded; these should be removed and put on one side, the hollow in the fish washed and the entrails replaced and kept in position with a wad of nettles. A heap of nettles should then be placed on a sheet of grease-proof paper, the piece of salmon laid on top and more nettles grouped about it, so that it is entirely surrounded by them when the paper is wrapped round. Outside this put a newspaper and finish off the parcel in the ordinary way.

Packing a whole salmon for transit is far easier. Special basses are made into which the fish is slipped, but, if these are not available, there is an excellent way of doing up a salmon in the tall rushes growing frequently and at times to the angler's confusion by the river's edge. Cut a good-sized bundle of these, choose the tallest, which will be from three to three and a half feet high, reverse some of them to bring the thin ends to the middle and

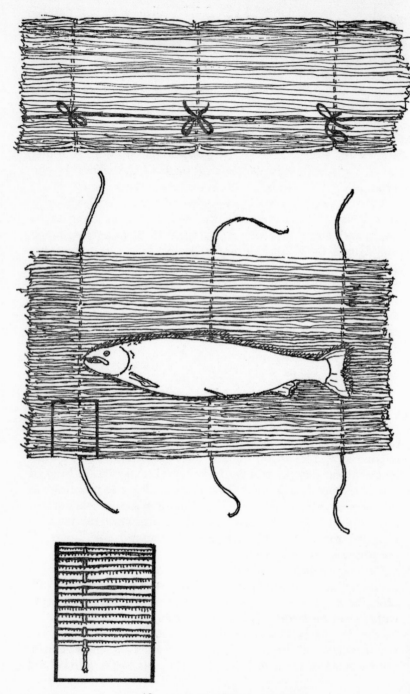

FIG 10   RUSH-PACKING A SALMON

make a carpet a little longer and wider than the fish. Lay the
rest of the rushes on top, bind round tightly at intervals of six
inches with stout string or, still bettter, with binder-twine and
cut off the waste ends with a sharp knife.

*Waders*

Wading trousers can cause discomfort sometimes amounting
to pain, or be so easy that one forgets their presence : it all
depends on the way they fit. Here are the points to be considered
in choosing a pair of waders.

First put on a pair of thick stockings and then get into the
waders. Be sure the feet of the waders fit easily, but not loosely,
and that the heels are in the right place and are correctly cut. If
the tread of the foot goes beyond the angle of the heel, the wader
will wear badly and, meanwhile, will be most uncomfortable. A
little above the instep, the wader should be cut slightly on the
big side to allow the high part of the foot to slip past; but this
allowance is often overdone. There should be a feeling of slackness around the thighs; but the legs should be cut high up into
the crutch, so that the angler shall not be hobbled on getting over
a stile. The only way to test this is see whether one of the knees
can with comfort be bent at right angles to the body. Waders
should be very wide at the top. Trousers fitting closely to the
waist make it awkward to get to the pockets of the fishing coat.

In any pattern of trouser-wader, the inside of the leg just above
the knee, the instep and the heel ought to be reinforced. If they
are usually worn with each side alternately next the water, the
sole should be doubled by placing two pieces of fabric together
better sides outwards. The very light waders now to be bought
are excellent for summer, but they will not stand much hard
work, unless they are reinforced above the knee and the feet are
made of *stout twill instead of the lighter fabric.*

Waders will last much longer if they are properly looked after
and, when they have been used, dried carefully, either in the
open air or in a drying-room, but never in front of a fire. A
weak spot, or a place where a leak is suspected to exist, ought to
be patched at once with a piece of fabric smeared with rubber
solution, having first removed with petrol the old rubber and
scraped away the worn threads of the twill. If the leak cannot
be located, dry and hang them up and fill them with water. The

water will soon trickle through the leak or small drops will appear in the porous area; these weak spots should then be marked with a pencil. Waders keep much better through the winter if they are hung up and not folded and put away in a drawer.

Socks to be worn over the waders ought to be chosen for their thickness and hard-wearing qualities; but, if they come well up the calf of the leg, they should not be allowed to drop down in folds over the ankle. A piece of elastic will hold them close to the wader, so that river-sand or fine gravel are unable to find a way inside the sock and then rub a hole in the wader-fabric, until a threadbare spot is formed.

For many years there has been a controversy about the right way to wear waders, tied in or open at the waist. One party maintains that to fasten waders at the tops is to court disaster, if the wearer falls into the river and be forced to swim for it, because the air in the waders will naturally go to the feet and support them at the expense of the head. The result of this would be drowning. The other side maintain that the tight cord excludes the water from the legs and therefore makes it easier to swim. The current school of thought is that it makes not the slightest difference but it is advisable to postpone falling into the river until your waders are already wet!

Latex rubber waders are excellent. They are easily patched, and dry very quickly, as they are not covered with canvas.

## Brogues

For wearing with trouser waders the best type of brogue I have found laces up the front with eyelets, and bears in front of, and to cover the lacing, a canvas tongue, held in position by two straps, which pass through loops on the tongue and which also act as ankle-supports. Do not have exposed hooks as a fastening for brogues—there is a danger of the feet being locked together, which might easily prove fatal, if the wearer was wading deep in a heavy current. This pattern is far and away the best; it holds up the foot, keeps gravel out of the brogue and shields the brogue-fastening efficiently. The next best has a solid tongue and is then laced up in front. Do not have anything to do with brogues that rely upon a couple of straps for their fastening; they are very dangerous, because they give no support to the ankles and destroy the necessary liaison between foot and boot, if stumbling and tripping over boulders is to be avoided. The easiest way to break an ankle is to wear such brogues! For this reason alone, I would strenuously oppose the use of low brogues, cut after the style of a pair of shoes. With light rubber brogues I have not experimented; I am told the main objection to them is their tendency to let their wearer slip about on the rocks that are at all greasy.

Where sliminess is characteristic of the boulders in the river, brogues should be soled with thick felt and only nailed in the heel; but they must be reserved for river-work, as the felt will soon wear out, if the fisherman walks in them to and from the river. Have the felt put on in two layers; the first attached as firmly as possible with glue or cement, the second or outer one lightly glued and sewn. As soon as a hole wears in the centre of the second sole, have a new piece of felt put on. Brogues treated in this manner last a surprisingly long time.

The problem of nailing is not at all easy to solve. Hobs fall out very soon; and yet the riveted kind should be avoided. If you go into a shop that deals in this kind of brogue, you will be told these nails never fall out, as they are riveted through the sole. Clearly you will ask how fresh nails can be put in. The answer is that the brogues will have to be resoled! If it occurs to you to compute the average life of a good nail at one month, before it is worn so smooth as to be useless for the purpose, you will discover the trap so neatly laid for you. Every month you will be called on to pay for a new set of hobs—and for new soles!

Use screw-shank nails, ordinary hobs, or a mixture of one of these with climbing nails round the edges of the soles; but never the kind that have to be riveted through the sole. There is one very safe type, known as the Wye nail, which is a large pyramid of hard-tempered iron or steel, screwed into a socket; and this, not the nail, is riveted through the sole. Nails of this design are easily replaced, but are expensive and only worth using in places, where other types have failed to give the fisherman a good grip.

Brogues must not be oiled or greased inside, as this will react on the rubber used in the manufacture of the wader-fabric and shorten its useful life. If they are stiff at the beginning of the season or in the morning, place them in a bucket of water before attempting to pull them on. See there are plenty of nails in the soles, as they are quickly kicked out, after a period of difficult wading. Buy a cheap shoemaker's last, a hammer and a supply of nails, so that you are independent of the cobbler. Never attempt to drive nails into dry leather; they come out in a very short time. Soak the brogues thoroughly and then put in the hobs.

Rubber thigh-boots are today generally preferred for normal fishing use. It is surprising how large an extent of water a salmon angler can cover with efficiency when wearing them. But these boots must be made of rubber of the highest quality. Lightness must be combined with strength, durability and pliability. Also the soles should be of synthetic material which does not alter in water; whereas leather soles shrink and soften, when soaked, and are distorted when dried. For these boots too I much prefer felt soles and well-nailed heels.

At the end of the day, turn back the upper portion of the legs to let the air circulate freely inside. Better still, use wicker-work or plastic boot-trees, such as are used to keep open Newmarket boots. Turn down the tops, insert the trees into the calf of each boot and then, if you wish, hang them up by the loop at the top. The inside of each boot will be bone dry in the morning. Before winter storage it is well worth while dusting the rubber with French chalk to protect it, and then hang up the boots in a cool, dark, dry place.

## Wading Staffs

A strong wading-staff completes the list of the salmon-fisherman's equipment. Some makers fit the top end of it with a female ferrule into which a detachable gaff, or a rubber button, may be screwed. An essential attachment is a wire loop whipped to a point within a foot of the top; to this is fastened a bull-dog clip secured to one end of a length of cord, which is long enough to form a convenient sling round an angler's shoulders. Thus the staff can be released and safely allowed to float a short distance downstream and yet be within easy reach, if needed, either in wading down or across, or as a gaff; in the meantime, both hands are free for the business of casting.

It is usual to fit the lower end with an iron spike; this makes a great deal of noise banging on the rocks. A quieter and equally efficient attachment is a thick rubber ferrule, which can be obtained from a stick-shop and riveted in place as well as glued.

## Fly Boxes

Metal fly-boxes fitted with spring-clips under which the bend of the hook may be slipped are universal. There are many other types on the market these days and becoming increasingly popular is the magnetic fly-box which has magnets in the shape of bars on which the flies adhere. The disadvantage of this type is that the magnets are heavy, and perhaps a better sort has bars of foam-rubber on which the flies can be hooked and detached with the minimum of trouble. If there is any choice, always pick a box made of blocked tin rather than one of aluminium, the difference in weight is negligible but should one happen to sit on ones fly-box the tin one comes out unscathed whereas aluminium bends irretrievably. If the edges of the two halves of the box meet properly no moth will ever enter and create havoc. But this will not necessarily eliminate the danger of rust.

I think the best way to prevent the hooks of salmon-flies getting rusty is to make an inflexible rule of putting used flies into a separate tin and to dry them carefully, after the day's fishing is over and clear the eyes of nylon (or of varnish, if the heads have been repainted), before replacing them in the fly-box. There will be thus no risk of the hooks rusting; the moisture will be taken out of the feathers (use blotting-paper or amadou for this purpose); it will give you a chance of inspecting and, if need be, sharpening up the points and of painting the exposed metal lightly with varnish, taking care not to allow any to get behind the barb; and, should you like to have flies arranged according to size, they can best be sorted out at your leisure after fishing is over for the day.

## CHAPTER FOUR

# FISHING

## KNOTS AND SPLICES

G UT has now been largely superseded by nylon, but for those reluctant to give up the old style a number of gut knots are included below:

FIGS 11 & 12   TWO FUNDAMENTAL KNOTS
The Thumb and the Figure-of-eight

*The Double Fisherman's Knot*

Place the two strands side by side and overlapping by four inches or so; with the right-hand end (which ought to be nearest the body) make a loop outwards and round the farther strand; complete the loop over the strand and back underneath it; repeat this, taking care to keep both loops open; thrust the end of the gut through the pair of loops, as though you were making a simple thumb-knot. Moisten the bent parts of the gut and draw

FIG 13   THE DOUBLE FISHERMAN'S KNOT

tight. Try to induce the knot to travel a little to the right, this will shorten the end that is subsequently to be cut off as waste. The left-hand half of the knot is to be treated in similar manner (Fig. 13). The two knots ought then to be soaked in water and pulled together; or they should be put in the mouth, lubricated thoroughly with saliva and then drawn up. The result is a neat barrel, from which the waste ends can be shaved with a safety-razor blade. Do not use this knot to join nylon.

## The Double Blood Knot

This is by far the best and safest knot for joining strands of heavy gut or nylon to make up a salmon cast. It was first described in print by Chaytor and has since been employed by numbers of grateful fishermen. The method is as follows:

Lay the two strands parallel together, one overlapping the other by about five inches; the short end of the left-hand strand should be next the body. Take three complete turns with this end about the long strand and towards the right; bend it back and slip it through the gap between the two strands, just short of the left thumb, the duty of which is to keep all secure (Fig. 14). This

FIGS 14 & 15    THE RIGHT-HAND HALF AND THE COMPLETED
DOUBLE BLOOD KNOT

is the first half of the knot. Reverse the strands and repeat the process; but, in poking this end through the strands, be sure it is pointing in the opposite direction to the other. The length of the strands thus pushed through is of no moment, as they will slip and shorten, until the knot closes up (Fig. 15). Place the knots in your mouth or in a basin of water; draw the coils together by pulling first on the long ends and thus shortening the waste; pull the waste ends in a direction at right angles to the lie of the main strands; and then draw the coils really tight, taking great care not to introduce any sharp angles into the cast that might develop into a "knuckle" or hinge. Shave the ends as close as you can and you will have constructed a neat and perfectly-secure joint that is as strong as the cast itself.

## A Dropper-Attachment

If you wish to use a second fly, an unusual thing in salmon-fishing, one end of either the Double Fisherman's Knot or the Blood Knot should be left long, so that a length of cast of about four or five inches projects from the top end of the knot; to this the dropper-fly is attached.

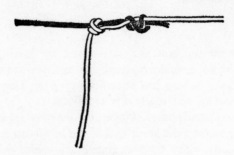

FIG 16    A DROPPER ATTACHMENT USING THE DOUBLE FISHER-
MAN'S KNOT

## Tying a Fly to the Cast

The Turle knot (Fig. 17), which is used so widely for tying on trout flies, is tied as follows : With the right hand bend the end of the gut round (away from the body) to form a loop, carry it over and round the standing part, under and round the loop and through to complete a thumb-knot in the end, through the standing part runs. Draw the thumb-knot tight, so that a slip-knot is formed. When the slip-knot is brought close up to the eye of the fly, the loose end should be tucked under the noose in the direction of the bend of the hook, so that it is held firm and the stream-line of the fly is maintained.

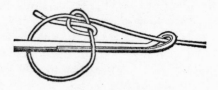

FIG 17    THE TURLE KNOT

## The Cairnton Jamb

This method of tying on an eyed hook is the most practical that has yet been discovered; it is safe, easily tied and quickly untied, when a new fly has to be put on. The single form of it, suitable to all flies dressed on eyed hooks smaller than 2/0, is made in this way. It is suitable for gut only.

For gut-loops and for large metal eyes the double form (Fig. 21) is safer and almost fills up the space in the wire loop. This is made by taking the gut round the neck of the hook an extra turn, which gives the necessary increased security.

FIGS 18 & 19   THE SINGLE CAIRNTON
First stage and second stage

 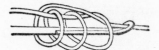

FIG 20   THE SINGLE CAIRN-  FIG 21   THE DOUBLE CAIRN-
TON COMPLETED      TON

## Fastening a Fly to Nylon

Pass the cast through the eye of the fly and slide the fly up the cast. Make two circles in the nylon laying one circle over the other. Then make an overhand knot round both circles and tuck the free end under the two circles. Slide the fly down the cast, put it through both circles and draw tight round the neck of the fly. Make sure the overhand knot is tight, and the free end under the two circles.

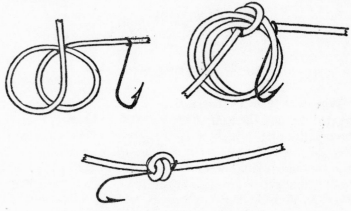

FIG 22   THE TWO-CIRCLE TURLE KNOT

E

## Chaytor's Reef-Knot Jamb

Pass the gut through the eye, round the neck of the fly and back again through the eye in the same direction in which it originally went. Let the short end be considered to be furthest from the body; bend it towards you; return it underneath the long or nearest strand; point it towards the eye; and push it under the coil that is embracing the neck of the fly. Draw all tight and hide the end amongst the fibres of the throat of the fly (see Figs. 23 and 24).

FIGS 23 & 24    CHAYTOR'S REEF KNOT JAMB

This is particularly good for securing gut-loops but not with nylon. For metal eyes there is nothing quite as convenient as the Cairnton knot.

## Fastening Gut or Nylon and Wire to Swivels, or Eyed Flies for Dry-Fly Fishing—the Half Blood Knot

Pass the end of the gut twice through the ring of the swivel; bring it round in a long loop and push the end back and round the standing part three or four times; pull this up tight and cut the cast, leaving an eighth of an inch of it sticking out (Fig. 25).

FIG 25    THE HALF BLOOD KNOT

Wire is very easily fastened to a swivel, if a strong pin is inserted through the loop of the wire. Lead the end of the trace through this ring; bring it at right angles across the standing part (Fig. 26); twist the two wires together three or four times; and then continue coiling the waste end down the standing part, taking care that every turn shall lie snugly against the preceding one (Fig. 27). With the flame of a match take the temper out of the end of the wire and roll it gently round. It is always worth going to the trouble of cutting wire with wire-cutters, as the hook on the end of it made by twisting catches in everything and often punctures the tip of a finger.

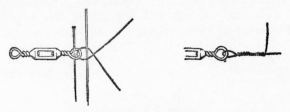

FIGS 26 & 27   JOINING WIRE TO A SWIVEL RING

### How to Make a Loop at the Head of a Cast—the Blood Bight Knot

The common method of constructing a loop by means of a thumb knot or a figure-of-eight knot in a bight of gut causes the cast to lie at an angle with the line. The knot shown in Figure 28 is safe for both gut and nylon.

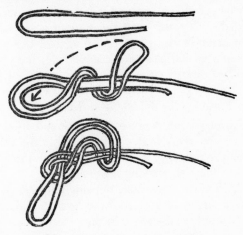

FIG 28   THE BLOOD BIGHT KNOT

### Methods of Fastening Off

The Whip Finish is a safe way of securing the whipping at the end of a rod or the tying-silk at the head of a fly; the "invisible knot" Chitty calls it (1841). When the silk has reached a point within six or three turns respectively of the point where the binding is to terminate, place the left thumb on the latest turn and make a long loop with the silk; bend this back and slip it under the latest turn (Fig. 29), which will, if strained, grip it securely. Continue winding with the silk of the loop for the required number of turns, taking care to push the loop every

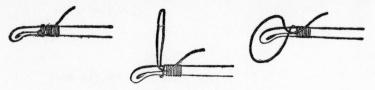

FIGS 29–31   THE WHIP FINISH

time over the end of the rod or the head of the fly (Fig. 30); this will ensure the bent-back silk lying under the new turns. Then draw the loose ends through and, in fastening off at the head of a fly, cut the silk off close (Fig. 31). There is a neat way of hiding the end of a binding on a rod. Strain the silk first one way and then the other, so that a tiny gap is formed between two adjacent coils. Hold the silk taut, insert the edge of a very sharp knife or of a safety-razor blade; press gently against the tension on the silk and the latter will be severed, so that the end cannot be seen, when the coils are pressed together again.

## The Whip Finish in the Middle of a Rod

The whipping is proceeding along the rod from left to right, over the rod and away from the body. Hold the silk, as it comes from under the rod, in a long bight and take the end of the silk loosely round the rod, working inwards.

Then work in close turns with the original part of the silk and pass the turns in succession over the loose end. Draw the waste through and finish as described in the preceding section.

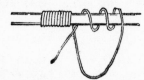

FIG 32   THE WHIP FINISH IN THE MIDDLE OF THE ROD

## *The Loop Finish*

Another way of fastening off near the centre of a rod is carried out by including in the last four or five turns a loop of strong, fine silk (see Fig. 33). Bind the turns of silk specially tight and then slip the end of the tying-silk through the loop, the closed end of which is pointing outwards (Fig. 34). Hold the coils in position and pull the loop and waste through. Finish off as above.

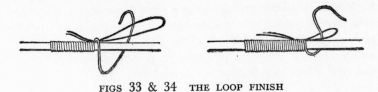

FIGS 33 & 34   THE LOOP FINISH

## *Attaching Nylon Backing or Collar to a Fly Line*

The attachment known as the Needle Knot or Nail Knot is the best I know. I have killed a number of salmon on it, and it never showed the least sign of slipping.

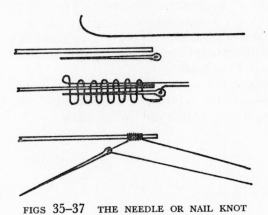

FIGS 35–37   THE NEEDLE OR NAIL KNOT

Lay the end of the fly line, the nylon and a bodkin, leaving a spare end of nylon to make the knot with. Then wind six to eight turns of nylon back towards the end of the fly line, and pass it through the eye of the bodkin. Then pull the bodkin to the left, slide the knot down to the end of the fly line, pull both ends of the nylon as hard as possible and cut off loose end.

A small eye whipped in the end of the line, within which the loop of the cast may interlock, is a practical way in trout-fishing; but I have not tried it with a salmon line. Alternatively, the line can be knotted to the loop of the cast by a figure-of-eight knot.

### Attaching Line to Backing and Splicing

Whip a small loop in the innner end of the foreline; whip in the backing a loop large enough to pass right through the largest reel you possess; pass the long loop through the small and over the reel; draw this up and the backing and line are securely joined and yet can be separated in a minute. By this means lines can be changed about with the least possible delay.

### Putting Rings On

See that the rod is facing in the right way and that the legs of the top ring are embracing the correct faces of the rod. Then tie down temporarily the rings throughout the rod and see they are properly aligned. Start whipping on the top ring, first with a number of turns of fine copper wire, then with the ordinary binding silk of the thickness of button-hole twist. The silk should be set in on the rod, below the ring-supports, and taken up to the last coil of wire; in this way the step between metal and wood is successfully spanned and the coils do not fall down and leave an ugly gap. Loop finish.

The intermediate rings are whipped on in the same way as the lower portion of the top ring; that is to say, the turns of silk are made inwards. Loop finish and varnish thinly.

## CHAPTER FIVE

# SALMON HOOKS

## Introduction

NOWADAYS the salmon fisherman no longer has the choice of the multiplicity of hook types with which our forebears had to contend. The Hamilton, Kirby, Kendal, Carlisle, Adlington, Kelson and other types of hook are largely museum pieces and of single hooks only the Limerick, Sproad and Round Bend, and to a lesser extent, the Sneck Hook are obtainable. Of these the Round Bend is by far the most popular for the Limerick and Sproad tend to be weak on the bend and Sneck Hooks are weak on both bends.

The material for hooks is now almost invariably a steel wire with a high carbon content, or a stainless-steel wire which has broadly similar properties. These materials have eliminated most of the problems associated with salmon-hook strength but one point of weakness remains in the making of the barb. For unless it is raised short and shallow, it weakens the strength of the metal beneath it. This is an important point for anyone who ties his own salmon-flies and has a number of hook-makers to choose from.

## Doubles and Trebles

For many years I have realized that the orthodox single hook was completely incapable of doing anything but a very poor job in the hooking of a fish. Apart from the unnatural angle at which a single hook swims, the chance of the "iron" going home is at best no better than even and, if the hook has an up-turned eye, probably 7 to 3 against. When a fish comes at the fly, it opens its mouth and, because the bend of the hook is vertical, tends in closing its mouth to turn the point outwards. Thus the moment a fish feels a pull, it has merely to open its mouth to get rid of a hook so situated.

Further, with a single hook it is very difficult to hook the "perfect taker". As we become better fishermen, we tend to meet a larger number of "perfect takers", because we are fishing the fly more slowly and without drag. It is a curious fact that the better the fisherman, the more offers he gets and yet the more difficult it becomes for him to hook a fish.

The problem of hooking a taking fish is in reality merely a mechanical one. Accepting the "perfect taker" as the normal, it appears there are two things you can do to make sure of hooking that fish. (1) Give plenty of slack line and hope the water acting on the belly of the line will pull in the hook. Yet that chance is never better than even. (2) Use a slack line and very sharp double or treble hooks rather than singles. Then at least one of the hooks will go home.

I do not think it unduly pessimistic to say that to hook 10 fish firmly on orthodox flies an angler may have experienced 30 offers and perhaps more. Using Waddington-type Elverine or Esmond Drury flies or tube flies with conventional triangles or doubles, he is doing badly if he does not bring in 10 fish out of 15 offers.

Although it must be said that tube flies have a horrid habit of catching in the cast, for they are so light that the slightest wind can cause such a snag.

Salmon fly fishing nowadays is largely a matter of small flies fished with a floating-line, and a very considerable school of thought, of which I am a member, advocates the use of the short-point double-hook, in sizes from No. 6 down to No. 10. These hooks are of various types. They are either finished in black colour or bronzed. The bronzed hook is the heavier, and so fishes a little deeper than the black, which is at times a great advantage.

Personally, I feel that a great many of the complaints made by anglers regarding poor hooking would die away were they to adopt the small, double-hook. I have always found that, provided the hook points were parallel to the shank, and the splay of the hooks not too wide, hooking was really good.

Some hooks are made double with the long, low-water shank. Personally, I can see very little advantage in this. I prefer the shorter hook. There is less leverage on the points when a fish is being played.

I am a firm believer in the motto of that great man, the late Alexander Grant, "let's see it working", and under the stern test of practice I am all for the short hook.

## CHAPTER SIX

# CASTING A SALMON-FLY

*Introduction*

UNDOUBTEDLY the best method of learning to cast is to watch a first-rate caster at the waterside and serve an apprenticeship under him; or to go to a teacher, receive a course of lessons, until you are proficient in handling the rod and in controlling the line, and then start practising the real thing by the river. The lessons learnt in a school of casting provide a good foundation for the lessons a man, if he is observant, will teach himself when he starts to fish. Casting is most certainly not fishing; but an angler with a grounding of what might be termed tournament-casting will soon be able to adapt himself to the particular kind of throw demanded by the occasion. If none of these advantages is to hand, recourse must be had to written instructions, a poor substitute at the best. And those offered here have been compiled with a full knowledge of the difficulty of describing in black and white the principles of casting, let alone the secrets and finer points of it.

For the purposes of this chapter, I have assumed you are fishing right-handed and are, therefore, standing on the left bank of the river. A current of moderate strength flows at your feet and there is little wind to prevent you getting and keeping full control of the line while it is in the air. You are imagined to have drawn off about eight or ten yards of line and to have worked it beyond the top ring and to have allowed it to come round and swing in the stream at full extension below you. This is the most favourable position at which to start the simplest form of cast.

*The Double-Handed Overhead Cast*

Before giving a detailed description of this throw, I want to insist on the supreme importance of getting the line correctly extended behind the caster's back. Most beginners look and pay attention to the result of the forward stroke alone; they judge the whole cast, in fact, by the way the line falls in the forward stroke; and they employ twice as much force in the forward stroke as in the backward, whereas the reverse would produce a far better result.

When the line is properly extended behind, the caster will feel a little tug and the forward movement will begin at that moment, instead of it being delayed until all the slack line behind him has become taut.

As soon as the beginner has grasped some of the details of the action of the overhead cast, he should ask his instructor to watch his back-cast and tell him when the line goes too high or too low, whether the rod-point dithers and does not yield to the tug, or is taken too far back to allow of an efficient delivery of the line. If the rod-point is permitted to travel back beyond the normal plane, the line, in coming forward, will be thrown upwards into the air and allowed to fall in curves across the water; this is an excellent cast, when it is desired to put a slack line across an intervening fast stickle. But it should be used only when the angler is proficient and perfectly capable of casting a long straight line.

I. Lift the rod-point with the suspicion of a jerk, which will raise the fly to the top of the water and will bring into play the middle joint of the rod. As soon as you are satisfied you can feel the weight of the line and that the line itself is following the lead of the rod-point, begin the upward stroke of the rod. There is no intentional deceleration of the motion of the rod after the jerk; the whole action is really an effort to overcome *inertia*, to get a feel of the line and then to make it move upwards and backwards, smoothly but at an increasing pace. This jerk and the subsequent upward stroke are known as the "recovery of the line", and it is part of the rod-makers' job to see that the middle and butt joints of the rod are properly built to stand up to the strain of withdrawing a heavy line from the embrace of water that seems unwilling to let it go. I do not advocate the withdrawal in this manner of a large length of line; it would be unfair on the rod. We have left the line travelling back in obedience to the lifting of the rod and moving at an increasingly greater speed towards its maximum point, which occurs when the tip of the rod is vertically over the right shoulder, or nearly so.

There are two distinct ways of lifting the rod. These are illustrated in Figs. 39 and 40. The former method is far less tiring and

gives a slightly better result as regards distances covered with
the fly. The other, I think, is far easier to adapt to casting in
awkward places; but without the slightest hesitation I advise every
learner to practise first of all that shown in Fig. 39.

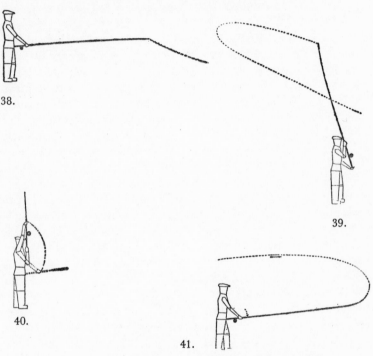

FIGS 38–41   THE DOUBLE-HANDED OVERHEAD CAST

In Figure 39 the motive power is applied by working the rod
almost as though the centre of the handle were able to rotate a
short distance about a horizontal axis. The upper portion of the
rod is lifted by the right hand pulling the top of the handle in
towards the body and by the left hand pushing the button away.
The right elbow should be extended as in the motion known in
the army as the "salute". After a pause (II), about to be
described, the actions of the hands will be repeated in reverse. The
right hand will push the rod away from the body and the left
will perform the task of pulling in the lower end of the cork-grip.

Throughout the whole process the hands have not been raised very much; and the work has been performed by this see-saw action with the centre of the handle as the "point of balance".

The second and older method is to carry the line well behind the caster's back by a corresponding lifting of the rod and by a full upward extension of the right arm. A full day's fishing in this manner throws a great strain on the muscles along the right side of the body; and it is doubtful whether as much finish can thus be given to the cast as with the newer style, especially when you are "cutting-down" against the wind. In each method the function of the left hand is for the most part to steady the rod, while the right hand does the larger share of the work of propulsion; in Figure 39 it may be seen helping to pull and then to push one end of the "lever"; in the other (Fig. 40) the butt is supported by the palm of the hand and is held quite loosely by the edge of the thumb and a couple of fingers. The left hand should not be allowed to grip the handle more firmly than is done in the new way, in which the duty of the slightly-bent fingers is to pull and, afterwards, that of the thumb and forefinger is to push.

II. When the rod has been lifted with an *accelerando* motion as far as the perpendicular, it should be allowed to follow through, until it is at an angle of about twenty degrees from the vertical. This is done by letting the left hand and arm come forward from the shoulder about two inches. The line will continue travelling back to its proper extension behind and in a slightly-upward direction. The point of the rod bends back a little also in answer to the momentum that originally lifted it and was not quite exhausted at the time the remainder of the rod was checked in its backward path. The carrying of the rod back and the flexion of the top preserves a control of the line and should eliminate all dither and forward lash, provided the caster is not too rigid and not gripping the rod too tightly.

Also, he knows that when he feels the weight of the latter, the exact instant has arrived to begin the forward stroke. If the rod-point be in any way prevented from following the line backwards a few inches the whole rod would vibrate, the rhythm and power of the stroke would be lost and the line would fall in front of the caster in a tangled mess. If you feel the pull of the line as it flexes the pliant point of the rod, you know that so far you have played your part correctly, and that you have merely to carry through

the forward stroke in continuation of the movement of the returning rod-point and make a reasonable finish to have completed
a successful cast. Counting time to produce the feeling of the
correct rhythm (which is identical with that in trout-fly casting)
is much inferior to waiting for the pull of the line at its proper
extension. Do not delay the forward stroke so long, that the fly
and line will have dropped and possibly have become entangled
in bush or tree behind you.

III. The forward propulsion of the line by the old method is
achieved by bringing the right hand down and slightly in front
of the body, so that the line is automatically thrown well out and
straight forward. If the timing is correct and the line and rod
are suited to each other, little more power is needed to put the fly
neatly on the water.

If the forward stroke is delivered too early, you will probably
hear a crack like that made by a whip, a sign that you should
be sure the fly is still there, by watching for a tiny splash at the
end of the cast as it meets the water. If you delay the forward
cast too long, there will be a danger of catching some obstacle
behind you; or, this risk avoided, you find you are apt to cast
high in the air, so that the line falls in a heap just in front of
your feet.

The forward stroke ought to be delivered from the position
some twenty degrees behind the vertical. It is a common fault to
find beginners allowing the rod to creep forward a little before
delivering the forward stroke. The inevitable result of this is a
weak and uncontrolled throw.

There should, however, be a small degree of wrist-flick to make
the cast extend itself fully; and, for long casting or if there is
anything approaching a contrary wind, strength proportioned to
the force of the latter must be put into the downward stroke of
the rod. How much muscular force is needed under given circumstances will be learnt by experience.

In the other method the forward stroke is delivered by forcing
out the right hand, which is gripping the upper portion of the
handle, and pulling in with the left, as described above. The
effect is much the same as that brought about by the old way,
but it is far less tiring and it allows of much long casting against
the wind.

The lifting of the hand in the back-stroke makes the old method very handy, when there is trouble in the form of bushes or low trees behind the caster's back, especially when he cannot use a Spey-cast or a switch (see p. 84), either of which would be preferable. An expert can, at will, cause a fly to ascend almost vertically in the back-cast, if he desires to clear some high obstacle behind him. It is often called the steeple-cast. Do not attempt this, until you feel you are proficient in the other throws. You will then achieve it by snatching the line off the water with an impetus, given at the start of the stroke instead of at the top.

At the same time, the right hand is lifted instead of bringing it back towards the shoulder. The forward stroke must be initiated immediately the rod has reached its topmost limit and the direction of the throw must be outwards rather than downwards, if the cast is to be carried through correctly. If a pause is allowed, part of the line will drop below the rod-top and, when the stroke begins, this slack will have to be taken up before the true cast can start. This throw should be used only with a short line, otherwise there is great danger of breaking the rod.

The forward path of the fly ought always to be different from that which the fly was forced to follow by the back-stroke, otherwise there is a serious risk of the line and cast being mutually entangled in mid-air. Some anglers control the movements of the rod, so that the fly follows a path like a figure-of-eight; some take the fly back over the shoulder and return it to the right of it; others throw the fly outwards and bring it back over the right shoulder. It is of no moment how it is done, as long as the two paths do not coincide.

As soon as you are confident you can manage ten yards of line, draw off another yard at a time, until you have reached the length of which for the moment you are master. Measure this and make a note of it, so that, day by day, you can check your progress. Try always to cast very neatly and to get the fly first on to the water—a most difficult thing to do, but very useful in greased-line fishing. As a rule, you will do well to aim at a spot a little above the surface of the river; this will assist very greatly in placing the line and fly on the water without undue disturbance. It is very common to see a man casting a line, so that it rolls along the surface, until it reaches its full extension, and then drops on to the water. This is a very untidy throw that may easily disturb fish lying in the vicinity; equally, it may call their attention to the fly. That is not a definite statement; but, if a line can be delivered in a more tidy manner, there is no earthly reason for taking the risk. If the trick of getting the fly in first can be cultivated, it will save you an immense amount of trouble when the time comes that, to avoid drag (see p. 139), belly must be kept out of the line.

When you can cast a short distance with the right hand leading, cross over to the right bank and begin throwing left-handed, before you find yourself acquiring a marked preference for fishing from an accustomed side. Form very early the habit of drawing in a short loop of line and of holding it with the lower hand in readiness to release it at the psychological moment, when the impetus of the line will carry the spare loop through the rings and the whole will be extended fully.

This is known as *shooting line* and is a handy method of casting rather more line than the rod will otherwise deal with in the air; and also it helps by taking up the slack line that all good fishermen draw in before making a new throw. In long casting, it is too much to ask of a rod that it shall recover from the water all the line originally put out, especially as some of it is sure to be *drowned*. A couple of yards and sometimes as much as five are pulled in and held fast by the unemployed fingers of the lower hand; this should be released at the precise moment in the forward stroke that can only be discovered by practice and experiment. It is hard to be much more definite than to characterize it as the instant, when the rod seems to give a kick and then straighten itself, and when the line can be felt pulling and straining to go yet further. A beginner must try this out for himself.

Cultivate the habit of holding a short length of slack line as soon as you begin learning to cast; after a short period practise releasing it; and, as soon as you hear the line going with a slap against the handle, you can be well satisfied with the timing. A great deal of the ease with which it is possible to *shoot line* is due to three main causes: the weight of the line, the alignment of the rings and their size and freeness from dirt or grease. It will be found far more difficult to shoot line with a two-handed rod than with a single-handed one. You will experience this, if you use alternately one hand and then two in controlling a twelve-foot rod. The secret is to prevent the top joint from bending unduly, so that the extra line is thrown across the water, instead of down at it. Also, the rings will be forced out of their *vertical* alignment and smooth egress will be denied to the line.

When there is strong downstream wind, casting over the right shoulder can be really dangerous. It is better to take the rod back over the left shoulder or to cast left-handed and put the line well inland, so that it cannot be driven by the wind at your head. As soon, therefore, as you hear the fly whistling uncomfortably near your head, you should adopt one of these methods and make use of the wind to a certain extent. If a tree or some other obstacle prevents this, you will have to employ the double Spey-cast, described on page 88.

In places where overhanging branches, fallen trees that have floated down and have lodged in the way of the recovery of the fly for the Spey-cast, or a lack of the right current to hold up the fly, all combine to present the luckless angler with abstruse problems, many times the way out will be found to lie in the use of two throws, where normally one would have been enough. First of all, a false cast is made with a shortened line in some convenient direction, from which it is comparatively simple to cast again in the right direction and to *shoot* the line at the right time. How many times this tactic has won me a fish from dense jungle-like places, where, by the usual methods, I should have gone home without ever having got a fly properly over the lie and only having lost several flies in attempting it? This method of double-casting is adapted to another purpose, namely, ensuring the straightness of a cast, in floating-line fishing (see p. 138). And in the same chapter is described the *mending* of the cast or *lifting over*.

There is a variation of the overhead cast often employed in a pool, where the backward cast is checkmated by high trees and where it is quite easy to throw the line upstream clear of the promontory formed by overhanging bushes. The rod is taken back along an almost horizontal path and in the forward stroke is manœuvred, so that the fly is projected outwards over the water at an angle of roughly forty-five degrees. Considerable effort has to be made to force the fly in its backward path to go outwards and clear of the bushes.

It is often more convenient to bring the fly near to the surface by raising the rod and then lowering it with a sweep which causes the line to belly upwards and drag the cast and fly up from the plane to which it has sunk. The line can then be recovered with far less effort and without any fear of straining the rod.

## The Single-handed Overhead Cast

In recent years there has been a growing enthusiasm for the use of single-handed rods for salmon-fishing, of some nine foot in length and generally used with a Forward Taper Line. While these rods, in expert hands, will put out a fair length of line, it is, I think, a mistake to use them on any but a small river. To cover all the water on a large river means deep wading and this, if carried to excess, can disturb fish especially in summer and low-water conditions.

Apart from this, a short rod is a great handicap when the line is on the water. It is very difficult to control the line so that the fly fishes properly, and, when a fish is being played, one cannot lift the line over rocks or other snags. A Double Taper Line helps line control but a Forward Taper Line with a short rod makes an almost impossible combination.

The *modus operandi* of single-handed casting is the same as double-handed. The right hand holds the rod and the left controls the line to be shot. Where beginners are concerned, I advocate holding the line under the forefinger of the *right* hand until that moment, during the forward cast, when the line is shot, thus:

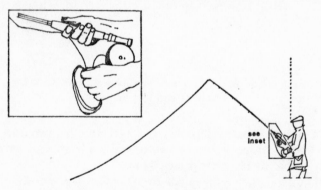

FIGS 42 & 43   THE SINGLE-HANDED OVERHEAD CAST
Holding the line

A common fault is to allow the left-hand to move upwards while casting and allow slack between the hand and the butt-

F

ring, which results in a weak and sloppy cast—hence the use of
the right forefinger.

The back-cast is the same as in the double-handed cast, and the
rod is allowed to drift back slightly beyond the vertical. The forward cast is made as soon as the weight of the line is felt to tug

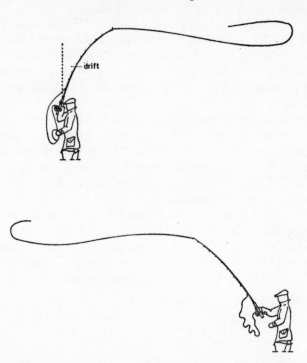

FIGS 44 & 45   THE SINGLE-HANDED OVERHEAD CAST
The back and forward cast

at the rod-tip. There is little difference between the two casts, and
he who can properly execute either will easily succeed with the
other as exactly the same principles apply.

Some readers may be small river anglers, and use short rods
with success, but I would again stress that, even on a little river,
a twelve-foot rod will do the work better, and fish the fly as it
should be fished, a much more important aspect than the actual
casting.

## Overhead Casting with a Forward Taper

The principle used in this cast is similar to that of casting a minnow, i.e. casting a weight attached to a fine line. The idea is to throw the short, heavy section of line at such speed that it will pull out many yards of the fine shooting line. To do this it is necessary to produce momentum. The caster has the heavy part of the line beyond the top ring, and the line ready to be shot either lying on the water or held in large loops over a finger of the hand which is lowest on the rod. The upper hand holds the line very tightly against the rod. In order to flex the rod as much as possible, the caster then makes several false casts, increasing the speed with each cast, and at the critical moment, releases the fine line. The result is that the heavy head flies away like an arrow, drawing out a long length of fine line behind it. After the cast is fished out the caster draws in the fine line ready to shoot on the next cast.

In making this cast it is important to avoid anything in the nature of a "thrash down". The line must go forward on a horizontal plane, so that it can draw the shooting line after it. The whole principle is that the heavy head must travel horizontally through the air at the maximum speed which can be obtained. This means that muscle enters into the matter. The caster has to put out a good deal of energy if he wants to throw a long line.

If, however, he is elderly, he probably would find the cast mentioned below more to his liking since it requires the minimum of exertion.

## Switch Casting in the Highland Style

This method requires a slow rod, preferably spliced, a Single Taper line, and oscillating rod rings. Thus equipped, the caster can fish all day with the minimum of effort. He does not shoot line; he need not worry over coils of loose line on a windy day, or when he hooks a fish. Everything is done for him by the rod and line; he can concentrate on the fly and the fish.

Let us suppose that our caster is standing on the left side of the river, and that the previous cast has been fished out, so that the line is straight downstream of the angler.

He raises his rod slowly into the position shown in Figure 46, and pauses.

He then describes an ellipse with the rod. This should be done comparatively slowly, but with gradually increasing speed, until the rod is against the shoulder (Fig. 47).

The forward cast consists of a short, sharp flip of the wrist, and away goes the line (Figs. 48 and 49).

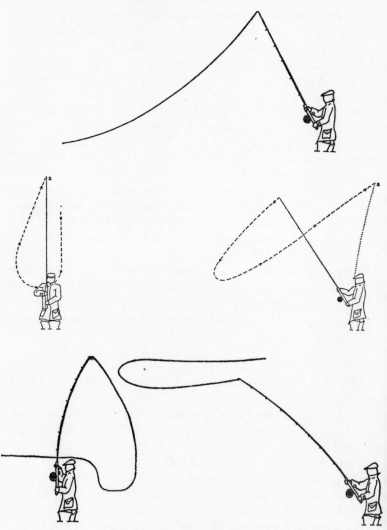

FIGS 46–49   THE SWITCH CAST

Note that there is no "thrash down", the line goes out as if cast overhead. In picking up the line, the first movement of the rod is *downward*; this throws an *upward* belly down the line and causes it to jump off the water. It is then pulled backwards as shown in the figures. There is no pause at the end of the back stroke and the forward cast can and should be made as soon as the rod tip has sprung back. Speed of rod movement during the pick-up of the line should be avoided, or the line will be sent too far upstream. Just an easy swing with no jerking. The whole cast should be smooth and effortless. One can cast all day, once the trick is mastered, and feel quite fresh at the end of it all.

As to distance, one easily can cast the following lengths of lines—assuming that the right tackle is used :

A 12-foot rod will cast 30 yards.

A 13-foot rod will cast 33 yards.

A 14-foot rod will cast 35 yards.

When I say easily, I mean that one can do so all day without tiring. Longer distances require more exertion, and a tall man will exceed these figures, so also will the expert.

This cast will work—after a fashion—with a Double Taper line, but the distances obtained will be less and the performance less finished. If once you have used a Single Taper line, the Double Taper will merely annoy you!

## The Single Spey Cast

This cast is really the same as a switch done sideways. The difference lies in attempting to place the fly outwards, over the river, instead of returning it to the same plane; also there is far more power put into the forward stroke, so that the fly and the line may clear the rod, when the last-named is brought downwards in the new plane, viz. outwards and across the river.

Of all casts this is by far the most difficult to describe. It has been attempted several times without much success; and these notes and diagrams are offered in the hope they will make more intelligible the teaching of an expert by the river, for that is certainly the only way to learn how to do the Spey cast. The analysis of the actions of the cast are not intended to supplant the instructions of the experienced caster, but are meant as a grounding in the principles that will relieve him of elementary explanations and will make his teaching the more valuable.

Imagine there are behind and a few yards above you trees, bushes, or other such obstacles that in the ordinary way would constitute almost insuperable difficulties, if you employed the overhead cast. For even if you were able to throw the line sideways upstream, you would find it no light task to place the fly across the water at the desired angle. It remains, therefore, to use either the Spey-cast or the Switch. Let us also imagine there is flowing at our feet a moderate current, which will make it possible to get the full extension of the line and to ensure the fly being near to the surface. The latter is a most important factor in the successful achievement of the Spey-cast; and lack of an adequate flow of water, from which the fly may be easily picked out, will make this cast most difficult and sometimes out of the question.

The first thing to settle is where you wish to place the fly and then to turn your body towards it. Let the inland foot be slightly advanced. Then lower the point of the rod, so that the distance travelling by it in being raised may be as great as possible and the maximum impetus imparted to the line.

As soon as the line is well extended downstream, place your left hand under the rubber button, so that, when the rod is in the upright position, it shall rest on the open palm. The right hand, which is to do most of the work, is to maintain a moderate grip on the upper portion of the cork-handle.

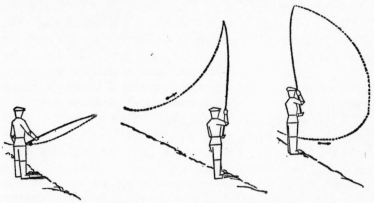

FIGS 50–52   THE SINGLE SPEY CAST
The line extended downstream—the rod in the vertical position—
the line travelling upstream

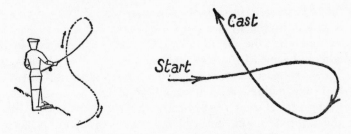

FIGS 53 & 54   THE SINGLE SPEY CAST
The downward finish—the track of rod point as seen from above

Then start lifting the rod into a nearly-vertical position, accelerating slightly to maintain the *pull* of the line at a constant strength. The line will at first follow in a downward-curving belly and the fly will be drawn to the surface and follow without actually losing touch with the water.

When the rod has arrived at a vertical position, incline it outwards and a little downwards, so that the belly receives a twitch that will cause an upward humping and the fly to leave the water and to travel just upstream and close beside the caster. Describe with the tip of the rod an ovoid path, the return portion of which comes back over the right shoulder and proceed outwards and across to the spot aimed at.

The outward inclination of the rod is made with the object of giving time to the fly to reach a position just upstream of the angler. From there the line and fly can be propelled across the stream without getting entangled; and the fouling of the line is a frequent danger against which you ought to guard most assiduously. You must satisfy yourself the fly is either opposite or above you, before making the cast, otherwise the hook will most likely take a firm hold in some part of your body, probably the ear. If the fly is not in this position, the line should be cleared downstream with a switch and the motions of the cast should be repeated.

It is a very common fault in those accustomed to overhead casting to raise the arms as high as they naturally would in that cast; but in Spey-casting, double or single, the upper hand should not be lifted higher than the ear.

The essential part of a really good cast is the maintenance

of the rod's motion throughout. There should be absolute smooth-
ness with no suspicion of a pause or a jerk; but the two essential
conditions are: the use of a suitable rod, rather heavy in the
middle and joined by splices, and of a line of a weight adapted
to Spey-casting, namely, one that has a steep taper and a moder-
ately heavy middle. Without this type of line you will find, in
throwing against even a light breeze, that the fly will be projected
in the right direction, but will fall short; and possibly both it
and the cast will be doubled back.

### The Double Spey-cast

When a strong downstream wind is blowing, it is dangerous
to employ the ordinary Spey-cast, as the fly is carried against the
angler's person when it is being propelled across stream by the
downward cut of the rod. If only his cap is hooked he is lucky!
The double Spey-throw has, accordingly, been devised, which
gives the angler the power of casting a fly under these disadvan-
tageous conditions and of casting it, if anything, often too straight
across.

If you wish to use this cast and are still fishing from the left
bank, you must place the left hand uppermost on the rod and the
right hand underneath the button. The left hand will do the work
of guiding, controlling and propelling. As soon as the line is well

The line extended
downstream

The rod coming to the
vertical. The line fol-
lowing upstream

The rod vertical. The
line travelling upstream

FIGS 55–57   THE DOUBLE SPEY CAST

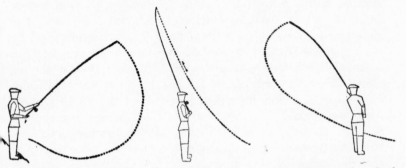

The rod over the stream but about to come back. The line still travelling upstream

The rod back over the bank. The line following it

The line coming back under the rod which is at the extreme left of the circular movement

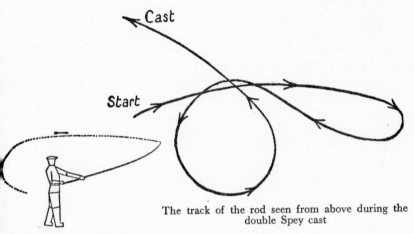

Cast

Start

The final cast in the direction required

The track of the rod seen from above during the double Spey cast

FIGS 58–62   THE DOUBLE SPEY CAST

below you, raise the rod exactly in the manner of the single throw, except that the rod-point comes round to the vertical, having followed an outward path. When there is a long line out, the rod should be brought into a plane much beyond the vertical and the hands and the elbows should be crossed, left over right.

It is then taken across to the left side and inland of the body and brought round to pass over the left shoulder until it is opposite the spot to which the fly is to be thrown. The rod is then brought smartly down and the body is again held back. The diagrams will explain the path of the rod-point far more lucidly than the most careful description in words could ever hope to achieve. It is worth noting that the fly never travels in the air above the caster; and that it touches the water just below and close to his left side, instead of just above him. The danger of his being hooked, therefore, does not exist. In this cast also the movements ought to be continuous with slight acceleration, as the point reaches the vertical positions over the right and over the left shoulders and in the finish.

If there is a really strong gale blowing downstream, which is making it an impossible task to extend the line behind in the overhead cast, a double Spey-cast, employed very indifferently, is infinitely better than the former, provided the angler can carry out properly the final movement of the cast.

In making the overhead cast the importance of feeling the *tug or pull* of the line on the rod-point was insisted upon. The essence of all forms of underhand casts, switch and both Spey-casts among them, is that the *tug* shall proceed from the line being held down by the water. The shorter the line to be thrown, the longer ought the caster to postpone the forward stroke, always long enough to allow the fly to sink a little in the water close to him and thus get firmly enough anchored to give the *tug*. This is of prime importance. I have mentioned it in the last paragraph of the chapter, in order to emphasize it.

## CHAPTER SEVEN

# WATERMANSHIP

## Introduction

"YE need na fash yersel the day wi' yer lang wand, for I wud na gie a pinch o' snuff for a' that ye'll get: there are too many pouthered lawyrs aboot." These ghillie's words of wisdom were quoted by Scrope in *Days and Nights of Salmon Fishing in the Tweed* (1843) and many must be the angler who has taken the tendered advice and turned away from a river for fear of earning the wrath, and total non-cooperation, of a Scottish ghillie. Yet would he have been right, and was the ghillie right? It is this perennial conflict between philosophy and experience and the glorious uncertainty of the sport—an uncertainty which I for one hope never ends—which is the charm of salmon fishing.

Over the years a salmon fisherman acquires a sixth sense about when, where and with what he will be successful. Salmon fishing is more often or not the chanciest of sports and the complete novice can at times succeed where the expert has failed; it is on average that the expert will come out on top. "Watermanship" is an art no one can learn from a book, nothing can compensate for a few hours on a river in the company of a knowledgeable fisherman. But in the following pages will be found a distillation of years of accumulated experience which will, I hope, be of use to the reader. And I start with a subject which is too often overlooked these days but which can make or mar one's own and other people's enjoyment of a day's fishing.

## Good Manners

The claim of good manners upon a salmon-fisherman is two-fold in character: thoughtfulness for the man who is fishing after him on his own bank and consideration for the man opposite. I write about manners with some diffidence, because it is assumed they go hand in hand with the good-fellowship of the waterside.

But alas! there is not always enough of the give and take in salmon angling that can make perfect the joys of fishing. Etiquette, as in other sports, is largely concerned with technique and consists of unwritten laws and of customs which are designed to make salmon-fishing more pleasant for everyone.

There is often a rivalry between those who fish fly only and those who believe in using fly, minnow, spoon, prawn and, in some instances, worm, according to the conditions present at the time. The chief arguments against the use of the spinning-rod run thus. Fish that have seen a spinning lure, or a prawn, and have refused both of them will have been frightened, so that they will not look at a fly for a considerable length of time afterwards. I am sure there are many anglers, besides myself, who could bear testimony to the falseness of that statement. The other is the suggestion that a salmon hooked on a fly fights far better than does one taken on a spinning-bait or on a prawn. This claim is hard to believe, especially when it is advanced so frequently by men, who religiously fish fly only and possibly have no skill what-soever in spinning or in prawning. But this class of fisherman is infinitely to be preferred to that composed of men, whose sole delight is in the use of the spinning-rod and who even go to the length of using a minnow, when the water has come into perfect trim for fishing with the fly. Under such circumstances, it would surely be more courteous to offer any fly-fisherman present priority in fishing the pool, to take advantage of, if he desire it.

To summarize good fishing manners: never enter a pool in front of a man. Move down one step before every throw when another fisherman is waiting to follow you. Do not spin a pool, when another is wanting to use a fly. On thinly-stocked lengths be content with one fish, leave the regular pools for an hour or two and try to catch a salmon in the more difficult and little-fished places. When you are fishing a river the banks of which belong to different men, cast as far across as you wish, but do not turn toward your own bank and then continue to fish.

### What Makes a Salmon Take

Here are two observations I keep by me and put to the test on every possible occasion:

When the river comes down after a spate, foam-flecked and

with bergs of white and yellow foam floating down at odd intervals, I am always very sceptical of the day's fishing and up to the present I have failed to take any fish under those conditions nor have I known others do so. Again, I had for years failed to raise a fish, when the river I know best was running stained with peat with a faint but unmistakable bluish tinge within its depths; but since then I have taken salmon on peat-water, which proves there can be exceptions to what I had imagined to be a local rule.

Every fisherman has surely noticed, from time to time, a sudden change in air-temperature, a warmth which to the salmon-angler so frequently means good sport, that it absolutely restores lost confidence, even at the end of a dull, cold and lifeless day, when it very often occurs. This natural phenomenon is a good augury upon which the angler may safely depend. Weariness, traffic and hunger notwithstanding, the salmon-angler ought never to allow the golden opportunity to slip by; it so frequently means the most glorious sport of the season.

Anthony Crossley in *The Floating Line for Salmon* (1939) made the interesting observation that, "if the water is very hot, a drop in temperature will have the same results". And writing of the Cork Blackwater "the temperature of the water stood at 14°C./57°F. The night after I arrived the wind went into the east and we had some days of very clear weather, warm in the daytime but bitterly cold at night. The water temperature dropped 3°F. The fish went mad for the fly."

Also I have discovered that rapid alterations in the level of the water, up one day and down the next, synchronize with an unwillingness on the part of the salmon to take any form of bait. There may be some connection, for salmon object to being unsettled and are extraordinarily sensitive to minute changes in water-pressure (which is the equivalent of water-level viewed from another angle).

Water-temperature also affects them, in that they are said to take a bait indifferently when this temperature varies considerably from day to day. One particular effect of very cold water in the spring is quite certain, namely, that running fish refuse to face it, but make their way extremely slowly upstream or wait in slack water in the lower parts of the river, until the snow water is out of it. It is also very noticeable that spring fish rarely show in the pools, and so infrequently do they jump, that the angler is almost tempted to suppose the earliest arrivals from the sea are yet below his stretch of the river.

The above paragraphs described the observations of an experienced salmon fisherman. The implications of what happened were reasonably well known, but the reason, or reasons, had never been scientifically explained; until in *Salmon Taking Times* (1965) R. V. Righyni developed the availability of oxygen theory as propounded by Waddington and other writers. Briefly this is that if the available supply be low the fish is not inclined to take any more physical exertion than is absolutely necessary. When the oxygen supply is correct, the fish feeling unsettled, is at the top of his form and will chase a fly.

Various biologists have stated that cold water, as in early spring, contains a good supply of oxygen, but that a salmon's breathing apparatus finds it more difficult to absorb. Later in the year the water is warmer and the oxygen is more easily absorbed. Under summer conditions, however, there may be less oxygen in the water due to evaporation, or other causes.

Another main cause of oxygen shortage is, of course, pollution, which, on some rivers, has now reached positively fatal proportions. It is, however, pleasing to see that conservation is now a familiar word to everyone, the movement is growing, and results being obtained.

Assuming that our river is unpolluted, and merely subject to the vagaries of the weather, the oxygen content of the water can, and does, vary to a great degree.

Wood sometimes caught salmon on the Aberdeenshire Dee with a floating line when ice was on the shallow water and there was snow on the banks. The water would be very cold, and, therefore, according to the Righyni theory, there would be oxygen available, but not too easy to absorb, and he quotes cases of similar conditions where a change of wind has brought a fall of snow and a rise in temperature sufficient to bring the fish "on".

He gives charts of taking times in March, April, late April or May, and high summer, which tie in, more or less, with the standard belief on many salmon rivers; and in the text he enlarges on many divergencies due to certain conditions.

In hot weather and low water the fish usually work into the

rapid water which is more aerated. If, however, strong wind or
rain develop, the fish will return to "lies" in deeper water.

The amount of evaporation depends, of course, upon the
weather. A soft, grey day with no glare on the water, and dew
still on the grass should give little evaporation; but hard, strong
sunlight certainly will.

Righyni is not entirely convinced by the theory regarding the
undesirability of fishing when the air is colder than the water.
But Wood, with his vast experience of Dee fish, had no doubt on
this point. Here we have a man who lived on his water, who was
very observant, possessed an inquiring mind, and killed hundreds
of salmon. I may add that I have never done any good, when the
water was warmer than the air, with a floating line. Even mid-
water fishing has not been very successful.

## Where do Salmon Lie?

The correct answer to this question is in any place between
the two banks where there is water enough to cover them. It is
easy to imagine they have some good reason in the selection of
resting-places and taking-places. But actually, I think salmon have
no real choice in the matter; it is the set of the current and the
shelter afforded by rocks that determine where they shall lie. The
existence of apparently-favourable lodges that always lack a
tenant is evidence that we do not understand the true nature of
protection given by rocks from the force of the stream. There
are, however, a few points on which we have scanty information,
enough on which to base probabilities.

The resting-place or lodge is often quite distinct from the
taking-place, or as it might more accurately be called, taking-
area. I believe a salmon occasionally leaves its lodge to go on a
short tour immediately upstream of where it rests and may rise
to a fly at any point on its cruise. But there are pools where, year
after year, unless winter or spring floods alter the bed of the river
to a very marked degree and favourite lies are covered with
gravel, fish take the fly in identical spots, or at most a foot higher
or lower (the level of the water being the same). There is an extraordinary constancy in this respect that is inexplicable in the case
of the salmon, which successively occupy these "seats", as Scrope
terms them. Where a trout is concerned, the explanation is easy :
food and the set of a current that brings the food; whereas a

salmon appears to select as its lodge a place in which the current is most favourable or demands the smallest expenditure from its store of energy.

Although salmon are very conservative in the occupation of their lodges, they will, in years when there is an exceptionally heavy run of fish, take possession of all manner of strange "overflow" lies. At such times, they may rest anywhere and often in the most surprising spots.

It is a general axiom that a salmon may often be taken out of shallow water, where the presence of one would hardly be credited. A well-defined stream flowing through the centre of a pool always holds fish, provided the river-bed is suitable; but often only local or special knowledge will give you accurately the position of the taking-area. Even a man of the greatest experience will, now and then, encounter conditions, in the face of which he will be helpless without the kindly assistance of a native or of one who knows the river by heart. Surface-indication is of some value, but it cannot supplant the more exact method of surveying the bed of the river in time of drought. This is only possible for an angler, who spends much of his time by a particular water, and he will need no assistance from others. Some men try and imagine how salmon could choose their lodges to best advantage. It is curious how common is the tendency to make a fish think as we might, were we faced with the same set of conditions; and often the conclusions drawn are substituted for what might have been learnt by accurate observation. Also, in flood-time on an unknown river, this method is unsatisfactory, because the surface of the stream gives no sure clue to the strength and direction of the currents at the bottom of the river.

When you are fishing a river for the first time, never be too proud or diffident to ask for help in spotting the lies; it will save you much unprofitable flogging of the water and a good deal of disappointment and prevent you forming an unjust opinion of it.

But as a matter of course a salmon fisherman ought to start learning how the current runs through the pools on the stretch he is going to fish and how the alterations in water-level change their characters. From a glance at the first pool he comes to on any day he should be able to say whether this pool will be in order and whether another will or will not be now too slack for ordinary fly-fishing. Those pools which are in order or *in ply* are said, in fisherman's language, to *fish* well. Another way of putting it is to say of a pool in good order that the fly will *fish* well in it. This really means there is enough current to hold the line taut, to cause the feathers of the fly to pulsate in a manner that suggests it is alive and to carry the fly down-stream fast enough to prevent it from going too deep.

In a slack pool both fly and line are soon drowned and come round very slowly to the angler's own bank, the fly losing thereby much of its attractiveness. When, therefore, a choice offers itself, the angler should always fish a stickle or a throat in preference to a sluggish stretch (cold water in spring-time excepted); but if he has only such a place in which to fish, he should either adopt another way of fishing, such as the floating-line or try other methods.

The length of a cast ought to be chosen to suit the clearness of the water, the light and the presence or absence of shade over the pool. Its strength is often governed by the size of the fly, because fine nylon will break under the strain of a large and heavy fly and also under that necessary to compel a rank or long point to penetrate beyond the barb. Therefore a given size of hook-point (which is almost identical with size of hook) demands a cast of a minimum tensile strength.

## Surface-indications of Good Salmon-water

By far the most reliable sign of a taking-area is the "V" caused by a division of the current. The flow of water is forced upwards and sideways on encountering the upstream face of a large rock that is resting on or is part of the river-bed. The true effect of this is uncertain, but it is likely that back-current is produced by some shapes of stones, the very bluff kind in particular. And it is certain that deceleration of the stream takes place in some part of the region in front of the stone, which would assist a salmon in stemming the current. Yet it is quite common for a salmon to lie against the side of a rock with its tail and part of its body in the lee of the obstruction, that is to say, slightly across the direction of the flow of water.

However obscure be the law governing the changes in direction or speed of the current in these circumstances, you may be perfectly sure a salmon takes full advantage of them. Salmon lie in

G

front of, or behind, or just at the edge of, a large rock. But the swirl or "V" caused by this obstruction is carried some distance downstream before it reaches the surface and, therefore, in estimating the true position of the rock, due allowance ought to be made for the speed and depth of the water passing over the top of it.

Along the edge or at the *cheek* of a stream or area of fast water is a likely spot for a salmon. In the slack edge of a really-fast and broken run, pouring out from the pool above, fish will, under circumstances best known to themselves, take freely; but, as a rule, there is only one side from which they can be fished for with any hope of success. This is possibly due to them lying only on one side of the stickle and being unwilling to follow the fly across; or because the fly cannot be presented in the right manner and held in position long enough for the fish to come up and *fasten*. This could only be a very special condition, as I have come across several heavy runs through which a fish has been quite keen enough to chase a fly. These heavy runs are not really worth fishing, until the water has *fallen in* and salmon have nothing to hope for, until the next spate brings a promise of freedom restored. Right in the current that turns towards one bank and flows gently round again is a fine place for a taking fish. Other spots are where the current, in the form of a crinkling of the surface, is suddenly generated, so to speak, and then bends or spreads into the draw of water at the tail; where the main current sweeps past a point above a little bay of slack water; and, provided there is depth of water, just below the point where the main stream comes across and hits a rock-wall. Fish often choose to lie in the area at the bend of a river and generally where a brook flows in; and are definitely held up for some length of time by the junction of a large tributary with the main, as though they were unable to make up their minds in which stream they were hatched.

The spreading tail of a long pool is sure to hold fish, unless there is some cause of which we are ignorant that makes it unsuitable. And, above all, remember that it is always worth-while fishing beyond the *draw* into the broken water below, especially when fish are running, or during hot summer evenings, when they will drop back until they are half in the rough, and also into the shallows, in order to secure more oxygen from thin and well-aerated water. Just behind the neck of a gourd-shaped pool, particularly if there are rock-slabs at that point and the river-bed shelves gently away to the lower half of the pool. In cold weather, during February and March, the deep dead pools are exclusively chosen as resting-places; but all positions taken up by salmon depend, to a very large extent, *upon the season of the year and upon the weather.*

All these places can, to a great extent, be spotted from the bank; the following, however, require a more intimate knowledge of the water, preferably acquired in times of drought. Salmon dislike lying on sand, mud and shifting gravel. They prefer to rest on flat slabs of rock or on a rocky bottom, if the latter provides them with shelter. A ledge in a rocky pool is a favourite lie, especially if the rocks are "skerry" or flat ridges arranged in layers. Another place is where the pool slides down into depth and convenient slabs of stone are present.

Do not be deceived by the pace of a run. The speed of the water beneath it and near to the river-bed is much slower and is probably much retarded by large boulders. The fish are not actually stemming the current at all, but are safely lying in the cheeks of the stream and in the shelter of the rocks and only enter the rough water when the game is afoot. And it is surprising to find, when she *falls in* and the fish in a pool can clearly be seen, how easy it is for a salmon to lie in the heavy *draw* of a pool, through which the river descends with power enough to make wading in it far from a simple matter. Yet a fish appears to use no effort at all in maintaining its position on or in the shelter of a rock, or upon large-sized gravel that affords no protection and, therefore, offers no respite from the labour of fighting the current. This, however, is an observation extremely hard to make, except in gin-clear waters, like those of the Aberdeenshire Dee. The shelter of a rock persists a considerable distance downstream; and that explains why a fish is able to lie in a place apparently unprotected from the force of the stream.

## In Times of Drought

As soon as the river falls below summer level, salmon move towards the middle of the shrunken stream in search of shelter and the necessary oxygen that the shallow edges no longer hold in solution. Also, they drop back into the draw of a pool, so that half the body is over the sill and is resting in the rough water, or make their way up to the thin sparkling water in the neck. There will they lie, particularly in the early days of autumn, with their backs almost out of the water; and, on a warm evening, it is always worth casting a fly into all the tiny pockets and stickles that are as rungs in a ladder to an ascending fish. These places ought always to be searched in times of very bright sunshine and low water at the back-end of the season, because salmon are then very apt to work well up the pool in readiness for the next stage of the journey. Fish the runs and stickles that in days of drought pass muster for the throats of the regular pools. The smallest run may be an attraction to a salmon cruising about dusk in search of well-aerated water.

This habit of salmon making an evening tour of a pool is very noticeable in days of low water and should be carefully studied. The area where the fly is should, therefore, be watched assiduously for the least sign of a flash, as a fish turns towards the fly or away from it. If the salmon refuses, I believe it to be a sign that the right moment has not yet arrived and that the best policy is to wait fifteen minutes or so before fishing again in the same pool. In the meantime, try another place, preferably where there is a little more stream.

### In Rising Water and Flood

The first half-hour or so after the water has begun to rise is traditionally a deadly period for salmon; and this time tradition is right! You will naturally go on fishing, until you find the salmon are not to be raised and the spate has definitely taken charge of the river. Chaytor's advice "On a rise in water—Go at once to fish all the places where lately it was too low to fish" is very sound.

When the river is dropping, but is still running bank-high, salmon will rest and often be hooked close in to the bank. As a rule, I prefer to fish the inside of the curve, as this offers thin and sheltered water to the salmon and an easy place for the fly to come round. Search very carefully the region inside the line of the fast current at a bend of the stream. This area is well-defined by two or three tiny walls of water pressed, as it were, towards the less troubled bay. Salmon often lie in the quiet water at the cheek of a current, if there is not too much depth. I have not found deep water suitable to a resting fish, unless the river is very cold.

The thin water at the tail of a pool also holds fish for a short period in their upward journey, especially if they have been running through heavy rapids and are very tired. They usually show in the rough at the very tail of the pool, often leap again just after they have entered the pool and are very likely to take a well-placed fly. You will probably be able to recognize these travelling fish by the poor fight they put up. In rocky pools salmon lie close in and rest on the slabs within a foot of the edge, just as they rest during a spate in places where normally you would wade ankle-deep or even where it would be dry land.

A good working-rule is to fish the flats rather than the regular pools; the former are far more productive and, on Association waters, are less likely to be in demand. And it is far better to fish the smooth glassy glides than the rough dubs and the broken stickles. In some instances, the current of a stream, as it is ebbing, swings across from the centre of a pool and hits the bank; this will alter the fishing qualities of the water and change the lies and taking-areas.

## In Time of Flood

I have been unable to obtain any evidence of the occupation of salmon during the height of a spate. Do they take advantage of the water and run up, as though there were no force in the current to hinder them? Or do they await the fall in level and the arrival of conditions that to us would undoubtedly be easier? Observations I have made from spate to spate were apparently contradictory at first; because one was apt to count the old fish with the new. In late years, I have looked more closely at the salmon I have seen show in the flooded pools and have come to the conclusion that old fish move slowly and without much enthusiasm. Those of us who are fishing some two or three score of miles from the limit of tidal water know well the joy with which we go home in the evening with the news that fresh fish are already up from the sea. It is an event in itself, comparable to the catching of a salmon. Those fish move fast enough without a doubt and are exceptionally bad takers; but, if you hook one at all, it is almost sure to be in a flat and not in a pool. I am thinking at the moment of the habits of fish in the upper reaches during a spate. Nearer to the sea, salmon are always more ready to take, although on the Annan fish run up on a high spate for several miles without looking to right or left, so that the lowest pools are left practically without any stock. It all depends on local conditions, the time of year, the temperature of the air and the water and upon some instinct of the fish.

As soon as the flood has begun to subside and the water to clear, a good fisherman has no need of any dove to tell him that the time has arrived to search thoroughly the edges of the river. This will probably mean fishing where, a day or two earlier, it was dry land, where grew mimulus, horsemint and other flowers that add their sweetness to the wonder of the river. The river will, at first, be turgid, but will, possibly, fine down in twenty-four hours to high water with a slightly-muddy tint; this is a favourable time for angling, as resting fish, not those you see leaping in midstream, will be close to the bank.

The presence of peat-staining generally means that fish are put off the take for two or three days, the duration depending on the extent of the peat-mosses, the intensity of the staining, the size of the flood and the time of year. On some occasions, there is high clear peat-water; on others, a mixture of washings from road and land with the peat colours the river a turgid yellow. As long as peat-water is present, there is little prospect of sport.

Early in the season, during a flood or a marked rise in river-level due to snow-water, which is often clear, salmon are to be caught in *dead* pools and in *dead* water, that is, outside the stream, in holes where there is scarcely any movement in the water, and in backwaters. It is not worth fishing in springtime near the stream.

It is one thing to hook a fish soundly and quite another to land it in time of flood. The only safe tactic to employ is to play the fish on as short a line and in as confined a space as you can. Let the salmon once get into the centre of the pool and it will ally itself to the racing flood and between them they will be more than a match for your tackle, no matter how strong it be. Use side-strain to turn the fish towards your bank, if it starts to run; hold it, as a last desperate measure, hard up against the bank, if you have a gillie or a friend with you who can gaff it

out for you, while it is held fast there. Once the salmon has got
into the draw of the pool and you cannot follow it down, the
game is as good as over. The last resort but one is give it a
slack line, but I doubt whether in a very strong flood a frightened
fish could help going down with the current. A better plan is
to lower the rod, hold the line firmly and walk slowly backwards.
Handlining will bring most fish to the bank, if the tackle does
not give.

Travelling fish appear to ascend through the heavy water in
shoals. They show at a gut in the river-bed, at a bend, in an area
of rough water or in a throat below a pool. It often pays, when
you see a number of salmon running through one pool, to go at
once and fish a convenient draw at the tail of an upper pool,
just where it runs into the throat. This is the kind of place that
one or two of the shoal might choose as a resting-place; and all
fish are likely takers as they enter a fresh pool. If the entrance
is narrow, so much the better; but the water will probably be
much more difficult to fish.

## In Days of Low Water

As the year moves on there will come a time when there is
no longer any current to keep the fly fishing and the line taut
and moving round towards the angler's own bank. The fishable
area has shrunk to the runs, of which there are in some
waters all too few. This is where the man who takes out
his ten-foot trout-rod scores, more frequently in the evening,
it is true.

A most fruitful time of day for low-water fishing with sunk
fly is the hour of dusk and the first hour of night, provided the
air is warmer than the water. Choose some small stickle leading
to a main pool, which several salmon are known to frequent and
cast into the stickle as well as out into the pool, wherever there is
enough current from the run to make the fly work. I do not advise
beginning in such a place, until it is certain you can wave the
rod over your head without a risk of being seen by the salmon
lying in the neighbourhood.

Be sure, in making a choice of your fishing venue, that the
moon is not behind your hand (whether it is hidden by a cloud
or is unobscured, it is equally noxious) and that you will not be
silhouetted against the evening light. A dark background of trees

is very welcome on evenings, when the clear and thin water allows the fish to see everything going on around them.

On sunny days I am sure it pays to get down to the riverside as early as possible in the morning, say half-past eight, Summer Time, so that advantage may be taken of any pools over which a shade is thrown by trees growing near to the water's edge.

What has been written above refers to open pools; fish lying in broken water or in stickles are affected in a different way. On several occasions, I have been surprised at taking a salmon on an exceptionally bright day when the sun was standing high, by casting a small dark fly across a stickle or into the thin clear water of the little runs at the head of a pool.

A salmon-fisherman well acquainted with the river he is fishing generally has the choice of trying for a known or for an unknown fish; that is, he may cast for a salmon he has seen that day or previously, he may fish the lodge he knows salmon are accustomed to occupy, or he may, as often happens in the spring-time when salmon show very little, be obliged to fish the quiet areas in the pools systematically and "on spec", much as a trout-fisherman does when he is "fishing the water".

## The Height of Water

Every river that fortune or goodwill has allowed me to fish I have found to possess certain marks sacred to those anglers who live by the banks of or who are able to fish regularly their favourite streams. A mark in this sense may be a stone, a tree-trunk, or the end of a wall that projects into the water; or it may take the form of a change in the direction of the current; but all of them have the same function, namely to tell the fisherman the height of the river or, viewed in the other way, to indicate where salmon are likely to take and roughly what size of fly to use. A mark may also denote the position of a "catch" or particular spot on the bank of a pool from which to cast. The most accurate kind is the water-gauge, an example of which is to be seen in front of Spey Bridge near Grantown; this in a cold unsympathetic way will tell the angler the exact height of the water in feet and inches. Without an accurate gauge, however, it is impossible to conduct investigations of real value into the relation of the temperature and height of water with the willingness of salmon to take a fly.

8 Difficult wading

9    A fine 36lb. cock fish from the River Avon

10 & 11  Spey casting

12   Time for fishing; the River Tweed in February

13   Time for fishing; low water on the River Garry, Perthshire, in August

At the moment I have in mind the kind of mark that told me what size of fly to tie on; such is the "salmon-stone" in front of Carrog Bridge on the Welsh Dee. When the river was running high enough to cover the stone, but clear enough for me to see the top of it through the water, I knew from experience there was a good chance of a fish, if I used a large fly in the edges or cheeks of the main current and in the resting-places frequently occupied by travelling salmon. As soon as the river had dropped, so that the top of the stone showed above the water, I knew that a large fly, such as 2/0 or 1/0, was the proper size to put up and that only the high-water pools would be then worth searching; and so on until the level of the water at the stone told me which pools were then in ply and which would have too little stream in them for ordinary wet-fly fishing. During my first visit to another river I was told a long deep pool did not fish properly, until the main current at a certain point deserted its central course and, striking diagonally across the river, hit the bank close to a low overhanging bush. I recall other examples from the first-mentioned river; the pool that was only worth fishing when the first of a group of stones put out its head from the water and was of little value when the whole group had appeared; and also the long shelving pool with a pronounced shingle-beach, by the width of which I could judge with considerable accuracy the right size of fly to employ.

It is clear, therefore, that the level at which a river runs and the quality (as well as the colour) of the water are matters closely bound up with success and failure in salmon-fishing. Equally important is it for the angler to observe the rising and the falling of a river, so that, from the outset, every opportunity should be taken of forming the habit of noticing them. Further, these marks tell a man who is familiar with the river, where it is safe to wade and whether he may at any point attempt to cross to the other bank.

The foregoing refers to a stream, swollen with rain and definitely known to be above its normal height for the time of year; it often happens, though, that a river begins to rise as one is fishing and it is part of a salmon-angler's education to learn how to spot it, since the finest of sport may often be obtained during the first half-hour of the rise in water-level. But afterwards, during the rise and until the river has settled down to a steady height, fishing is likely to be unproductive. It is quite easy to cultivate a habit of watching the river for signs of rising or falling, until this branch of watermanship becomes instinctive.

Here are a few hints that will make it easier to keep a check on the level of the river. As soon as you reach a pool, take particular note of the margin of the water and see whether the edge of the water, where it embraces a small pebble, appears to have shrunk back within itself, forming a tiny wave that has failed to roll forward and has expended part of its energy in swelling upwards, until its top is almost convex; this is a sure sign of rising water.

A rise in water after a prolonged drought is well marked on the shingle of a pool, as the river will be flowing over a strip of bleached stones which, a day or two before, were lying naked under the sun. As the river clears, you will see deposited on these stones fine brown *detritus*, brought down by every flood, as part of the process of denudation and rebuilding. And, if you are curious enough to look under some of these stones, you will be surprised at the way the long-barren area has received back again its population, caddis and loaches predominant among them.

If, however, you fail to find any direct evidence of a rise in the water, make a mental note of the height of the river, using as your mark a stone, a submerged limb of a tree, or some other convenient object; or force a stick into the bed of the river or within the fissure between two stones, until the notch cut in its bark is level with the surface of the water. Care should be taken to select a mark sheltered from any waves that might be raised by the wind, as their action would soon destroy all the value of the stone or stick as a water-gauge. It is extraordinary how simple all this is in practice and how useful are the results, both on the actual day and for purposes of comparison afterwards. Every fisherman ought to make a habit of marking the height of the water at a certain point, so that he may keep in touch with the river from day to day and judge the size of fly to use and where fish will probably be lying.

Very often one can distinctly feel the water, when it rises rapidly, creeping up the waders and, if trout have previously been taking the natural fly freely, it is quite certain they will suddenly leave off feeding.

The way in which a river like the Wharfe will come down in sudden spate, carrying all before it, is well known. The water comes down in a wall as solid as the bore or "eagre", which, sweeping up the Trent, denotes the return of *Aegir*, the ancient god of the Norseman, to his Mercian dominions. One is prepared for that emergency after a cloud-burst on the moors; but the stealthy and silent rising of a great salmon-river is just as dangerous to an angler, who has incautiously adventured himself upon a "whaleback" surrounded by deep water.

The height of a river will remain near to its peak, for a greater length of time than it otherwise would, if there is near to the river's source a lake that acts as a reservoir and holds back a part of the heavy surface-drainage of the upper basin. If, during the days succeeding the spate, there is a strong wind against the stream, the storing-power of the lake is considerably increased and the river will run for some time at an even level and then drop very slowly; this is a very happy arrangement both for the salmon and for the angler. The fish find good and dependable "running-water", which gives them every chance to distribute themselves evenly over a wide stretch of the river; and it greatly extends the period during which the pools remain in good order.

## Wading

*In an unknown river, always use a staff when wading; if, also, the river is in high flood, do not wade at all.* The depth of clear water is often very deceptive. On the other hand, the ruffle of the water due to the wind or mud-staining during the early days of a spate may hide pike-holes, knife-edges, or difficult rocks, the presence of which you could not suspect. A series of knife-edges is the most treacherous form of river-bed you are likely to meet. The water has, in past ages, cut through a system of laid rocks, thereby exposing the edges of the *laminæ*, which most dangerous when they are canted obliquely downstream and invite a man to step on them, but allow him no foothold to prevent him sliding off into deep water. Further, it is characteristic of these rocks to be undercut. If you are wading out into a river and encounter a band of rocky bottom covered by little more than shoal water, exercise the utmost care at every step and use a wading-staff to help in sounding the depths all round you. The presence of cleft rocks or boulders, in the gap between which it is

very easy for your brogues to slip, is another danger, especially
when there is a strong stream pressing at your back, or when
a boulder to which you have entrusted your weight betrays you
and rolls over. I have been unable to make up my mind which
feature of the middle Spey I disliked the more : the boulders
that held my brogues firmly wedged, as though in a blacksmith's
vice, so that I floundered in the water and at times almost sat
down, or the washing away of the sand and fine gravel from
under my feet, while a treacherous current conducted an insidious
attack by pressing steadily against the back of my knees in the
hope of lifting my legs from under me. The force of a river is
one thing, but the part of the body where it presses is quite
another; and under the knees is the very devil!

Sometimes a good knowledge of a river makes it possible to
wade into and fish a pool in floodtime that, from soundings with
the foot close to the bank, appears far too deep. There is a scour
near to the bank, but beyond it there extends downstream,
parallel to the bank, a "whale-back", along which a fisherman
can wade in safety. But should he wish to come ashore to adjust
tackle or to play a salmon, he must remember not to strike straight
across the deeper portion behind him; otherwise he will be sure
to ship some water over the wader-tops and possibly be washed
over. The way out of the water is downstream along the "high
ground", until he reaches the "col" connected with the bank.

There is little point in wading out to a greater depth than will
assist a fisherman in covering the salmon-lies efficiently and with
greater ease. The whole object of getting into the water is to clear
obstacles in the back-cast and to cover a fish without using a
long line, or one that is too far off to reach from the bank, even
with a long line; it enables an angler to fish more effectively
and often to present a fly in several different ways to the same
salmon.

During the first two or three days of a flood, much *débris*
comes down and you will probably think it barely worth while
fishing, until the river is clear of it. The rising water carries a
short distance, and a quick fall in level leaves stranded, many
derelict branches, as large as saplings, that a more prolonged flood
would have carried seawards; and a succeeding flood completes
the work. It needs but a moderate rise in level for the river to
bear down the flotsam left behind; and this arrives in the lower

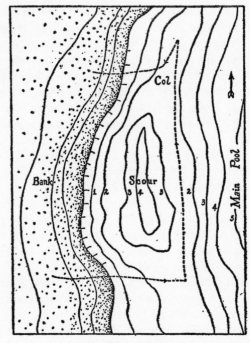

FIG 63   WADING
The dotted line denotes the track of the wader. To come into the
bank across the scour is to ship water over the waders and perhaps
to invite disaster

reaches, at a time when the water is beginning to fall. The fisherman is thus taken unawares and may be struck in the back by
one of these large branches, before he has any reason to expect
the danger. I have had two narrow escapes from being knocked
over by stray trees floating down and have made a habit during
a flood of occasionally looking upstream for their approach. Also,
look out for ice floes during springtime fishing.

The crossing of a river, when it is running high, demands much
courage and experience. Do not attempt a passage unless you
have a staff or a stout stick cut from out of the hedgerow, to act
as a prop on the lee-side of your body; and it is foolhardy to
start, unless you know approximately where to expect the deepest
part of the crossing. What chances, after all, will you have of
getting across, if you find yourself compelled to get on to tip-toe

(a fatal thing in fast water and when the bed is uneven or rock-strewn) and the worst part is still to be reached? When the wise man finds this happening, he turns back, seeks another ford, or gives the venture up. While you are crossing, turn the side of the body to the force of the stream and work slightly upwards, as this will allow you to lean against the water and increase your steadiness; only move one foot when the other is *firmly* planted. If you have an inexperienced or weaker companion with you who wishes to cross, wade just above him with your inside arms across each other, so that your body deflects the full force of the current and, if no staff is available, instruct him to carry the rod horizontally in both hands to act as a balancing-pole.

Take great care as soon as you have traversed a strong current and are entering a zone of quieter water. Your foot apparently weighs so little in water, that with the resistance of the stream gone you are, in taking a step, apt to kick out rather violently and, if your foot strikes a big stone, over you go!

It is very bad practice to wade, when no wading is needed, and especially to wade right on top of salmon. I have often noticed anglers, in certain pools well known to me, wading down a pool along the edge of which fish are wont to lie. In such places, do not enter the water, but, first of all, search the nearest zone of water by casting a short line from the bank. Work down the pool in this way and then enter the water and fish the remaining area.

To summarize: in wading the most vital points to remember are: Use a staff in an unknown river, especially when it is in flood. Never move when you are fishing out a cast: fishing and wading deserve separate and exclusive attention. Keep an eye well-cocked for floating branches and for a rise in the river. Crossing a swollen river is not lightly to be undertaken. Enter the water warily and know exactly how you can best get out of it.

## The Fishing-Log

Opposite is the form of fishing-log I use. I treat it purely as a record of success and failure; as a clearing-house of ideas that occur to me the season through; and as a record of the times, ways and places of the taking of fish. I have noted down the height and condition of the river and anything that might serve

| Date | River | Pool | Lure | Fish | Weight | Remarks |
|------|-------|------|------|------|--------|---------|
| 20.6.68 | *Dee* | *Willow* just above wicket-gate, on far side L. | Turkey *Jackson* 2/0 14' Split bamboo 12 lb. B.S. | Salmon 37 ♂ | 20 lb. 8 oz. 1530 to 1551 | Dull with bright intervals, but there was a little mist clinging to the hills all morning; this went away later. No fish had been showing in any of the pools. It grew much warmer in the afternoon. Water lower today (up to an inch below the salmon-stone); yellowish but much clearer. No foam coming down. Conditions very like those of 7/7/62 when I got a fish in Little Pool, so I put on same size of fly. Saw a distinct flash and tightened; did not feel a pull. Fish did not fight well at first, as it would come close in to me. Much helped afterwards by the current. Condition first-rate; gill-arches very pink; no parasites; small "seal-mark" under chin; and small hook. George (the bailiff) came along, as I was leaving, to say two fish had been taken in Top Pool on a spoon; evidently salmon like something more showy there than in the Willow. They were taken at 1515 and 1540. Pied Flycatcher has arrived after all; heard but could not spot Grasshopper Warbler. An awkward branch in Enchanted Wood Pool ought to be sawn off; it stops back-swing in spinning. |

Length: 40″
Girth: 18″
Scale-result: 2·3+
Temperatures: Air   at 09.30 hours 65°
            Water  at 09.30 hours 56°

gaffed by self

to identify a subsequent set of circumstances with those then present, my idea being to try and discover why salmon should take on some occasions and at other times refuse. Whenever similar entries are made by those fishing up and down the same river, it will often be well worth taking the trouble to find out and compare those experiences with your own.

In making entries in a fishing-log do not stint yourself in the matter of space or detail. The description of an incident, written shortly after it has happened is always more valuable, as well as more vivid, than your recollection of it, put on paper, some years afterwards. Make a record of the bank from which you were fishing when the salmon was taken; this is judged by turning your back to the source of the river and looking towards the mouth and recorded as L. or R.

If you hear an interesting angling experiment retailed by the riverside, or a trick that might help you to fish better or to improve your tackle or your technique in any branch of the wide subject of fishing, write it down in your log in full detail, so that other men may benefit.

### Recovering a Fly from a Tree

Whenever I hear a fisherman talk of rescuing a fly from the

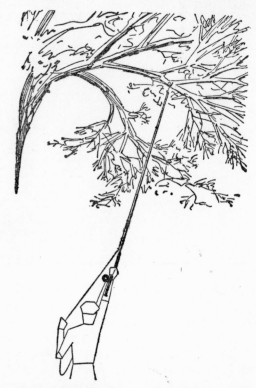

FIG 64   RECOVERING A FLY FROM A TREE

topmost branches of a tree, my mind instinctively turns to a
painful incident that happened to me on an otherwise delightful
morning. I had been disgracefully broken by a fish through
striking too hastily and was vowing to make a better show of it
next time. When, as ill-fortune had it, a small piece of a common
alga green flannel weed floated against the line, this so much
astonished me that I struck violently again and flicked the fly
up into the branches of an over-hanging tree. The rod was put
on the bank, while I surveyed the position of the fly. As soon as
I was satisfied that I might succeed in extracting it, I took up
the rod and then dropped it with extraordinary alacrity, for with
the cork handle I had included in my grasp a wasp, which quite
rightly resented the treatment. I also was very much hurt at the

reward dealt out to me for the exercise of most commendable
patience in recovering the fly! However, the fly did at length
come away from the branch as soon as I had pulled the line
through the rings, until the tip could reach the fly, so that by
keeping the line taut, I could lift the hook off the twig that
was holding it.

The trick will only succeed when the tip of the rod will reach
as far as the fly. If the rod is not long enough to unhitch it point
the former towards the snag, draw the line taut and pull on it
slowly, until the fly comes away, the twig breaks or is bent low

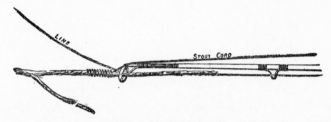

FIG 65    The forked stick is held in the top by tension on the
cord until it is placed in position

enough for you to get hold of it, or the cast snaps. This handling
is more effective than straining with the rod and does little harm
to any of the tackle.

If the fly is within reach of the rod, but will not yield to the
lifting of the rod-point, cut a small forked-stick, leaving one leg
of it longer than the other. To the middle of the long leg tie a
length of stout string, pare the end of this leg until it fits in the
top-ring of the rod and place the crook of the stick over the
branch on which the fly or bait is fast. As soon as the hook is
in position, take away the rod and haul on the string, until the
branch is depressed far enough for you to reach it.

A projecting bush on the angler's own side which hangs low
down, almost to the surface of the river, often catches an ill-
thrown fly or bait. The best method of recovery is to tie a stick
or bottle on a bight of the line, allow it to float downstream,
pick it up below the bush and then pull from that side. This
generally succeeds, where a direct pull would have only tightened
the hold on the hook.

H

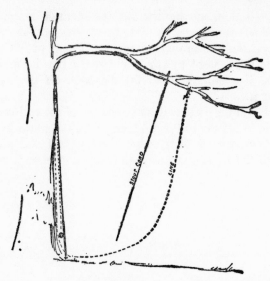

FIG 66   The branch is pulled down by means of the cord until the fly can be reached

Whenever your fly or bait is held up in some snag, do not start pulling hard, until you have sat down and thought out the problem. There is in these difficulties much room for ingenuity. But, if there is another who wants the use of the pool, do not disturb the water without his consent. Very often it will be better sportsmanship to break the line and lose the bait or fly.

*Salvage*

A very ancient way of releasing a bait from the bed of the river, where it had become entangled, was an iron ring large enough in diameter to pass over the rod, which was tied to a length of strong cord. The ring was allowed to slide down the line and, as soon as it reached the obstruction, the cord was pulled until the snag gave way.

The modern way, when all other forms of persuasion have failed, is to try and float it off. An empty bottle, well-corked, is tied by a noose to the line and allowed to float past the point where the bait is held; it may be necessary in order to get a direct pull downstream, to throw the bottle well beyond the snag. In a very strong stream and if the bait is only lightly hooked, the

bottle-trick will often succeed; but as a rule it fails, because there
is not enough resistance offered by the bottle to produce the
required pull to effect a release. Instead of the bottle I have used
a stone, which I have attached to the line with a running noose
and have thrown it across and beyond the snag. A sharp pull
on the line will sometimes loosen the bait, when the stone is on
the far side of it.

It is a good rule to try to get a strain on the line from the
opposite bank and therefore the arrival of anglers on the other
bank ought to be hailed with delight, because it is a comparatively simple feat for one of them to throw a fly or, better still,
a minnow or spoon, across your line, draw it in to their side and
pull the bait away from the rock or whatever the snag may
happen to be.

As soon as you realize you are fast in a rock, let out some
slack until there is a good bight in the line downstream and by
giving several sharp tugs at the line see whether the head of water
will release the bait. Do not try a direct pull that may destroy
all hope of your succeeding when other methods are brought into
play. If you are forced to break, make a mental note of the
approximate distance the snag is from the opposite shore and try
to get two objects that will give you a line on it, so that you will
stand a chance of recovering the bait when the water has fallen
far enough to enable you to wade across and search for it. It is
not worth risking a soaking or worse in attempting to cross a
swollen river.

One day I was held fast by a particularly tenacious rock and
found myself without the customary length of string. Accordingly

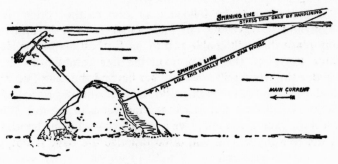

FIG 67   THE OTTER IN ACTION

I placed a small branch of a tree athwart the line and floated it down below the snag, so that a pull might be administered to the minnow. I succeeded so well that it was but a small step to the adaptation of the poacher's "otter" to serve the same purpose. This consisted of a short piece of driftwood to which a piece of smooth cord was tied. In the end of the cord was made a fixed loop which ran upon the line. The cord was so tied on the wood that the fatter end of the branch was nearer to the point of attachment than the other; this ensured the "otter" shooting diagonally across the current as soon as the force of the water pressed upon it. The chief difficulties were at first to prevent the loop being twisted and closing on the line and to ensure the "otter" working in the right direction. The latter was overcome

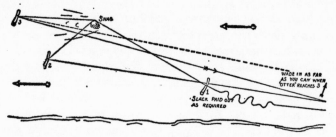

FIG 68    The method of using the Otter seen in plan

by placing the wood carefully in the water in the right way and maintaining a steady pressure upon it while it was travelling. The pinching of the line was partly cured by using thicker cord, although some men have, since then, tried chicken-rings, key-rings, paper-clips and other such devices.

The procedure to be followed, as soon as the "otter" is in position and is travelling out and across, is to walk upstream to any place that will enable you to get furthest across the river, because the more the strain upon the line comes from there, the better the wood will cross and get beyond the snag (see Figs. 67 and 68). The "otter" is then allowed to float down some yards, while line is paid out and eased by undulations of the rod. When you feel the pull of the line, give a good jerk—with the hand, not with the rod-point. This will often dislodge the bait. If not, try all you can to persuade the "otter" to go yet further over and repeat the jerk when the drag on the line reaches your hand.

The weight and length of the wood are important items, as they must be adjusted to the flow of the river at the time. A heavy "otter" in floodtime will strain a line beyond recovery; a light and short one where there is only a slack current will present adequate surface to the water.

By this method and by adapting it to circumstances, I have accomplished some extraordinary feats of salvage; and all the fishing friends to whom I have explained the technique have had similar success.

## CHAPTER EIGHT

# SUNK-FLY FISHING

*Introduction*

BEFORE the advent of floating-line fishing, dry-fly and very fine low-water fishing, the accepted method of fly-fishing for salmon was one which demanded a river flowing at a minimum level, and equipment suitable for these conditions, i.e. all the heavy wet-fly tackle still thought by many to be essential to the sport, and a fair knowledge of where fish might reasonably be expected to lie and to take. In trout-fishing terms, it was wet-fly fishing downstream and largely "chuck-and-chance-it". It is still in wide use today, and in certain conditions and in some rivers it is the only practicable method of fishing for salmon with the fly, especially in the early part of the season. But to digress for a moment.

*Fishing a Pool*

Imagine you are sitting on a rough seat by the waterside in the company of a beginner and of another angler, who has promised to guide him through the early stages of learning to fish for salmon. The latter is tying on a fly and explaining why this particular pool has been chosen, as one well suited to a beginner, and exactly how he wishes him to cast and where he thinks a fish ought to be raised.

At the risk of being tedious I will repeat some of the wisdom that was poured into the ear of that novice, as he and his companion sat on the bench in the forenoon of a warm day in June many years ago.

"We are on the right bank of the river," said the seasoned fisherman; "and I chose this side on purpose, because here you will have to fish the water, which is flowing from left to right, left-handed instead of right-handed, which comes more naturally to most men. I have generally found that, when a man gets accustomed from the outset to fish entirely on the left bank, casting over the left shoulder is difficult to get into afterwards. Now for the fly. I have picked out a simple pattern in size No. 2, which is about right for the height and colour of the water, because the river has, after last week's flood, been running for twenty-four hours or so without any noticeable drop in level or 'falling in'. It is first-rate salmon-water and there is a full stock of salmon in every pool and also in the flats. I want you, therefore, to wade in gently and as far up into the neck of the pool as you conveniently can—go as far as you are able without losing your balance in the current—and start casting across the stickle at an angle of forty-five degrees or so downstream."

The novice, accordingly, waded in as he was told and, after drawing off line and working it through the rings, made his first cast across to the slack water on the far side of the main current. The pool was on the narrow side and therefore he could, without spoiling it, fish the whole width at the first time of going down. But he noticed at once that a belly formed in the line immediately it touched the water, which brought back to him the hint, given but a moment before, on the best way of "mending the cast". He had been told to lift the point of the rod and with a twitch cause several yards of the line to fall upstream, so that the belly in it was straightened. By this means the fly was allowed to fish properly and not dragged across the surface of the pool.

The effect of allowing the downstream bow to remain in the cast is discussed elsewhere. He found, however, the current in this particular pool was too strong for the manœuvre to be successful; but he made the discovery that, by throwing a longer line and at an angle that placed it further downstream, there was less tendency for the fly to *skirt*, that is to skid along the top of the water without sinking, and that it would be more likely to go straight under directly it touched the water. His teacher, sitting on the bank, noticed with approval the change of tactics, for it meant that his pupil had the gift, as valuable to a fisherman as to anyone else, of thinking for himself and of acting.

Some men fish a left-handed pool by casting over the right shoulder and then either keep the rod in the right hand or change it over to the left. I think this practice is a mistake, because a belly is thereby put into the line that cannot easily be taken out. But when one is fishing from the right bank, the upstream throw over a favourite lodge or catch is more effective when it is delivered over the right shoulder than when it is made over the left and *vice versa*.

The beginner thus fished down the stretch, moving, as he had been instructed, one step at a time and being extremely careful to fish every cast out fully, before taking a step forward and making a new one. He had been warned of the danger of moving down-stream, while the fly was passing over the fishable part of the pool, because such a movement meant the line would cease to be taut. If a fish should choose at that moment to seize the fly, he would have only a small chance of hooking it.

Thus he continued systematically down the pool, taking care the line should always be free of the handle of the reel, holding the rod in the orthodox fashion and, where he had been previously told there was sure to be a salmon, *hanging* the fly in the current, so that the fish might have every encouragement (see p. 127).

Before beginning he had been advised not to work the fly but to keep the point of the rod steady, while the fly was travelling round in the current, and only to give any motion to the fly, when it had reached a point directly below him and was being allowed to hang there. This was done as a final inducement to a salmon to come up to the fly. More often, however, he allowed the fly to hang and obtain its movements from the stream. A further attempt to persuade a hesitating fish was then made. The fly was drawn up a couple of yards in little jerks, by taking in with the right hand that length of line, before making the next throw. This also helped the recovery of the line.

In this way the whole pool was fished out to the tail, the very end of which, even the rough water just over the sill, might easily prove the only part to yield a fish; but there was no response to the fly, nor did a fish show. He returned, therefore, to the seat to receive the just criticism of his efforts, which he knew was awaiting him.

"I was glad to see," the experienced angler said, "that you took advantage of the passing clouds, when you began to cover the most likely bit of the water; it would have been a pity to have fished that piece with the sun shining down at its brightest. But I think you hardly gave the fish, which is generally to be found lying close under those overhanging trees, a fair chance of securing the fly. I know you cannot cast underneath the branches without running a risk of being caught up in them; but you can fish that part, if you cast a long line well on the upstream side of—in fisherman's language, above—the first of the branches and then trust the current to carry the fly underneath. It entails long and accurate throwing; but this is one of the occasions when it is worth going to the trouble of making a dozen casts or so, because fish that lie in such places are apt to snap at the fly and argue about it afterwards!"

When the learner showed very plainly he was a little disappointed in failing to raise a fish, his companion told him he should find consolation in not having seen a salmon show, for when they do "come on to the take" sport is all the better. A salmon that is disporting itself in a pool is not generally a taking fish.

"Besides," said he, "there are always far more fish in a pool than would be guessed from counting those that actually have shown. At the height of the season, there are certainly five fish in the river for every one that is seen. Few opportunites occur in the rivers of these islands, as they do in those of Canada of counting the actual number of salmon in a pool or stretch; but when conditions make this possible, you will be amazed at the large number present."

He next explained why he thought the occasional upstream cast paid so well. A fly cast upstream to a fish sinks more readily than does one cast downstream, because the latter is being dragged by a cast that is under considerable tension due to the weight of the water and is, therefore, kept near the surface. It searches places denied to the fly fished in the normal manner.

"There might appear," he said, "to be little difference between the fly fished upstream and that which is dragged down by the belly in a line; but the essential difference is that one is swimming down and a little across at approximately the same pace as the current, while the other is being dragged rather more across than downstream, and at a speed far greater than that of the river. And, further, the attractiveness of a fly, intentionally pulled through the water across a salmon's nose, consists largely in the speed, which makes the fish think it is going to lose its prey. This is quite different from the *drag* of a taut line pulling a fly skidding across the surface of the water.

"I see," continued the experienced angler, "that you are proposing to sit here, smoke a pipe and give the pool a rest. I do

not believe in hammering the fish too much, but I am sure you
will stand an excellent chance, if you go in again at the top and
go down the stretch again carefully. See the point of your hook
is still there—I should not otherwise change the fly—and fish
just as eagerly and keenly as though you were going down the
pool for the first time. Watch the water, the surface as well as
the region a little beneath and you may see the cast draw as a
fish takes, or spot the flash of a fish turning away or passing
near the fly to make an inspection. And if you should fail to raise
the fish I saw show its nose just now in a very hopeful way, you
can leave it and come again and see whether 'such a change may
have come o'er the spirit of his dreams as will give you cause for
joy'."

## Hooked!

It was very fortunate that the beginner looked at the fly, for
he had been fishing part of the pool with a broken hook-point.
This had clearly been caused by allowing the line to go too far
behind him during the back-cast. The fly had touched a stone
and the point of the hook had snapped off without making the
little tinkling crack that usually gives the angler warning. The
fly was quickly changed for one similar in size and pattern; and
he began fishing the water above the spot where the salmon had
been seen. If it is true, as my experience leads me to think, that
a salmon, which has risen, is cruising about the pool; it may be
some little distance from the spot where it showed, by the time
the angler can get his fly there. It is always better, therefore, to
start higher up, in order to make sure of covering the salmon,
for, even if it has moved lower down the pool than the place
where it rose, the angler is creating a sort of screen between it
and its lodge, so that it is almost bound to see the fly. One does
not want to run the risk of putting the fly right on top of the
salmon; it is therefore better to bring it, cast by cast, nearer to
the place where the fish showed.

Step by step, the fisherman brought the fly nearer to the place
where the salmon had shown and, just as he had reached a
point from which he was covering the lie, he was observed to
draw the rod firmly back over his left shoulder, until it arched
beautifully under the strain of a heavy fish. He immediately placed
the butt of the rod against the top of his left thigh, slipped his

left hand up to the extreme edge of the cork-grip and started to back slowly out of the pool. For an instant, the fish lay inert and unresisting, as though it did not yet realize that the hour had come for it to fight for its life. Then it turned and went downstream at a tremendous rate, taking out line rapidly, right down to the backing, while the angler was anxiously making his way backwards out of the pool trying to keep the line as taut as he could. He had been specially warned that, on hooking a fish, his first care should nearly always be to get out of the river. If the river is in flood it is dangerous to remain in heavy water, while you are straining against a fighting fish. You may have to follow a fish and should at once get ashore, so that you may be ready for this manœuvre. Whichever way a fish moves, it is good tactics to keep opposite; this can best be done by walking up and down the bank and swinging the rod-point inland and slightly downstream, so that side-strain is applied with the shortest possible line. On the whole the danger of having the line drowned is less, when you are on the bank, especially a high one; and this is worth some consideration, because a drowned line frequently means a lost fish.

There is a tremendous advantage in knowing beforehand where and when a salmon is likely to take a fly; although every fisherman, at first, feels on that account a kind of nervous excitement, which can only be controlled by experience and firm determination to be absolutely calm when the moment comes to tighten on the fish. Some salmon, when they take the fly, do so in a violent manner that, on occasions, upsets the nerves of even the most expert fishermen; but it will be discovered that every season brings its increase in calmness and the realization that normally the hook will go well home without any conscious effort on the angler's part. The true advantage lies in being able to take the precaution of seeing that the line is clear of the reel-handle and of adjusting the hold of the finger upon the line so that a sudden strain may not break the latter. And remember that as soon as a salmon has recovered from the shock and surprise of being hooked and decides to run for it, allow it to do so, because this is the essence of the game itself, is very tiring to the fish and "is doing your business for you". The exceptions to this rule rarely occur.

In the tail of the pool the fish jumped into the air; the angler responded by lowering the point of the rod, so that the hook should not be torn out nor the line broken, should the salmon in descending fall upon it, when it was under tension. So much line had, in this instance, been taken out, that it was doubtful whether the lowering of the point was really necessary. Save at that moment, the novice was most particular to keep his rod well bent, so that the strain might be maintained and the line kept taut. This should always be done, under the penalty of losing a fish. When you are at the water's level and are following a salmon downstream, keep the rod-point up, even if you should happen one day to have an experience similar to mine, trip on a stone and sit down in the river, with the water up to your armpits! Under those distressing circumstances, you must endeavour to hold the rod-point high, keep a steady strain on the line and all will be well. In the early stages of playing a salmon, see that the rod is well bent; the flexibility of the top will save the cast from sudden strain and the hook-point is bound to keep its hold, as long as the tension of the line is maintained. In playing any game fish, and no doubt many others, even unrelaxed tension is the ideal, but it is sometimes hard to apply.

We left the beginner in the throes of playing his first salmon and, on the whole, dealing very skilfully with it. He had got below the fish, so that it should not have the assistance of being held up against the current, because it is all to the angler's advantage to make the salmon draw heavily on its strength in resisting both the strain of the line and the force of the stream. Also, it is far easier to put side-strain on from below than from above; and side-strain is a most potent and effective weapon in the hands of a capable fisherman (see p. 231).

There was only one snag in the pool that could with certainty be called a danger-point, an overhanging tree, the lower limbs of which had, through the subsidence of the trunk, dipped down into the water and become a menace to any angler who allowed a hooked fish to go inside them, so that the line was entangled, possibly beyond any hope of recovery, or at least long enough for the fly to lose its hold through the struggling of the fish. The novice had been duly warned of this snag and, rather than hazard in such a jungle the first salmon he had hooked, he held on and turned it, when it made as if to go towards the branches, preferring (and I think rightly) to lose a fish through having the cast broken in a good cause than to suffer the ignominy of being hung up in submerged branches and broken. "When a salmon is going," had said his instructor, "either in the direction of a snag, or out of the pool into one below, where it is difficult or impossible to follow, and you have failed to turn it with side-strain or by throwing it slack line, there is only one course left: hold on. Lower the point of the rod, which will materially augment the pull you are able to exert, if the need should arise, hold the rod horizontally and hand-line the salmon, a procedure few fish can withstand for long; and, if any part of the tackle gives and the salmon goes free, I should be willing to bet that the cause would prove to be due to the hook having been torn out of the flesh, having been opened out by the pressure, or having been broken at bend or barb."

The experienced angler stood, gaff in hand, behind his companion and *in low tones* gave him advice that enabled him to bring in the salmon at the right place for gaffing. Here we will take our leave of them and consider in detail several points that have been raised in this section.

## Spring Tactics

If conditions in the early part of the season are such as to require a deeply sunk fly, then the most practical way of fishing it is to use one of the modern sinking lines. These lines go deep and they take a big fly down with them. Their use is, however, limited to the early days of very cold water and weather, just as the modern spinner gives up his very heavy baits as soon as water and air begin to warm up. In the early season, the water is not only cold, but often very heavy. Admittedly the angler does not then fish the fast water, but even the slacker parts are moving much faster than one would think, and, in a river like the Spey, there is a very great weight of water coming down—the angler who has only fished little rivers can have no idea of the force behind such a river.

Now our springer in the early months is a leisurely gentleman, and if he is to take the fly at all, then he requires it to be served up on a plate, so to speak. In others words, the fly must go down to him and swim across his nose within easy taking distance. In many pools fish lie in the slack at the cheek of a stream, and the only successful way to cope with these gentry is to cast into the stream and let the fly fish round into the slack. The problem is to get the fly deep enough.

At this time of year, therefore, fishing resolves itself into (a) fishing as slowly as possible, and (b) as deep as possible. The best answer is to fish as long a line as you can achieve, casting well downstream. After that, it is a matter of faith and hope. Keep slogging away until you feel that beautiful firm, solid, downward pull that only a salmon can give. Then give him what a Speyside ghillie calls "a right bash". Half measures are no use where 4/0 to 6/0 doubles are in use. Bang it into him! Lie back on your big rod, hold the line tight, and double up the rod—a real hefty pull.

## Fishing the Sink-Tip Line

As the water warms up, the sinking line is changed for a floating one which has a sinking tip. This is a much more pleasant line to fish with, as the heavier part—the line being, I advise, a Double-Taper—is floating, and therefore easily lifted for a cast; and, equally important, can be controlled by "mending".

I use a double-hooked fly with a bronzed hook. Bronzed hooks are heavier than black ones and so keep down to the level set by the sink tip. The fly therefore fishes at about the same level as would a wooden minnow.

Fishing in this manner when the water is about 35–45 degrees F. is quite good fun, and is productive. The line can be controlled even though its tip is out of sight. I usually cast downstream at an angle, according to the speed of the current, of from 30–40 degrees. If necessary, I "mend" to keep the line straight, and fish with my rod-point raised to about 45 degrees from the vertical. This gives enough slack line to ensure the hooking of the fish, and is, of course, slack in the air as opposed to slack in the water, which would be the case if the angler was using a Single Taper line, when the rod-point would be kept low.

When the water temperature is in the range 42–48 degrees F. there is often doubt as to the level at which the fly should fish. Personally, I never go over to the fully floating line until I find that other anglers are being successful with it, but continue to fish the sink tip.

Also, when I find that the air is colder than the water, as it sometimes is in June, I bring out the sink-tip line, and I think it pays to do so.

During the spring the average angler is fishing a fair-sized fly, say No. 1 to No. 3, if fish do not respond, he should, I think, cast at a wider angle so that the fly comes faster across the fish.

## Holding the Rod

As soon as a fisherman has completed a cast, he drops the rod into rest with the button against the top of the thigh. If he is fishing on the left bank, he will have made the cast with the right hand leading and will thus naturally place the button against the left thigh, holding it there with the left hand. But the main work of supporting and manipulating the rod and of lifting it in the act of tightening on a fish is performed by the upper hand, which should hold the rod at a point near the top of the cork handle. It will be found quite simple, by holding a loop of line lightly between the index and middle fingers, to exercise the proper measure of control over the running of the line, so that there shall be enough resistance to pull the point of a hook into a salmon's jaw. Alternatively, the line may be controlled most delicately by the disengaged hand. And this is better.

When a fisherman is on the other bank, the principal rôle naturally falls to the left or upstream hand. Some men develop the lazy habit of swinging the rod-point round too quickly; this accentuates the belly in the line, which causes appreciable delay in gaining contact with the fly. The correct presentation of the fly is a very complex matter. The best rule is always to try and judge from the set of the current how best to arrange that the hook shall be pulled into and not out of the mouth of the fish. When the fly has arrived under your own bank, raise the rod a little to avoid the probability of disaster, should the rod through-out its length be pointing directly at the fly, and the compensating action in the top of the rod thus be at zero at the moment when a salmon takes the fly.

## Hanging the Fly

"The place is a favourite and most deadly cast if the fly is allowed to hang beside the current" : in these few words, often I am sure passed unnoticed by most readers. Chaytor gives expression to a great truth worth many salmon the seasons through. I do not know the point in the stream he writes of, but I can see in my mind's eye similar places, where the hanging fly is the deadliest, and on occasions the only, method of raising a fish.

A hanging fly is one that is held by the rod-point and allowed to swing in the play of the stream, or in the gentler current at the cheek of a run. In either instance, the rod should be pushed well out over the river and be kept low; but, as soon as a fly has been hanging half a minute or so at the edge of a stream, the rod should be raised slightly (not higher than to an angle of sixty degrees) and line taken in jerkily, a foot at a time, until two yards of it have been drawn in through the top ring. It is then time to make the next throw and "shoot" the slack line. During the time the fly is darting upstream, a salmon, timid and hesitant before, will often throw all caution aside and take a fly that has already been refused as it came round in the current. If you have failed to raise a salmon from one side, cross over and hang the fly on the other side of the stickle, provided a bridge or a ford make it physically possible to do so and you have the right to fish from the other side. It is usual to find fishing a stickle from one side far easier and more productive than from the other. A fly cast from the wrong side is washed away from a salmon and quickly hidden from its view by the white water; while from the other it is carried to and hangs above the salmon, but this does not apply to the same degree in floating-line fishing.

To fish a fast run properly the fly should be forced down and be made to swim at a good depth, the line being kept as straight as possible. A line thrown across a stickle bellies at once and drags the fly rapidly over the surface, unless it is straightened by lifting the belly upstream by a special movement of the rod-point. (see p. 140). But whenever it can be done and will not disturb the salmon, the better policy is to wade in as far as the edge of the current, where it issues from the pool above, and cover the water by holding the rod well out across it. This solves the problem of sinking the fly and, to a small extent, of controlling its movements. On the whole, I find it pays to put the fly only a short distance beyond the stickle and not to cast into the slack water on the far side of it, unless the fast water is narrow enough to be spanned by the rod; this allows greater control.

14 & 15  Contrasts in water: *above*, spinning on the Yorkshire Esk at Glaisdale; *below*, fly-fishing on the Scottish Dee at Dinnet

16 & 17  Contrasts in water: above, the famous Bridge Pool at Grantown on the Spey; *below*, the River Slaney, Co Wexford, Ireland

## Pulling in the Hook

There is a school of anglers who hold the opinion that fish hook themselves, because the weight of the line and the resistance of the water to it provides force enough to "pull in the iron". It might therefore be deduced that fish are more likely to hook themselves in heavy water than in slack, which is undoubtedly true. And certainly salmon do for the most part hook themselves; but it depends on whether the point comes in contact with a soft part of the mouth, whether the current is powerful enough, what size the fly is, how well-constructed is the barb and how sharp the point. In my opinion, it is abundantly clear that a large hook (No. 1 and bigger) does need some help from the angler in penetrating far enough into the flesh (and sometimes gristle) to secure an adequate hold, that is to go in right over the barb. But, nine times out of ten, the sharp point of all but the larger hooks will go home unaided by the fisherman. In springtime or when the water is high, a large fly is indicated by conditions; this in turn compels the use of a large hook, which needs no little assistance to effect penetration beyond the barb. Nowadays the angler would probably be using the Waddington or other treble-hook fly.

Throughout this book I have adhered to the rule I laid down elsewhere of using "tighten" rather than "strike". The act ought to be deliberate and yet determined and its spirit is well expressed by the description I have adopted. But "strike" calls aloud for sharp, almost violent, action, a fact of which many beginners will bear testimony in the shape of the disasters they attribute directly to the use and influence of the word. So always *tighten sideways and with the point of the rod almost downstream, and above all, wait until you feel the pull.*

In fact, I believe the best advice that could be given, when fishing in clear water, is : if you see a salmon coming to the fly, close your eyes and tighten calmly and sideways when you feel a tug. There is nothing more unnerving than seeing a salmon as it approaches the fly, especially when you are fishing from a rocky ledge into the water below.

Do fish really come short? Or is *feather-drag* due to the fly having at a critical moment been snatched away from the salmon by the angler? Or is it due to bad presentation of the fly? If a

I

salmon takes wholeheartedly without being hooked, reel in and examine the point of the hook. If this is sound, look at the fly and you will often find the ends of the feathers forming the wing well chewed and possibly showing signs of having been nipped by the jaws of the salmon. *Feather-drag*, in this instance, has clearly been caused by a fish having taken endwise-on a fly it has followed; this is incorrect presentation of the fly and, there-fore, the fault of the angler alone. Controlling a sunk fly, so that it shall come broadside-on to the fish, is a far more difficult matter than floating-line fishing. An alternative is to change the fly for one dressed on the same size of hook, but with shorter wings and body, in taking care that no belly that can be straightened shall be allowed to remain in the line and in keeping the rod-point up a little as the fly comes round. If you feel the tug of a fish, swing the rod in towards the bank, preferably on the downstream side, and tighten with deliberation. Above all, *do not strike* !

## CHAPTER NINE

# FLOATING-LINE FISHING

## Introduction

IN the 1930s, when the first edition of this book came out, Floating-Line fishing for salmon—or greased-line as it was commonly called—was synonymous with the Wood technique. This method of fishing still has its adherents, and accordingly a description of the Wood floating-line technique appears later in this chapter, but the majority of salmon fishermen today use developments of pure Wood.

## A Critique of the Wood Technique

That Wood was an able fisherman there is no doubt. He lived on the banks of the Dee during the season and he really studied salmon and their ways. *But*, and it is a big *but*, his beat, Cairnton, was, in his day, probably the most prolific beat in all Scotland. Further, Dee fish are very free-rising, and in my opinion it is the easiest river in which to kill fish. Fresh run Dee fish will "have a go" at nearly any fly presented in almost any way. It is, therefore, the ideal river on which to experiment. Again, Wood had stone jetties built out into the river from which he could cover all the best lies very easily. It was, in fact, the beat of one's dreams.

Starting with this great advantage, Wood developed a technique which killed fish, and, more important, which satisfied himself, and suited his theories. Basically, he liked to show his fly as much sideways as possible to the fish, to let it drift down unchecked, and to let the fish hook itself. All these things could be done at Cairnton, but on heavier water—such as parts of the Spey, for example—they were very difficult to carry out. That is why I, for one, preferred the techniques of Alexander Grant and Percy Laming, with possibly a little of Wood's style used here and there, as occasion warranted.

Wood adopted the floating line in 1903. Percy Laming was

using a floating line in 1897. Alexander Grant was fishing an oiled line even before Laming used grease to float his line.

Wood's technique consisted of a small, single-hooked fly fished just below the surface, and supported by the floating line. He insisted on allowing the stream to hook his fish, and, for that reason, confined himself to single hooks, his idea being that a double-hook would be ejected by the fish before it had taken hold in its mouth.

This method delighted Wood, so much so that he used it even under conditions basically unfavourable to floating line. Fish caught under bad conditions—cold air and water—especially delighted him and he would smile happily as he played the fish! Wood was an artist who liked to do things the hard way.

What do we really owe to Wood? I think we owe several things. Firstly, the publicity which his methods received brought salmon fishermen back to the knowledge, long neglected, that a small fly fished near the surface in summer and in low water would kill fish. Secondly, that salmon could be killed on light rods—Wood's twelve-footers were light, and his casts tapered, in summer, down to 1x. Thirdly, he added a new interest to fishing the fly by developing the *mend* and the *lead*, so making control of the line on the water a very real thing. Fourthly, he produced an artistic way of hooking fish.

But, as I previously mentioned, there are very few Cairntons in the world, and very few anglers with the time available and the enthusiasm to reach Wood's high standard of skill. The well-to-do professional or business man is tied to office, conference or business for some eleven months in the year: how could he hope to equal a man like Wood who lived on the riverbank and fished every day?

So some of us looked for simpler, but effective methods of summer fly fishing. Three methods seemed to fulfil the necessary conditions. These conditions were:

(1)  The fly must fish close to the surface.
(2)  The fly must—except in hot weather—cross the fish slowly.
(3)  Hooking should be as certain as possible.
(4)  The line must be controlled while it was fishing.
(5)  The technique must be reasonably easy to master.

The first method is that which many people have adopted. It consists of a floating line, a three-yard cast and a fly size, say 6 to 10. Personally, I use a short double-hooked fly. The trick in fishing this method is to use a long line, as the longer the line, the slower the fly swings across the river, like a long pendulum. The speed depends also on the angle to the stream at which the fly is cast—in fast water, of course, a more downstream angle than on a slower stream, so as to give a fish time to turn after taking the fly, the angler either (a) holds a yard of loose line under his forefinger which he releases when the fish takes, or (b) keeps his rod-point raised to provide some slack in the air. Both methods are equally effective.

There is also the Laming method of controlled drag and, last but by no means least, Alexander Grant's oiled line technique, the forerunner of them all. These "simpler" methods are described later in this chapter; two of them are older than Wood's system. But both Laming and Grant disliked publicity, and I believe that their highly successful methods were unknown until the publication of *Fine and Far Off* in 1952.

That well-known sportsman the late Ernest Crosfield used to say "if you see your rises in early spring you are fishing too shallow, and if you don't see your rises in summer you are fishing too deep". He used to keep his fly near the surface by pulling in line by hand. This, of course, gave the same effect as floating the line, so far as depth was concerned. He killed hundreds of fish in this way.

Over the years several anglers tried to find ways of dealing with summer fish, and as Wood received most publicity, most anglers tried to imitate his method. But, in actual practice, very few did. Most of them misread his instructions! As I have said, his method was complicated and required a high standard of skill and self-control. Nowadays many people will not take the trouble to learn a difficult art, or have not the time. I am afraid that fishing, like many other things, is becoming mechanized. Personally, I am not attracted by a sport where skill is not needed; that is why I prefer certain ways of fly-fishing to spinning.

So I think we may say that Wood started the floating line as a popular method. It would catch on among south of England fishermen because of its resemblance to dry fly *à la* chalk stream.

In its way, the Aberdeenshire Dee is the chalk stream of Scottish salmon rivers, as—spates excepted—it is gin-clear and comparatively gently flowing. The south country angler is brought-up to regard drag as the ultimate sin, but one of their fraternity thought otherwise, as do Spey salmon. Of this, more anon.

I should like to emphasize the fact that, nowadays, floating line is *the* method once the early months are over, and the water temperature is in the upper forties. But there is a nasty transitional period when no one is quite sure how to fish. To be honest, most anglers seem to spin until they are dead certain that other people are taking fish on a floating line. After that happy day arrives quite a lot of them still go on spinning! In fact, many spin all through the season.

### The Wood Technique—by A. H. E. Wood

One afternoon in July 1903 I was fishing an Irish river. The weather for some time past had been exceptionally hot and dry, so that the river had dropped considerably and was very clear. I had had no sport all day and sat down to think beside a pool full of salmon that had steadily refused to look at a series of flies, presented to them, as I thought, in every possible way. Shortly afterwards, I saw one fish and then another rise to something floating down on the surface of the water. This continued at irregular intervals; and at length I was fortunately able to observe the cause, namely, a sort of white moth similar to those often seen amongst the heather.

I went to the head of the pool, which consisted of an eel-weir, and there found a number of salmon lying with their noses pushed right up to the sill. As luck had it, I happened to have with me a White Moth trout-fly; this I tied on the cast and sat on the plank-bridge over the weir. Then holding the gut in my hand, I dibbed the fly over them. After some minutes, one of the salmon became curious enough to rise up to examine the fly, but at the last moment thought better of it; this I believe was due to its attention having been distracted by my feet, which were dangling over the plank, barely six feet away from the water. I changed my position, knelt on the bridge and let down the fly. This time the fish came more boldly at the fly and it was followed by others; but I had pricked several before I realized that, because I was kneeling directly above them, I was, in striking, pulling the hook straight out of their mouths. So I changed my tactics and, by letting go the cast at the right moment, succeeded in dropping the fly actually into the open mouth of the next fish that came up to it. I then picked up my rod, ran off the bridge, and made all haste downstream. All this time the line and cast were slack and floating down; yet when I tightened on the fish, I found it had hooked itself. By the use of this trick I landed six fish, lost others and pricked more than I care to say, all in a few hours. After that experience, I discovered myself fishing on the surface or as near to it as I was able. The final advance came, when I started using a greased line to assist in keeping the fly in the right position, and I thus evolved out of a simple experiment what has become a most interesting mode of salmon-angling, the greased-line method.

Further, my experience of greased-line fishing has shown me that a salmon is more ready to take a fly on or just under the surface than at any other level, except very near the bottom. I therefore aim at keeping the fly at the surface, or sink it right down to the stones; and I have entirely forsaken the ordinary practice, which causes the fly to swim in mid-water.

## Greased-Line Fishing

Fishing in the usual way with a sinking line and a sunk fly you lose control of the fly, more or less, once it is under water, and hardly know where it is or what it is doing. With the greased line you are able to control the position and *angle* of the fly in the water and also, to a very great extent, the speed at which it travels; for you can nearly always see the fly, or, at any rate, know exactly where it is. In all water, slow or fast, the fly is on or only just under the surface, and you seldom fail to see any fish that come to it, and, in doing so they generally make a head-and-tail rise. Therefore, I fish the fly on the surface or as close up to it as I can; but only if *the air is warmer than the water*. This means that even with ice and snow about, there is a better chance of getting fish with a greased line and a No. 1 to No. 4 hook than with an ungreased line and a sunk fly, provided the sun is out or the air is warm. And, in addition, I have all the fun of seeing the game and of fishing light, as opposed to the "chuck and chance it" method. Many have said that the pleasure of fishing with a greased line is the thrill of *seeing* every fish

raised actually come at the fly; and those who really follow carefully what is taking place can learn a great deal from what they
observe. For instance, what is the favourite angle at which salmon
go for the fly? Why do they sometimes miss it? Do they *ever*
come short? These are some of the questions which the use of a
greased line helps you to answer.

It is best to grease the line thoroughly before starting every
morning. If it is for the first time, spend some time in rubbing
the grease well in. A good grease sold by any tackle-maker is
suitable, but I prefer a thick one, such as Cerolene, well rubbed
in with a wash-leather pad. Occasionally I treat the whole line;
but every morning I make a point of greasing about thirty-five
yards. Rub it well in, do not leave more surplus than you can
help to come off on your rod or hands and, as far as possible,
keep the rod-rings free from grease. After the first application, do
not again grease the last yard or so next to the cast, as so much
grease gets on to this bit in actual work; but if you find the knot-
attachment to the cast sinking, you should give the last yard some
grease, but *never* grease the cast. In cold weather, one application of grease in the morning should easily last the day; but, in
summer or hot weather, it is often necessary to grease the line
again, at lunch- and tea-time, or whenever you find it does not
float easily in reasonably-quiet water.

In slow-running water there is *little difficulty* in keeping the
line floating. The trouble is that the grease soon gets on to the
gut, which then floats, and so does the fly. If you want the fly
to sink, a sharp jerk will generally pull it under the surface. If this does not succeed, rub lightly the cast and the last
yard of line with a bunch of dead grass; this usually cures the
trouble.

In strong oily water you will not find much trouble, but watch
carefully for a sucking eddy or swirl and prevent your line getting
into it, by lifting either up or down stream, whichever suits you;
otherwise you will get a drowned line and lose control. Your
ability to forsesee the effect of eddies and currents depends upon
your watermanship.

In strong broken water make your cast nearly square across,
then, before the line becomes tightly held by the eddies, lift it
upstream, without moving the fly. When you see all is right with
the fly, lead the line downstream, just holding it with the point

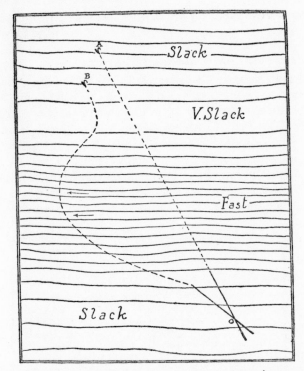

FIG 69  The result of casting across a fast current into an area
of slower water and leaving the line to look after itself

of the rod enough to prevent it going as fast as the current, without actually drowning it. As soon as the fly gets round to your
side, it may then pay you to keep the rod behind the line and
gradually lift the point; this prevents the sudden snatch that
occurs when a fish lying below you takes the fly when the line is
taut. But only lift the point high, if a shortish line is out or if the
water is strong. Always allow for a certain slackness in the line
out of the water and be on your guard against a drag or the
drowning of any part of it. Try to anticipate what the eddies are
going to do. It does not matter how slack the line is, so long
as the fly is fishing as you want it, for you can always ensure
enough movement in the fly by giving a free hand to the surface
eddies and by letting the line guide the fly where you want it
to go. There are very few idle moments with a greased line; but

a great deal depends on yourself, if you are going to make the most of it.

*Double or false casting and lifting line over*

If I am fishing in warm weather, I usually make a double or false cast every time, as it is not easy to lift a long line from its position downstream and all in one cast place it upstream and across, if there is a high bank behind. By pulling in some yards of line, then lifting and making a short false cast square across, it becomes easy to lift the shortened line high behind and to shoot a great length of it upstream and across. By this means also I am very much more accurate in placing the fly where I want and can be sure of placing it lightly enough to float on the surface.

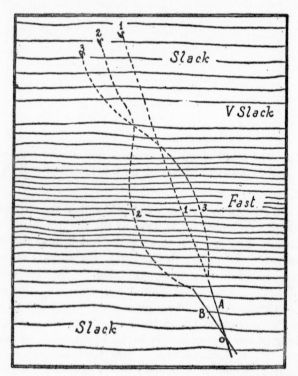

FIG 70   Cast to 1. The current acts on the line and 2 is formed. Lift over to straighten, as in 3, and repeat this as often as it is needed

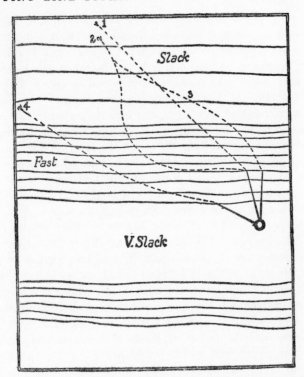

FIG 71 Cast to 1. Do not allow the line to get into position 2, but mend it to 3 and prevent fly being pulled upstream. Follow line round with rod so as to get into position 4 as soon as you can

When making a cast to this or to any other place, do not aim the fly at a spot in the water, unless a gale is on, but try to place the fly a foot or two in the air, over the spot where you want it to fall, and let the line drop lightly on to the water.

Even in February, except in flood water, I do most of my fishing with a greased line and a No. 1 *Blue Charm*. In broken water, I cast rather more upstream than the orthodox cast of a salmon fisherman, then lift my line off the water and, without moving the fly, turn over a loop of line upstream and *across* to prevent any drag on the fly.

The lifting-over of a line is done to correct a fault, namely, to take the downstream belly out of a line and thus relieve the pull or pressure of the current on the line, which is communicated to the fly and exhibits itself as *drag* (Fig. 69). But if the line is proceeding at an even pace and shows no sign of going to drag, there is no need to mend the cast. On the other hand, if the current continues to belly the line, but before it gets a drag, lift again and continue to do so as often as you can see a drag forming (Fig. 70). Do not on any account acquire the *habit of mechanically lifting over*, no matter how the current runs. Always have some reason for doing it : to prevent drag or, more often, to control the speed of the fly across the river. A few examples of its use are shown diagrammatically in Figs. 69 to 73.

This mending or lifting is effected by the raising of the elbow and by a turn of the wrist, which makes the rod follow evenly a semicircular path, point and butt moving in unison. It is a lift, not a back-cast, and its direction should be across stream as well as up. The line should be removed from the surface of the water by raising the rod almost horizontally and keeping the arm stiff, that is, the point of the rod should usually be no higher than the butt. It should then be swung right or left with a gentle circular sweeping movement and put down where desired. If there is much rough water or a strong stream, it is useful to start lifting the line by a slight movement of the rod downstream, this prevents drag or friction, which would move the fly, and the line comes off the water more cleanly. If the water you are fishing is fast enough to need it, the first lifting of the line should be made immediately the fly has settled and without losing the fraction of a second. At first you will find that, in doing this, you will pull your fly through the water, but with practice you will soon be able to lift a long line right down to the cast without disturbing your fly. And even if you do pull it, the effect will only be felt while it is travelling a foot or so and it will then begin to fish properly. Whenever you feel the pull of the line on the rod, you know that drag has been set up; something is wrong and needs correcting, because drag prevents the fly from fishing in such a way that a salmon can take it without *coming short*.

In some kinds of water, particularly where the speed increases evenly from where you are standing to where the fly falls, you need not mend the line at all. You will find that the fly fishes for itself, provided you are casting downstream as well as across. But you should never cease watching your line. On the other hand, in very quick or broken water, you may have to mend twice, or even three times, as the fly comes round. All this you will discover by practice and, if you are like me, you will also find that you have added a fascinating series of experiments to the pleasure of

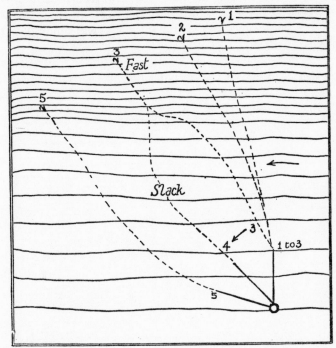

FIG 72   Cast to 1. By the time the fly gets to 3 there is an up-stream belly in the line; correct this by mending it to 4 and then continue to bring rod round to 5. Maintaining tension on line will help to keep the line moving down faster

fishing and will get fish, when anglers using the old methods do not.

By "mending the cast", I am able to check the speed of the fly all the way across and to bring it round as slowly or as quickly as I like, close to the bank or into dead water near the shore. The slower the fly travels in cold water (1° C. to 10° C.),* the more chance there is of getting the fish to come out of the deeps;

* 33° to 50° Fahrenheit.

and the same is often true of shallow pools. But when the water
is warmer, the question of the speed of a fly is not important;
even then I rarely fish a fly fast. In February and March when
the water is cold, fish are generally to be found in the dead deep
waters or in slow-moving streams. If in these places the fly hardly
moves and begins to sink, draw in line with your fingers very
slowly and keep the fly as near the surface as you can, but do not
be in any hurry.

At any time when you see that the fly is going to drag or the
line is getting below the fly, lift your line off the water to a point

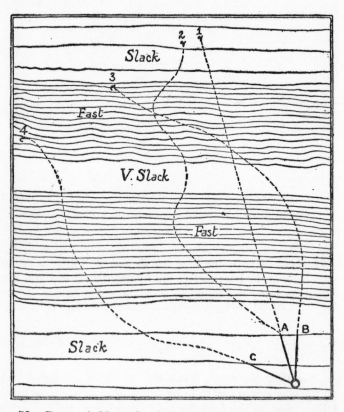

FIG 73   Cast to 1. Never let the line get into position 2 and keep
on mending it so that it is in position 3 most of the time. When
you get to 4 hold rod at C, and let the fast water pull the fly
over the slack water

beyond where the drag starts and place it again upstream of the fly. With practice this can easily be accomplished by a circular sweep of the rod as described before. In fact, the line can at any time be lifted, unless it is held by an eddy you should have noticed beforehand and have made allowances for, by placing it upstream or downstream and thus controlling the speed and position of the fly.

When I am using a light rod and finest tackle, I often cast rather more upstream and across, as in dry-fly fishing, and let the fly and line float and drift down with the current. If the fly floats and skims when the line is fully extended down the pool, straighten the line on the surface and give it a sharp jerk, which should put the fly under; then fish it round to the bank at whatever speed you like. A jerk on the line, before the line is straight, will make it sink in the nearest eddy and have no effect on the fly. In this way, the advantages of dry-fly and wet-fly are combined, for in the early stages the fly fishes dry and finishes up sunk, just below the surface.

## Sizes and Patterns of Flies

There is probably more controversy over the size and pattern of flies than any other aspect of salmon fishing. I would not contemplate for a minute any idea that my own ideas are an infallible way to success, but I have tried them for many years and personally done well with them. In February and March I usually fish with a No. 1 hook, ordinary dressing; as the water gets warmer or clearer I use smaller sizes down to No. 6. In April, as weather and water become still warmer, I have to use even smaller sizes, No. 6 to No. 12; but as long as the fish will come for a No. 6 I do not go lower. I only reduce the size of fly as the fish becomes shy of the larger sized hooks.

In really warm weather, in May and sometimes even in April, these ordinary hooks and flies, No. 1 to No. 12, are from my experience too heavy in iron and dressing for clear water; I then use summer flies tied for me with an extremely sparse dressing; no part of it going beyond the point of the hook. The hooks have a long shank and are made of very fine oval wire. They swim well and in a stream do not hold the water. The older the fly and the thinner the dressing becomes through wear, the better the fish seem to like it, provided the weather is hot and the water clear. I have caught fish on a practically bare hook, on which there was left no body and only the head and four fibres of the wings; and quite a large number on a hook with only the body of the fly left on it. The body of such a fly decreased in size every time a fish was taken out and yet it still proved attractive. I sometimes wonder what a salmon will *refuse* to take and whether this is not, after all, *nymph-fishing for salmon*!

The question is often asked what pattern of fly (No. 1 hook or smaller) should be employed for this method. I have come to the conclusion that it does not matter what pattern is used. Formerly I possessed the usual collection most beginners like to look at, a great many of them on double hooks; but all those are now discarded, as a salmon feels a double hook too soon for my liking. I only use three patterns now. *Blue Charm* and *Silver Blue* are my stock, simply on the principle that one is more or less black and the other white and so give *me* a choice. But some five years ago, a friend seeing my box and, hearing that I did not think colour mattered at all, offered to bet that I would not use a *March Brown* for the rest of the season to the exclusion of any other pattern. I took his bet, on condition that I could use any size I wanted. I did not, on any occasion, find the change of pattern made the smallest difference. I got my share, and more, of the fish caught. Since then, the *March Brown* has been added to my collection and so forms the third pattern. *Blue Charm* and *Silver Blue* I have in all sizes from No. 1 to No. 12, ordinary weight of hook, and *March Brown, Blue Charm* and *Silver Blue*, sparely dressed on No. 4 to No. 10 light low-water irons. The last three I only use in warm weather and clear water, starting in some seasons as early as April. I always begin fishing with a *Blue Charm* and only change it when all the sizes I think right for the day prove no good. I then try a *Silver Blue* in the size I think will suit the conditions. But if the water is very clear and the weather bright, I use a *March Brown* and pick out a fly that has very little dressing left on the hook. In these summer hooks dressed short, a No. 4 is equal to a No. 6 (ordinary fly) in length of dressing, but not in thickness, and so on down the scale. If you raise a fish on, for example, a No. 6, change it to a No. 8 and try again and you should get it; if it does not come again, go on fishing with a No. 8, for that fish has shown you No. 6 was on the large size for that pool or place.

18 & 19   Contrasts in water: *above*, the River Namsen in Norway; *below*,
Loch Naver in North Sutherland; a good salmon, sea trout and brown
trout loch

20 & 21  Contrasts in style: *above*, worming on the River Lune, near Tebay, Westmorland; *below*, fly-fishing on the Spey

Be careful to employ a cast the nylon of which is suitable to the thickness of the hook and the fly in use.

## Presentation

I find the best angle to present the fly is that which shows it broadside on to the fish; the latter invariably comes some yards to meet the fly, which is taken by it across its mouth. This is the ideal and in straight-forward fishing usually happens; the result is that, as the fish is travelling upstream and across, it takes the fly with it (See D in Fig. 74) and the cast and line continue to travel downstream. Consequently, in less than a second or so, you have the position shown in figure E which means that, without your having tightened the line or moved the rod, the fish has hooked itself, for the hold of the water on the cast has pulled the fly across and well into the angle of the jaw. You will find the point of the hook has gone well home and that there has been no need to strike. *Wait till you see the line being held or pulled on the surface of the water* and then tighten, but do not on any account strike. In doing this, *do not lift the point of the rod*, but keep the line all the time on the water and move the point of the rod towards your bank at whatever level it was when the fish took. In other words, continue fishing as if no salmon were after the fly.

There are, of course, all sorts of eddies and places where fish lie and all have to be fished differently, so as to present the fly to the fish at the angle at which it is best able to see the fly, most likely to be tempted and not "come short". As there is little a fish does not see, the fly ought to behave naturally all the time, as an insect or other live creature would do in the water. Avoid, therefore, any unnatural drag and let the fly move with all the eddies it meets, as will any living thing that is trying to move in the water *with the stream* and across. If you swim across a river, you have to swim at an angle to the stream and make use of all the eddies. Let the fly do the same and act in a natural manner, not as if it were attached to a rope. The floating line, if fished properly (and this is by no means so every time), has no drag and often is all slack and crooked; but, nevertheless, you are controlling the speed of the fly and the angle at which it crosses the stream. Unless you have lost control of the line, you can at any time lift the line off the water and place it where it should

K

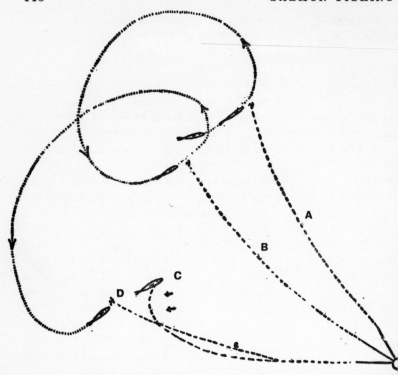

FIG 74   A fish has missed the fly at A, has swum round to take
it at B, has again missed it and only succeeded in taking properly
at D

be; you can thus put the fly where you want and make it *swim*
properly.

When you are wading down a long pool or are in strong
water, take up your position and start with a short line. Continue
to pull off a yard or so every throw, until you have drawn off
all the line you can comfortably cast. Reel up more than half of
the line and then move to a fresh position about half-way down
what you have already covered, start again with a reasonably
short line and progressively cast as far as you can. Continue doing
this all down the pool. The advantages of this method are mani-
fold. It is so much easier, when you are wading in strong water,
than is taking a step or so between each cast, and the fly is shown
to the salmon at different angles; you can fish more accurately

and with less trouble; and it is more interesting, for I find nothing more dull than the "step and cast" method.

## Hooking

When using fine tackle, take great care the rod, line, cast and fly shall all balance and work together for accurate and long casting. Of course, these small flies and hooks do not hold all the fish you hook; indeed, it is surprising that with such small hooks it is possible to land salmon at all. However, as the fish takes the fly on the surface, you can see exactly the manner of its taking and that is a great help in learning how to hook a fish. You can almost always hook a fish where you like by controlling your nerves and the fly. For instance, when you are fishing a streamy bit of water and a fish takes the fly, you will, if you move or strike at once, most likely pull its nose; but if you wait until it goes down (and even a little longer), you will find every time you have hooked the fish in the angle of the jaw.

With a No. 1 hook down to say, size 4, it is necessary to tighten *fairly* quickly *when* you feel the fish; or, if your line is slack, when you see that part of your line near the fish begins to move. The reason for this is that the fish feels the hard iron of the larger of the small-sized hooks and lets go sooner. This is not so with the smaller summer-sizes, unless the line is being dragged. I have often landed a fish and found the cast through the mouth and gills and the hook in the side of the fish. The chewed fly had been ejected through its gills; a clear proof my line had no drag and was slack. This fish generally takes somewhere downstream of me.

After you have made a cast and when all is on the water and to your satisfaction, lead the line with the point of the rod. The height of the rod-point above the surface of the water should vary with the strength of the stream and the size of the fly. With a No. 1 hook, hold the rod-point from three to six feet above the surface, the higher distance for a fast stream, the lower for a slack one. With a hook from No. 4 downwards, hold the point still higher, varying with the strength of the stream, and the size of the fly even as high as twelve feet or more when fishing a very small fly in a very strong stream. Under all conditions, always keep the point higher with a short line than with a long one.

When a fish goes for the fly, continue moving the point of the

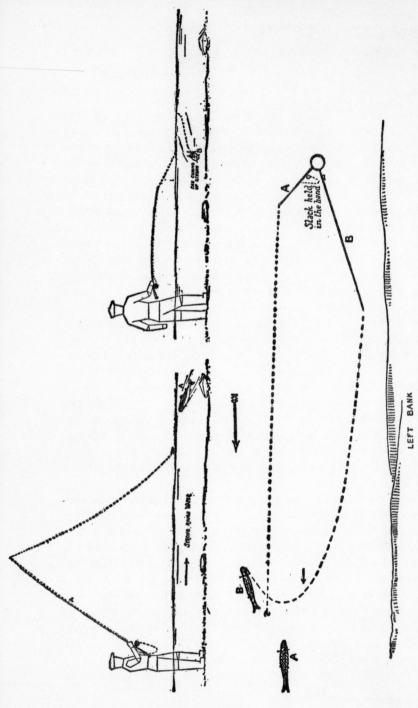

FIGS 75 & 76   The rod is held very high, A, so that if a fish takes the fly, when it has arrived below you, slack may

rod round as if no fish were there. With the point of the rod three feet or less above the surface, move it round at the same level; when it is above three feet drop the point towards your own bank, but continue moving it. Do nothing more until you feel the fish, which will already have been hooked, because the stream has done the trick for you. If a fish misses the fly, I have often seen it come at it a second and a third time in the same cast and finally hook itself. Had I struck or pulled the line, this would not have happened. As you are clearly seeing all this taking place in front of your eyes and are in consequence very apt to pull at the fly or increase its speed, keep your head and force yourself to pay no attention *until you feel the fish*. When a salmon goes for the fly more than once in the same cast, it swims in a kind of loop downstream and comes round to take the fly broadside on; and does the same again and again if it misses (see Fig. 74). All this takes place just under the surface of the water. You can see it all, and it is very trying to your nerves; but you must keep them under control, until the iron has gone home. I have often seen fish going through these manœuvres, before taking the fly, and a number of my friends have told me of the same experience. In every instance, the fish appears to have acted in the same way.

There is another difficult fish to hook, that is the one straight below you or that takes the fly at the moment when you begin to draw in the line, after a cast has been fished out. A salmon often takes you then, as though it was urged to do so, because it thought the fly was running away. There is a snatch and a grab, and it is often done like lightning. If you ask an old hand at the game the most difficult position to hook a fish, or where he most often gets a pull without hooking a fish, he invariably answers "straight below me". You can, to a great extent, overcome this trouble, when you are employing a small fly, by keeping the point of the rod up in the air, as I have just described. This gives the fish a slack line. If the stream is *very* strong, and I am using my twelve-foot rod, I sometimes hold the latter perpendicularly. I hold it at this height, in order to give plenty of slack line in the air when, owing to the pace of the stream, there is no slack on the water, and, whenever I see the fish or any movement near the fly, I immediately drop my rod downstream and towards my own bank. If this is done quickly enough, the fish will have a slack line and can take the fly and turn before it gets the pull; and then the drag of the line from below pulls the hook back into the angle of the jaw. The result is generally a firmly-hooked fish. I do not believe any fish intentionally comes short. The fault lies with the way we fish. When you are fishing slow-moving water and have a very long line out, keep the point of the rod a foot or less above the surface of the water; there will already be plenty of slack line on the water. You may not be able to see the fly when the fish takes it; but, if you watch the line near the cast, you will see it stop or being held. With only a short line in slow water, keep the point of the rod about three feet above the surface; but, in fast streams, hold it very high, in order to get a slack by making a belly in the line in the air. When you see the fish take, drop the point of the rod downstream towards your own bank, which will give the line a good chance to go slack. Do this quickly and only then feel for the fish; more than likely it has already been hooked and, thanks to the pressure of the current on the line, it is likely the hook has already been pulled home.

### The Time to Fish with a Floating line

Many people seem to think that surface-fishing is no use, except in shallow water and during hot weather. Experience has shown that it is equally good in icy water, as long as the *air is warmer than the water*. It is also good in all depths of pools, if the water is reasonably clear. My favourite pool in February and March is a slack water on the edge of a strong stream and that pool is twelve to fifteen feet deep. At that time of the year, I usually use a No. 1 hook. Later in the season and in warm weather, the fish lie in the strong stream of this pool and deep as it is they often take a summer hook No. 8. Every day I fish, even in February, I start by using a floating line and only when it fails do I use a sunk line and a big fly. As a result my fishing book shows that forty-three per cent of my fish caught in February in the last ten years were taken on floating line and small fly, sixty-five per cent in March, ninety-four per cent in April, and ninety-eight in May, and so on. I used to think it was no good fishing the floating line and small fly except in warm weather; but some years ago on an opening day, the 11th February and very cold, by late afternoon my sunk line was frozen up in the rod-rings. As a last hope to end a good day's fishing, I tried my floating line and small fly No. 1 hook, as the floating line does not freeze up so quickly, and managed to get two more fish. That made six; four on a big fly and two on floating line, the last two both caught after four o'clock. Since then I have always fished floating line in all weathers and under all conditions, even in snowstorms, and it rarely fails or is beaten by a sunk line; but I like to know that *the air is a bit warmer than the water*, for then the fish are undoubtedly more willing to come up to the fly. In early spring when the temperature of the water is more often under 4° C. (38° F.) that of the air is generally higher. On the other hand, the air may well be colder than the water on a May evening, when the water is as much as 15° C. (59° F.) and over. This does seem to put the fish down. I use, therefore, a big fly under those conditions; and this accounts for the occasional fish caught by me on a big fly, as late as April and even May.

In hot weather during May, June, or July, when the water is really warm, it pays always to cast across and upstream and to let the fly float and drift down, as it likes, and at times to lift the line upstream to prevent a drag. For three-quarters of the distance the fly travels, it will float on the surface, practically dry. Under these conditions, you will get a lot of fish to take the fly in this position, although it lies flat on the surface and does not ride high on its hackles, as a well-cocked dry fly will. When, however, the line reaches its full extension downstream, give the line a jerk or two to make the fly and part of the cast go under; this will prevent the fly skimming across the surface of the water. You can then fish the fly across the pool towards your own bank.

There appear to be two almost-distinct periods when salmon have different ways of taking a fly. Until the water and the air get continuously warm (say 13° C./55° F. or over), the fish do not come freely to the drifting-down or dry fly. Therefore, when fishing early in the year, do not waste time casting downstream or even square across; but put the fly rather more upstream than is usual in orthodox methods. Occasionally try the upstream or square-across cast, as you never can tell what a fish will do. If fish start taking the floating fly, continue making the upstream cast, as there is nothing more deadly than the use of a floating fly and the practice of *dibbing* for salmon. We do not often get the right weather in this country at the time the fresh fish are up. If we did, we should get more fish than we actually want to give us good sport.

## Sundry observations

Contrary to old ideas, I do like a very sunny day for taking fish, even when there is no wind. I like to see the fish and go for it, because this provides far more fun than does the sunk method, and gives more chances of making the most of what I observe and of developing my skill at the game. When you are fishing a greased line, pray for an upstream wind or no wind at all. A wind, blowing contrary to the general flow of the river, makes it very easy to lift the line off the water and place it upstream wherever desired. Another and more important point is, an upstream wind checks the line and keeps it from travelling downstream too fast, which helps you to fish more slowly and to control the fly more easily. Even for an old hand, a strong downstream wind is always awkward in greased-line fishing, for it takes a lot of practice to lift against it, without disturbing your fly, although with experience it can be done, unless a gale is blowing. The only way is to hold back the point of the rod and not follow the line so much, and then make little lifts upstream whenever you can manage them. If you can get into the water, much of the trouble is avoided by fishing more downstream and by keeping above the fish.

To most fishermen the greatest advantage in greased-line fishing is, perhaps, that the head-and-tail rise made by the majority of fish in taking the fly can clearly be seen in quiet waters. The rise is normally slow and deliberate; but, in a stream, it is done in a quick yet casual manner. The sight of the fly being taken makes the pulse beat more quickly and most people take a long time before they learn how to get under control the habit of striking. This causes the fish to miss the fly, or it only gets pricked.

Moreover, you can fish properly many places you could not so fish with the ordinary methods. Take, for example, a bit of dead water on the far side of a stream. You can place a small fly in this dead water and, by lifting the line upstream above the fly, the latter can be kept for some time moving along the edge of the dead water; and often the line can be lifted several times without perceptibly disturbing or dragging the fly (see Fig. 77). Also in fishing an eddy behind a rock you can place a fly on the

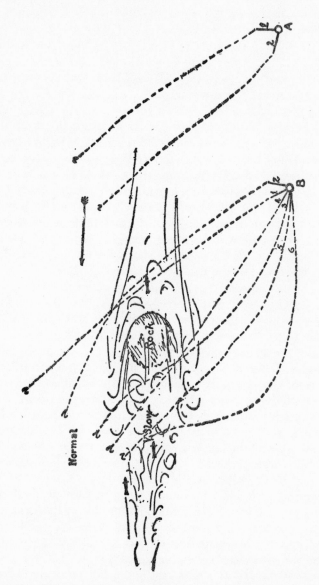

FIG 77 Showing how the difficult area beyond a band of quiet water can be easily covered. B1. Cast and mend to B2. Mend again from 3 to 4. Allow fly to be drawn gently from 5 to 6 by letting rod swing round. Compare the diagram with figures

edge of the stream on the far side of the rock and, as soon as it has settled, you can lift the line again and place it upstream. This allows the fly to wander about behind the rock and, by the time the stream on your side of the rock has got hold of the line, so that you cannot lift again, you will most likely find the fly is held by a fish. Often in this circumstance you will not see the fish take the fly, as the latter has been sucked down by a back-eddy behind the rock. *Watch the line*. You can continue all down that eddy, fishing in the same way and, as soon as you begin to cover the water below the rock, you will very likely see one or two head-and-tails rises at the fly. By this I mean that, as you begin to search the water below the rock, you will meet other fish, which will show with this head-and-tail rise, because the fly has not been sucked down by the eddy and is travelling near the surface. How far below the rock you may expect it to happen depends upon whether the rock is showing above the water or how deep its top is below, or how strong the current is. But this type of rise will often be observed near to the point where the two streams widen, converge and join the general flow, that is, where the water between them begins to move downstream and gets free of the influence of the eddy or reverse current.

Another great advantage is that, if you can get at the head of a pool well out in the stream or on a jetty, you can fish the water as far as you can cast. After that and without stirring from the place, make as long a cast as you can across the stream, then pay out another yard or two of line and let that fish right down and round. You can, if you wish, repeat this cast from the same place, shooting all the line you can, paying out an additional two yards of line every time and allowing it to float away downstream. Of course, you will lift the line, as often as necessary, off the water and mend it again upstream of the fly, without interfering with the progress of the fly. By continuing this method you can cover forty to fifty yards without moving down. You will probably be able to fish it better than if you had moved down lower and had started casting again, because a fly travels slower across the water at the end of a long cast and a fish you have covered a few times before, as the fly was floating down, may be tempted by seeing it pass so often.

In conclusion, I might remark that some fishermen imagine this method is only good in certain places, such as in the Aberdeenshire Dee; but many friends have told me they have found it more than useful in most other countries where the Atlantic salmon is caught and in rivers of this country too numerous to name. Others who have adopted the greased line write and say that in the old days, in hot summer weather and low water, salmon-fishing was given up as hopeless; but now this method has given them (not the salmon) a new lease of life.

*Wood brought up to date—a Modern Floating-line Technique*

It is indeed remarkable that so many people, who have read all about floating-line fishing, have built up a technique without realizing its object. How many of them know that floating a line, and taking the *belly* out of it as it comes round, are means employed to bring the fly to the salmon as slowly as possible. Few anglers can make a *mend* without moving the fly or know it is essential to push the rod-point out over the water, when making a lift. Three or four little jerks given to the fly during the time it is *fishing* are, to say the least, not very helpful.

An angler ought to have a clear picture in his mind of what he wants to do, before he sets out to do it. With some men it becomes automatic, after the line has gone out, to *mend* it, probably in an upstream direction; whereas it may be there is no need to interfere with its natural progress. If the river at the middle is flowing more gently than at the sides, the correction ought to be not up but down stream. Also, a wind blowing against the line at the time of the *mend* is very difficult to outwit. That and other vital points need careful thought before casting begins.

A friend of mine who fishes the Dee put the whole matter very succinctly. His method, which certainly has brought him a great many fish, is to cast as long a line as can comfortably be done and at an angle that will allow the fly to start *fishing* as soon as it pitches. If he is compelled to *lift the line over*, he makes a large *mend* straightaway and then leaves well alone. Of course, he may have to lift and place the line once or twice during the fishing out of the cast; but that entails minor adjustments, which are far less likely to disturb the fly.

The whole essence of salmon-fishing is the slow speed of the fly, which, if big, ought never to be travelling at more than $2\frac{1}{2}$ miles an hour and, if a small one, no faster than $1\frac{1}{2}$ miles an

hour. On the assumption that a fly represents a small fish, it will
be realized that such an animal, an inch or so in length, is hardly
likely to be swimming briskly across the river at 10 miles an hour;
and, if it is coming across the river, it must keep its head upstream
and slightly turned toward the bank it is making for. If it does
the former or fails in the latter, it will appear unnatural and will
not be touched.

Deliberately induced *drag* (see below) does occasionally pay
a dividend; but it is unwise to do this, unless there has been
formed a very clear picture of what is intended. When a fly is
being fished across the stream toward your own bank and a small
belly forms in the line, the whole line comes round to about 70°
down stream and then steadies and swings slowly round. Very
often a fish will take just after the fly has straightened out. I
used to think a fish took at that point, because it thought the
fly, having suddenly straightened, was attempting to escape. I
was wrong. What really was happening was that when the fly
was coming round with the belly in the line, it was swimming
too fast for a "fish" of that size. It was *dragging* and acting
unnaturally. At the moment the belly came out of the line, however, the fly fished properly and naturally and it was taken.

The angle at which a line is thrown across a river often affects
the speed at which the fly can be brought down. By far the best
way of fishing with a sunk line or a floating one still remains (a)
to wade out until you are just upstream of the salmon-lies nearest
to your own bank and (b) then to cast a long line at about 45°
down stream. Then make one mend and let the line severely
alone to come round as evenly and slowly as possible. Some will
say that the great Arthur Wood cast at right angles to the stream
or even upstream. There was, however, deliberate method there,
since he did not wade and therefore the nearest lies were probably 10 to 15 yards out from his own bank. Thus he cast dead
across and *lifted over* so as to slow down the fly as much as
possible, that is, though the bank-speed of the fly was still high,
the water-speed was virtually nothing. This meant that he fished
only the first ten yards or so properly. After that, however much
*mending* was done, there was always a small belly in the line. Of
course, Wood did what he wanted to do magnificently—cast to
taking fish and controlled his line for the first 50° of his cast.
He cared little what happened to the last 40°, as the fish were

not as close in to his bank as that. If he had been wading, I am pretty sure he would have changed to casting as far as he could at an angle of 45° down stream, mending and letting the fly come round slowly.

In my opinion, floating-line fishing is used with far too little careful thought; and the shadow cast by a floating line is calculated to distract the attention of the fish. But my main difficulty has always been to cast a long enough line to be hidden and yet, on a narrow river, to present the fly roughly beam on.

## Controlled Drag

I feel that, owing to the dry-fly man's horror of the word *drag*, it has become a dirty word with the angling public. Salmon, however, are not chalk stream trout, and they can, on occasion, behave in a way to scandalize the South Country fisherman.

It was that very experienced and able fisherman, the late Percy Laming, who invented controlled drag. He was a very well-known angler, both for salmon and trout; he leased a beat on the Spey for many years, and also was the owner of part of the Itchen. He killed some 4,500 salmon during his fishing career, and made some enormous one-day bags—21, 19, 17, 15 twice, and many double-figure days.

When the water was low and warm, he used drag with great success. He used a 14-foot rod and a double-hook fly, and did not grease the last two yards of reel line.

He cast down and across, and in easier water, nearly square across, and let the fly fish itself. He told me that the fly coming down and across was taken by the fish when a fly swimming in the conventional style did not interest them. Now this method worked in practice, not in theory only, in spite of theories that a small creature could only swim at $2\frac{1}{2}$ miles an hour, and so on. It does work.

The drag can be controlled by varying the angle to the stream at which the cast is delivered, by mending, or paying out a little line by hand. The drag can be short or long; the turn-round at the end of the drag can be done in front of a known fish—thus producing flash—in fact, the fly can be shown at various angles, and at varying speeds.

### The Oiled-Line Technique

The late Alexander Grant was, to my mind, the greatest salmon fly fisher of them all. A man of great manual dexterity, a student of nature, a mathematician of so high a level that he and Professor Einstein corresponded on such abstract maths as the fourth Dimension, and, in addition, possessed sound common sense and vast practical experience of salmon fishing. His rods, lines and flies were designed on scientific principles, based on mathematical formulae, and I have never seen any rods and lines which produce the same effect.

His rods became famous as the Grant Vibration Rod, but the Vibration line which goes with it is not so well known. As it forms the basis of the method I am describing it must be mentioned. It consists of a square-plait silk line dressed with linseed oil, and tapered evenly from tip to butt. The taper is continuous all the way up the line, with no breaks in the taper at all. The load on the rod is thus exactly proportionate to the length of line being cast.

Now a line floating on the surface was anathema to Grant, as he said, it throws a shadow over the fish, and, if there is a breeze, it causes a ripple as it floats along (see below).

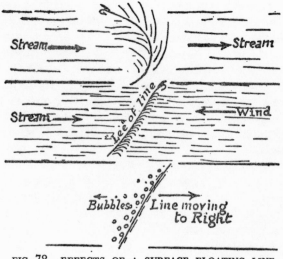

FIG 78   EFFECTS OF A SURFACE FLOATING LINE

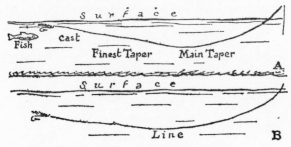

FIG 79    FISHING SMALL AND LARGE FLIES

In summer and low water it is vital to keep the line as unobtrusive as possible, and on the same level as the fish, but upstream of it. The front end of the line is not doing anything to alarm the fish when it is in the water, and when being cast, it drops like thistledown on the surface. The two sketches above show how the level at which the fly fishes can be varied by looping an extra-fine taper on to the end of the line. In high summer the finest taper would be used, in spring the main line only.

As to fishing the fly. As long a line as possible should be thrown, so that (*a*) the fly swings very slowly and (*b*) it keeps the angler well away from the fish's eye.

Before commencing to fish, the line is rubbed down from end to end with a rag soaked in refined, but not boiled linseed oil. This helps to prevent the line becoming soaked, and also acts as a lubricant to the line, both in the water and in the air. It also prevents bubbles adhering to the line when fishing and glittering in the sun. The bubble must have somewhere to lodge, and as the surface of the line is liquid oil, the water just slides off without leaving air-bubbles which are caused by the oxygenation of water as it ripples over a rough surface.

The fly should be fished slowly, so the angle should be fairly acute. The reason is that the fly should travel slowly. The biggest angle shown below is 35°, and this is on an easy, even-flowing pool tail. Grant used to say "keep the line straight and vary the speed, if you wish, by varying the casting angle, within limits". By limits he meant such angles as to let the line fish straight.

As to hooking fish, I have seen him hook a fish at 50-yard range, and both hooks of the double-hook fly were buried up to the bend. He always said "the surest hooked fish, all else being

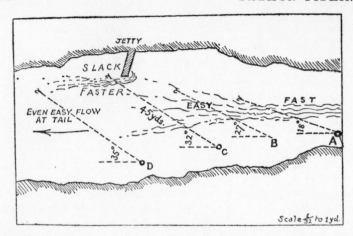

FIG 80   Casting angle on varied water to give slow speed to fly
and prevent drag.

equal, is with a long line". In case any reader imagines that
"50 yards" is a misprint I should say that, in 1895, Grant switch-
cast a distance of 65 yards in a tournament, and without shooting
any line. That is equal to the present overhead cast record, where
about 30 yards of line were shot. So much for "progress". But
Grant based his technique on obeying the scientific facts governing mechanical movements; modernists either do not know these

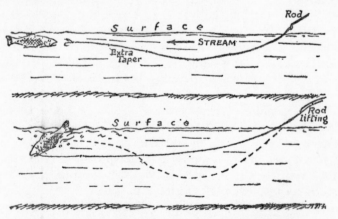

FIG 81   Showing the vertical sag in a Grant line which allows
the fish time to take the fly before the line tightens.

principles or choose to ignore them. Be that as it may, Grant habitually hooked fish at from 40 to 50 yards' distance.

The good hooking was the result of the fish pulling against a long line *in* the water, now, although the line was straight, it had a vertical sag due to the tapering of the line. This allowed a little slack for the fish to turn after taking, as figure 81 shows.

When fishing out the cast in this style the angler should keep his rod tip low—almost on the water—so as not to destroy the vertical sag in the line, and when a fish takes do *nothing until a pull is felt*. Then the rod should be raised steadily, and the fish played in the usual way.

As to flies, Grant always used double hooks, and, in summer sizes 7 to 9 or 10. In early spring he went up to 2/0 or 3/0, using only the main part of the line, i.e. with the finer end of the taper taken off as shown in Fig. 79.

As to the effectiveness of this method. The first day on which I tried it was on the Ness. It was a sunny day with the Ness at summer level. In two hours I hooked six fish and pulled a seventh. That is good enough for me!

## CHAPTER TEN

# DRY-FLY FISHING

### *Introduction*

SOME few seasons ago, Gerald Curtis, who had experimented for some time on the Wye, invited Lee Wulff, the American author and angler, to fish on the Aberdeenshire Dee at Aboyne. Much to my pleasure, I was invited to join the party for a week, and so had an opportunity of witnessing the latest dry-fly techniques as practised in Canada.

### *La Branche*

The method of dry-fly fishing for salmon as perfected by La Branche in North America relies on three points for success : *The fly must float high; it must be placed close to the fish; and drag must be avoided.*

The first point was covered by tying the hackle of the fly at right angles to the shank of the hook. The second was ensured by having the fish see the fly. The third depended on casting and this meant to La Branche the *curved cast*. The curve to the left is comparatively simple, that to the right is more difficult.

### *La Branche—The curve to the left*

When the angler has fixed on a fish and has selected the spot on which he is to direct his fly, he must take up a position so that his objective is not at an angle greater than forty-five degrees, but he should not attempt to cast with more line than can be kept alive in the air without effort.

It is important that the angler should learn to judge distances as accurately as possible. Until he can do this he should cast the fly straight upstream and allow it to fall upon the water at a point which is assumed to be the correct distance. Being satisfied as to the distance the angler makes a cast towards the fish, but not directly at it. About three feet more line should be used than is calculated would reach the fish and the calculator should direct the fly about three feet, or even more, upstream from the fish and as the line is about to straighten he should pull or hold back the top of the rod enough to stop the fly. This will throw the fly out of the direct course and will impart to the line, and obviously to the fly, an impulse to return as it would if being retrieved. If this check is timed properly the fly will be thrown downstream and the leader and forward part of the line will fall where they are, a sharp curve will be the result. The length and diameter of this curve depend upon the degree that the rod is held from the vertical, the horizontal or side position throwing the greatest curve. The angler will be less likely to become discouraged if he makes his first attempt from the horizontal position as nearly as possible, as the curve will then be more pronounced. It is rarely that anglers are met who are able to throw the curve with the rod at an angle of less than forty-five degrees from the perpendicular.

In throwing either to a fish that may be seen or to one that is not visible no change in principle of the cast is involved.

Salmon love to lie in narrow deep eddies or stickles against a ledge past which the river races madly. Unless one is very expert a wet fly is whisked away so rapidly by the pull of the water on the line that it rarely reaches these fish. With the dry fly, however, these places are not difficult because the angler fishes upstream and across and with the curved cast the leader which is in the current and upstream from the fly does not exert any drag until the fly has had quite a long drift. If some obstacle prevents the proper handling of one's rod to throw the curve and forces the cast to be made with the rod in a perpendicular position the loose cast can be very effective when drag must be overcome, especially where the fish cannot be reached from below and the fly must be drifted down from above. The loose cast is accomplished by casting in the ordinary overhead manner with more line than is required to reach the objective and draw the fly back sharply just before it alights. This is not over-pretty, for it causes the leader to fall in rather ragged shape, but until it is straightened out by the current the fly is not greatly interfered with.

*La Branche—The curve to the right*

This cast is not so simple because to execute it correctly the angler must deliberately lose control of the line and therefore it cannot be retrieved if the fly appears to be about to fall improperly. It has, however, the added advantage that it may be thrown from almost any angle, and it calls for nothing more than the ordinary manner of handling the rod except at the moment of the actual delivery of the fly. The usual false casts for measuring distance and direction may be made, but a much longer line than is indicated by the position of the point being assailed must be used.

No deviation from the usual false casts should be made except that while keeping the line alive in the air the fly in its forward flight should bisect an imaginary line drawn from the bank to a point in the stream about eight or ten feet from where the fly is to be dropped. It is helpful to imagine that the casting line has neither fly nor leader attached to it and the cast is delivered as if the object was to drop the end of the line at the point where the imaginary line on the surface of the water has been bisected. When it is determined that the line in the preliminary cast is over this point and the final fishing cast is to be made instead of permitting the live line to exert this full energy upon the line released from the hand, this energy is deliberately killed by prematurely delivering the line that is held. This action results in depriving the forward part of the line and leader of the life which, should the line have been held, would have been imparted to them. Thus that part of the line which is free of the top and which is exerting the pull will use up all of the energy and the line beyond that point will die and fall where it is. If the release is timed correctly the energy fails when the line is still in the looped position it assumes in the forward cast before the line has straightened out, and if these directions are correctly followed it may be made to fall on the water as gently as in any other cast. The curve described is greater in scope and hence more effective than the left-hand curve, and I think it is almost as easily executed.

### General procedure

As soon as the fly alights the rod should be held in a horizontal position pointing directly at the fly for as long as the fly is floating naturally. The rod should be held in the right hand alone and the butt should rest against the body. As the fly drifts downstream the slack line should be taken up by stripping it in with the left hand. The action of stripping in the line should be free and determined so as to keep place with the fly, but it is not to be jerked. The recovered line should be held in loose coils in the left hand, where it is ready for the next forward cast. Thus the line which has been gathered will have shortened the casting line so that it may be lifted from the water preparatory to another cast without difficulty.

The fly should not be retrieved until it is below the angler or until it is no longer floating straight downstream but is being swung across the current under the influence of the drag.

When a rise comes, by allowing some of the loose line to pass back through the guides the rod may be raised to the vertical—the correct position as the hook is pressed home.

## Modern Techniques and Equipment

La Branche used a double-handed rod of fourteen feet in length, weighing seventeen to eighteen ounces. Nowadays in Canada the tendency is to treat salmon as though they were large trout, and use single-handed rods. One reason is that, while the fly is fishing, and line is being drawn in by one hand, it is easier to hold a single-handed rod with the other hand than to hold a longer weapon. Again, long casting does not seem to be required, as the fish can be approached quite safely by wading or the use of a canoe. I am told that a cast of fifteen yards is all that is required. The rods used by the majority of dry-fly men are from eight to nine feet in length, although Lee Wulff uses one of only six feet.

Lines are the multi-taper type. The most expert of the dry-fly men are now using a semi-floating line. This sinks a little in the water, and does not ride on the surface-film as does a greased line. The reasons underlying this choice are—the line is less visible to the fish; and, owing to the resistance of the water, it helps to hook the fish.

I saw this latter point well-demonstrated on the Dee. Lee Wulff had made a cast well up and across stream, and his fly began to float down. At this point his attention was distracted by an onlooker, and he turned his head and began to answer his remark. At this moment a black nose appeared, and quietly engulfed the fly. There was hardly a ripple in the water. Down

went the fish, the line tightened, and Lee Wulff came to life
with a rush as he felt the pull. In this case the resistance of the
water had set the hook, and set it well. The fish was a nine-
pounder, and the stream fairly slow.

The cast is now of tapered nylon, knotless. The angler knots
on a point to suit the conditions, and renews his point as necessary. The breaking strain of the point varies from ten pounds
down to two and a half pounds.

Reels are usually three and a half to three and three-quarter
inches diameter, and of medium width, and the backing of nylon-
monofilament or woven.

Flies nowadays seem to be breaking away from the original
all-hackle, barrel-shaped type. The fly is longer and thinner, and
the latest tendency is to design flies which sit well down into the
surface-film of the water, and do not ride high on their hackle-
points.

The Wulff flies, for example, have plastic bodies, hair hackles
and wing, and sit right down on the water. These flies have a
hackle tied so that its axis is at right angles to the hook shank.
The White Wulff has a split wing like a conventional *V*-wing
trout fly.

Hair is obviously ousting feathers as a wing and hackle
material, and the flotant generally used is a soft-line grease. The
leader is not greased.

*Fishing in Canada*

Most anglers in Canada, I am told, believe in working hard
over a fish that has been seen to rise, in fact they try various
flies and variations of drift for a far longer period than a British
fisherman would consider suitable. The old idea of resting a risen
fish does not seem to apply in Canada.

It must be realized that the Canadian season is very short,
and is in the height of summer, probably averaging only the
months of June, July and August. The stock of fish is also, by
our standards, very heavy. The combination of very clear and
low water, high temperatures, fresh-run fish and many grilse
make ideal dry fly conditions. Further, the Canadian is by law
confined to fly fishing only, as no form of bait fishing is allowed.

The angler in Canada does not face the wide variety of conditions which are found, say, on the Spey. In Scotland one begins

the season with frost and snow; follows a spring of variable weather and a summer which may well be bitterly cold. What are the chances of the dry fly succeeding in Great Britain?

*British Conditions*

Salmon *can* be caught on the dry fly in clear water. In spite of a very cold wind, Gerald Curtis and Lee Wulff between them landed four fish on the Dee. However, there is no doubt that they had to work very hard for their fish. Where peaty rivers are concerned, the chances of the dry fly are less. Lee Wulff tells me that he prefers clear rivers for dry-fly work. It is only fair to say that, during his time on the Dee, a spate coloured the water for two or three days, during which period conditions were hopeless.

It must never be forgotten that the dry fly was first used for salmon on the Hampshire Test in 1906 by Major J. R. Fraser, and, later, by G. L. Ashley-Dodd. But the Test is a chalk stream and usually very clear, and cannot be compared with a Highland river which is often peat-stained.

The situation requires thorough exploration, and there is only one way in which this can be done. If a number of salmon fishermen would seriously try the dry fly on their respective rivers we should soon acquire sufficient data for us to answer certain queries, such as—will fish take the dry fly in peat-stained water? What is the most favourable water and air temperature? Will "potted" fish take a dry fly? Are there any conditions under which fish will not rise?

My experience on the Dee leads me to think that the dry fly could well become a useful method in this country, on certain suitable beats. It will, however, require a great deal more practical experience before a confident answer can be given.

The range of water covered by a dry-fly cast is very limited compared with greased-line fishing or the traditional wet-fly cast down and across, as shown in the sketch below, and it means many more casts per day.

The dry fly fisher has to select a fish, and fish for it exclusively, while the wet fly covers an area containing, maybe, three fish. The more fish which see the fly the better, one of them may be the "daft 'un or the blind 'un" Chaytor's keeper spoke of!

Another factor which acts adversely to the adoption of the

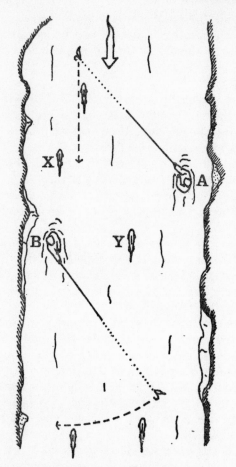

FIG 82    DRY-FLY *versus* WET-FLY :
the dry-fly man (A) only covers one fish at a time, while the
wet-fly man (B) covers two. Note that fish X and Y are not covered
by the dry fly.

dry fly in Great Britain is the modern desire, not to say economic
necessity, for a big bag. The angler in Canada has a different
approach. He has gone in for trout fishing methods, which the
conditions allow him to adopt, and, as bait fishing is barred, he
quite naturally tries any and every variation of fly fishing that
occurs to him. In any case, the law sets a limit to the number

of fish he can kill per day, so that record bags are out of the question. That being so, the field is open to the ingenious angler who can invent a new fly, or way of presenting it.

In this country, the angler can try fly, minnow, prawn or worm, and the law allows him to catch as many fish as he can. So the angler here usually is a general practitioner, and his Canadian counterpart a specialist.

Apart from any question of technical suitability, I very much wonder whether dry fly will make an appeal to the British salmon fisher. His temperament is widely different from that of the transatlantic angler, and he may well remain uninterested. There are, of course, many waters in Scotland which would be very difficult to fish with a dry fly. The beat which Messrs. Wulff and Curtis fished is an easy one, but I could take them to many places which would tax their skill to the utmost, and which might even prove completely impossible.

I recently spoke to a well-known American angler who, having seen many British rivers, confirms this view.

The future of dry fly now becomes one of great interest. We know that it will hook fish. If sufficient interest is forthcoming, the next edition of this work could well require a lengthy chapter on the dry fly.

## CHAPTER ELEVEN

# OTHER METHODS OF FLY-FISHING FOR SALMON

*Loch-fishing for salmon*

THE practice of fishing in the sheets of water into which salmon run hardly differs from that in the river; but it is certainly not very remunerative, except in a few instances. One of these, the fishing in Grimersta, is famous for the number of fish it yields. Angling is there conducted in a chain of four lochans, which are joined end to end by short lengths of river and the lower of which is connected to the sea-loch by a mile of river. The small pieces of river point to all the most successful fishing being done in the lochans themselves. These sheets of water are shallow and have a gravelly bottom; these circumstances induce fish to rise freely. Generally two flies are employed on one cast and most of the fishing is done from a boat. The Grimersta chain of lochans is typical of a Hebridean loch in which salmon and seatrout abound, but there are few others approaching it in the possession of such a prolific stock of fish. As grilse are more numerous than the other classes, light tackle and a twelve-foot rod will serve.

When the water is rough, it pays to cast well into the waves, close inshore, where salmon are likely to show; to throw over any rising fish; and to search very carefully the neighbourhood of any submerged reefs of rock. Try to persuade fish that are hooked to keep clear of weed-beds, especially if you are employing a dropper. If the fish is to be gaffed and lifted in a boat, keep the dropper well away from the side.

Other lochs where fishing for salmon is regularly practised are Loch Lomond and Loch Maree. In the former in February, March and April fishing is done by trolling a minnow, natural or phantom, at the end of a trace and thirty to thirty-five yards of spinning-line. From May onwards, fly is employed in certain areas in which fish are still in shoals; later, they scatter and lie in shallow places and they "are generally found closer to the shore and in shallower water than seatrout. They like to lie in water four to six feet in depth, with a sudden dip whither they can retire when disturbed. They are certainly partial to places where large blocks of rock rise from the bottom" (*Fifty years with the Rod* : John Stirling).

Whatever rod is employed, care should be taken that the tackle is in due proportion, one part with another. Stirling recommended several patterns of seatrout flies as leader and dropper on the cast. *Mallard and Olive*, *Teal and Olive*, etc., in sizes 7 and 8, and also a few larger should there be waves or strong ruffling of the water. The depth and clearness of the water in which you are fishing, will, to some extent, influence you in choosing the size of fly to put on; and I think you should always take into account whether you are likely to meet salmon or grilse, because the latter are said to swim higher and may, therefore, be raised by a smaller fly. It is as well to carry some small *March Browns* (or any other fly you particularly fancy), lightly dressed on fine low-water hooks. In Loch Lomond, there is a stock of salmon that may be relied on to show sport by rising to the fly, a very unusual state of affairs in loch-fishing.

On the other side of the picture, there is Loch Lubnaig in the Forth basin, which salmon enter as early as the 15th of January, the Falls of Leny notwithstanding. The bed of the loch is irregular, but two-thirds of it is covered by water less than fifty feet in depth. A few salmon are taken here on the minnow by trolling; but, wrote Stirling, "I have never heard of a Lubnaig salmon being taken on the fly".

Lough Conn, the Connemara loughs and Corrib, all yield salmon to minnow and fly; a few salmon are caught in time of spate as they enter Llyn Dinas from Glaslyn in Carnarvonshire; but it is rarely worth fishing specially for salmon in these large sheets of water, if a river is available. It is better to go in quest of seatrout and be thankful for the happening salmon.

Dapping for salmon with a blowline and a live Mayfly has become, more and more, a popular method in the south-western districts of Ireland; and both seatrout and salmon fall victims to it. After the Mayfly season, or where the Mayfly does not occur, the live grasshopper and the daddy-long-legs are used. Corrib is a great centre for this mode of fishing and so is Lough Currane (Waterville).

Blowline fishing needs much experience; and to me it is, at present, far more difficult than using the artificial in the normal way. The live grasshopper, daddy, or Mayfly must be kept dancing or resting *on the surface*; if it sinks, it is drowned. And, when a fish comes up, you should not strike, but wait until it actually takes the bait down and then tighten. The fish often play around and splash about the bait, before they decide to take it. And it can be imagined what sharp eyes and steady nerves are needed, when the line is bellying out and the 'hopper is far away from you.

*Harling*

The lower portions of great rivers, such as the Tay and the Shannon, as it was before the hydro-electric scheme was carried into effect, are too wide for anglers to cover wading or casting in the usual way from a boat. A special method was, therefore, devised of trolling the fly astern of a boat and steering a course that ensured a large area of water was being thoroughly searched. One of the Shannon methods was very much the same as that used today on the Namsen and other broad Norwegian rivers. Harling was formerly common on the lower Tay, but, in recent years, it has fallen into disuse. I am, therefore, taking as a standard the Norwegian method.

The stream in rivers on which harling is a recognized mode is generally very powerful; and heavy flies and baits are needed to get down to the level at which fish are running. Flies of the necessary weight would be difficult to cast and this way of presenting them to the salmon is the only one that is practical. When, however, the Namsen, for example, drops considerably, there are stretches where the fly can be cast in the normal way with fair prospects of success.

Three rods are employed at the same time. They are spread out at an angle of forty-five degrees from one another and held in position by small brass castings fitted in a board at the stern of the boat. The reel lies flat on the board and the line is prevented from going out by the pressure of a small weight or flat stone resting upon it. Rods for this type of fishing must be stout enough to withstand the strain of resisting the current and long enough to spread the baits well. Eighteen and sixteen foot is the recognized length for the rod. The reel is chosen to suit; a diameter of four and a quarter or four and a half inches will provide ample room for the necessary hundred and fifty yards of level line. The casts employed are of 20 lb. breaking strain or more.

The baits vary according to the season and the height and temperature of the water. Early in the season, dace and golden sprat are taken well, although this varies from year to year. Also there has been specially designed for the Namsen a spoon called after that river; it is used as large as three and three-quarter inches and as small as two inches, the size being chosen to suit the level and state of the water. The colouring of this spoon is silver on each side, silver outside and copper inside, or silver outside and gold in. Flies of standard patterns, but of large size, are also used; and special flies are also sold, to the heads of which are fitted tiny propellers to break up the water and cause "flash".

As soon as the boats, which, on the Namsen are rowed by two boatmen, are under way, the flies or baits are let out until they are trailing about twenty yards behind. The course of the boat is straight across the river and back again, dropping about two yards every harl. It is very heavy work for a single man to keep the right course, as the current is so strong. For this reason it is the custom to employ two; and the second man has the additional duty, when a fish is hooked, of winding up the line of the third rod. The recovery of the other lines and baits is the first duty to perform, directly a salmon is hooked. The next is to get to land and allow the angler whose rod has become attached to a fish to go ashore and play it. Sometimes two fish take the bait almost simultaneously and, I am told, three have on rare occasions been played at the same time. It is very unlikely that all three would keep clear of one another long enough for them all to be played out and brought to gaff.

The salmon of the Namsen and other large Norwegian rivers have a reputation of being very heavy fish; and it is the playing of them which undoubtedly provides the major part of the fun of fishing for them. The hooking of salmon by the method of harling depends entirely upon the skill of the boatmen. If they know the river and the habits of the fish, they can steer a course that will introduce the baits to the maximum number of fish. Whether the fish will come at the bait and fasten is a matter that rests with the fish alone.

## CHAPTER TWELVE

# SALMON-FLIES

*Introduction*

THE practice of salmon-angling has undergone a remarkable change during this century. Apart from developments in tackle and the advantages it has given, Wood at Cairnton on Dee, La Branche and Hewitt both of the United States, Waddington, Righyni and many others, have successfully experimented with the presentation of the fly. They in their day did, and other fishermen are now doing, much to redress the balance between the mechanism of angling for salmon and the philosophical approach.

Philosophical sounds a pretentious word to employ in this connection; but I can find no better way of describing interest or research associated with the fish itself, its habits, its senses and its environment.

The salmon-fly, also, has recently come very closely under review. It is the traditional lure, the origin of which is not understood. It may have had prototypes in nature. More probably, men took the trout-fly and dressed it in a size they considered commensurate with the greater bulk of the salmon, for the early patterns were certainly very large. The multiple-winged patterns of Venables demonstrate that. How the brilliant plumage described by Franck, leading in due course to the gaudy fly of Irish dressers, came to be added we have no idea whatever.

Anglers have in late years been seeking as never before for the true meaning of the so-called salmon-fly, wondering why it is taken by that fish. That a salmon's memory goes back to the duns and sedges of its parr-days is unacceptable. That a fly suggests forms of marine food is the happiest guess. But what are they?

*What is a salmon-fly?*

A modern salmon-fly is not regarded as an imitation of the natural fly, upon whatever it may primarily have been based.

In fact, the word *fly* is given by courtesy; it is a title earned by the manner of its construction and origin and academically is entirely wrong. But what else can it be called? Lure is at present earmarked for the spoon, the artificial minnow and other baits.

What then is a salmon-fly? Or rather, why does a salmon take it? It is not a conscious imitation of any form of food taken by the salmon in the sea; the nature of the marine food of salmon was unknown when flies were first invented. But to rule out imitation is to state only half the case. The fly may be a suggestion of some form of salmon-foods. The possibility that salmon feed regularly in fresh-water has been ruled out of court. The evidence of scale-reading and other scientific research has settled that point (see p. 245). Can the fly have some resemblance to a marine form of food? A likeness due to colour, shape, size, or behaviour? Here we are on less slippery ground; suggestion is always a safer word to use than imitation, because the closest imitation to human eyes is from a piscine point of view, probably quite unlike the real object. The *Silver Grey* has been described as a marvellous representation of a shrimp; and some men associate brilliantly hued patterns with similarly coloured forms of marine life and attribute the success of these flies to that resemblance. Personally, I think curiosity is a solution more likely to satisfy that branch of the problem.

There is also the theory of anger and of the desire in salmon to seize, kill, or destroy anything that annoys them. I wonder what happened when there were no flies to bother them. Did they wander sullenly about a pool, seeking a victim, and, finding none, go back to the lodge and await a return of a state of peace with the world? In disproving this theory it is tempting to recall William Scrope's magnificent sophistry and to suggest the angler as the salmon's benefactor, because he relieves the monotony of life in the pools by providing objects, upon which they can vent their feelings!

Another suggestion put forward is that a salmon takes a fly, because the latter is suggestive of a small fish in difficulties and presumably unable to look after itself, or struggling violently and therefore disabled or even deformed, and, in consequence, an easy prey. If this is the impression given by a fly, a salmon ought every time to take the fly in obedience to the natural law that the

22 & 23   Contrasts in style: *above*, coracle fishing on the Welsh Dee at Llangollen; *below*, using a floating line on the Clay Pool, River Awe

24    Tailing a salmon; on the River Dee

25    Nearing the gaff; on the River Dee at Banchory

weaker shall not survive. But in most rivers where salmon are found, they live in a world of such impressions and, for the most part, disobey the law, as well as many others laid down for their observance! Also, I suspect the latest ideas concerning the proper presentation of a fly would not allow it to give the impression of being in difficulties, but rather of having enough control to make for the side. That, at least, is the idea given me of a fly fished in the floating-line manner. If a salmon thinks the same, it takes the fly, presumably, from fear of missing something!

In fresh-water, the habit of feeding is not lost by a salmon; it sleeps soundly, until it is fully reawakened by the resumption of sea-life. Occasionally the appetite breaks out during the descent of the fish as a kelt, but only to a very limited extent. Undoubtedly fish in the sea are often led to their food by the flash emitted by their prey, or by it they induce their prey to come to them. This instinct to seize something that flashes becomes dormant when the salmon enters the river, or upon leaving the feeding-banks; but a salmon's reflex is ready at an instant to react to the old stimulus, should certain conditions obtain. Of the nature of these conditions we know practically nothing, but in fact it could be said that a salmon takes a lure from habit.

A suggestion that fish are influenced by the presence of high water at the river's mouth is hardly worth considering, when the pools under consideration are far up the river and separated from the direct influence of the tide by several weirs. If the word moon is used instead of tide there may be something in it. Yet tides certainly can affect fish, but this I have observed only where the river flows out into the estuary.

The sea-pool of a West-Highland river I fished during June held a fair stock of salmon, seatrout and an occasional estuary trout. These fish were not to be taken at all, except at a certain time : for a period of twenty minutes beginning at twenty minutes after half the tide had ebbed. Nor was there any record of salmon having been taken at any other time of day in the sea-pool. I thought I would test this, but found that, directly the psychological moment arrived, fish that had previously ignored my fly went for it with extraordinary promptitude. Whenever it was my turn to fish the pool at this time, I hooked a fish and the other fishermen did so in their turn. If the period occurred about mid-

M

night and there was no moon, fish took just as well. Within one such period of twenty minutes I hooked a salmon, a seatrout and a slob or estuarine trout; I fished on for an hour or so, but had no more offers. This phenomenon may not be due to the tide, but to the degree of salinity of the water. If so, the same conditions would be expected to begin forty minutes before the tide had half-flowed; but no one who had fished that pool at such times had found it was so.

Suggestion and the excitement of a salmon's reflex appear to me, at best, only half-truths, which need a mediate cause to explain why so many fish, widely separated, are simultaneously affected. There are several entries in my diary stating that suddenly the air grew warmer and fish, which all day long had seldom showed, started breaking the surface of the river with nose-rises and with little explosions like kisses. This note is always accompanied with the story of one or two salmon raised, hooked, or landed. The temperature of the water or of the air have, *by themselves*, no influence we know of. Salmon will take in all temperatures of water within a definite limit. Nor is the change of water-temperature itself considered to be important. But observations over a prolonged period of these two temperatures and their comparison have produced evidence that salmon take freely, when the river-temperature is lower than the air-temperature, and are extremely loth to rise, when the air is colder than the water.

### Selection of a Salmon-Fly

The chief reasons that lead a fisherman to select a fly for any given pool or flat are, according to current theory, three : *the pattern* ought to be suitable to the colour of the water or to the light; *the size* right for the height and temperature of the river; the *style of dressing* adapted to the way he wants to fish the pool. One style will cause the fly to swim high and another will make it sink down amongst the stones on the bed of the river, where salmon are usually wont to rest. Style in this sense means the ratio between the quantity, not length, of dressing and the length of the hook, or the fullness or spareness of the dressing. These factors largely control the tendency of the fly to swim high or a little below the surface. Although style, the weight of metal in the hook and the manner in which the fly is fished play a part, the extent to which a fly can be compelled to sink does not amount to very much, unless a weight is attached to the cast, or a piece of lead wire has been coiled round the shank of the hook, before the fly was built on it. But the modern lines will put a fly well down.

Every fisherman is agreed on the importance of discovering the right size of fly for the pool at a given height of water. But it ought always to be kept in mind that a size of fly may take a fish in one pool and be far too large or small for the next pool, or for the flat or the stickle adjoining.

Wood of Cairnton had an alternative view on the matter, which was decidedly original. By swinging the rod-point towards the bank, so that the current pressed harder upon the line, or by taking in a little line, he made a large fly travel noticeably faster through an area of slowly-moving water. The effect was almost the same as if he had fished a smaller fly at the normal pace. This tactic Crosfield called *pulling through* and he employed it in summer, whenever he wished the fly to swim close to the surface. Of course, Wood used this trick only when conditions were suitable and as an alternative to changing to a smaller fly, a subject he studied very closely. Thus the speed at which a fly travels is a new factor to consider in deciding the right size to use.

The temperature of the water is often of great assistance in determining the size of fly; but pattern and colour are usually negligible quantities, compared with the consideration of size. When the water of the river is very cold, fish lie low and the fly should be big and heavy (6/0 to 4/0) to get down to them; but, again, account will have to be taken of the strength of the current and the depth of the water, or else there will be a great risk of a very heavy fly getting foul of the bed of the river or, at least, of the point of the hook being blunted against the stones. It is possible to avoid this, without changing the fly, by fishing it rather faster, that is, by taking in a little line, so that the fly swims at a higher level. It should be borne in mind that, when conditions indicate the use of such big flies, salmon are sure to be lying in quiet water; thus the controlling of the level at which a fly swims is more important than when the streams and stickles are being searched.

Any directions I could put down on paper to assist in the selection of a fly would be perfectly useless to the man at the waterside.

With all the conditions of wind, sun, barometer, thermometer, water-level known, it is often very difficult, even for a master of angling, to choose with any real confidence the right fly for a given pool. If he had been told the size and pattern of the fly on which a salmon had, five minutes earlier, been taken by a man fishing from the opposite bank, he would find the problem little easier, unless his experience had taught him always to put on a smaller or a larger fly than had succeeded opposite. It is very common to find the size of fly that takes a fish from one bank will not succeed, when it is used from the other. Sometimes a fish will not take a fly it has seen on many occasions and in several sizes, until a favourable moment has arrived. But there are a number of points about fly selection which are worth recording :

The current opinion is that flies bearing colours of the red end of the spectrum should be used in thickish water and those of the blue and green end for clear water. It is important also to make sure that the colour-tone of the fly be correct for the day. Another way of saying "bright day, bright fly and dull day, dull fly" :

Bright day                   silver body
Medium day                   yellow body
Dull day                     brown, black or grey body
Very dull day                black body

The four patterns of tube-flies used under normal circumstances are: *Silver Grey*, *Logie*, *Blue Charm* and *Thunder and Lightning*. Alternatives for the first two are *Torrish* and *Lady Caroline*. Occasionally I put on a tube-fly dressed purely with stoat's tail, when I want to fish something very small. And I am a strong believer in the value of adding tiny jungle-cock cheeks to a lightly dressed tube-fly.

The whole question of the right size of fly to offer a fish is extremely complex. It is probably best to start with a medium-sized fly—unless you are a follower of the Exaggeration Theory. This theory, which was first put forward by Kelson in *The Salmon Fly* (1895) was for several years tried with considerable success on a stretch of the Welsh Dee. And the employment of a large and extremely bright fly prior to fishing down with one of a more moderate size and tone probably took more fish than ordinary methods. I have also personally had success with the Exaggeration Theory on a smaller scale—say a No. 3 first time over and a No. 6 or 7 the second time.

Of local patterns there are or were hundreds; but many of them have strangely lost their parochial appeal and have been invested with general effectiveness on rivers, far from those for which they were so exclusively designed. Also, there is the opposite process to be seen on the Spey, the Eden, the Chester Dee and many other famous waters. The old sombre local patterns have been driven out and the invading gaudy flies, to use a time-honoured epithet, are taken quite as well. The value of local advice about flies was brought home to me when first I fished the Taw in spring. In water that elsewhere, particularly in the

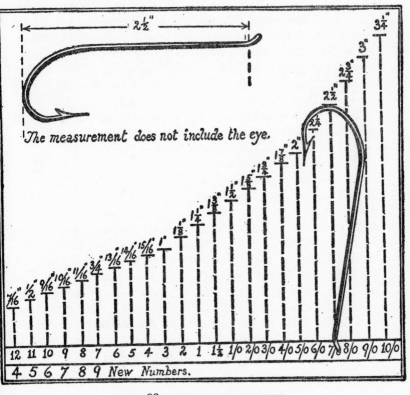

FIG 83   SALMON HOOK SIZES

Welsh Dee, would have required a fly of No. 2/0 or 1, I was told that nothing larger than No. 3 was needed; and after some doubt and much experimenting I found that it was so.

On another occasion in a certain year Lochy salmon at one period of the season were only to be raised by a *Canary Fly*. The next year, that fly was generally ignored; which suggests a change in the colour of the water. On the Carron, *Green Highlander* has long been a favourite and local men demand some green in the patterns they employ.

## Other Views

Modern writers have expressed views ranging from the wide choice offered by R. V. Righyni to the school which believes that only size matters.

Righyni divides floating-line flies into four main groups, Silhouette, Translucent Illusion, Normal Image, and Flashing Illusion; also two subsidiary groups. If the fly is fishing in a strong light which could dazzle a fish he argues that colour cannot be seen; all you need is a dark fly which will show up as it comes between the sun and the fish's eye. Hence the Silhouette type such as the *Blue Charm*.

The Transclucent type is, for instance, a *Silver Grey*, which, under a sun shining down river obliquely, will look more attractive and not so solid as a silhouette type.

The Normal Image, represented by such a fly as a *Hairy Mary* or *Thunder and Lightning* is, he says, a dull-weather fly.

The Flashing Illusion, e.g. a *Silver Doctor* he regards as a last resort.

But one should, I think, refer to the other side of the coin. The late A. H. E. Wood used only two patterns all through his season; and for one season he used a single pattern only, and still caught as many fish as usual. He varied the size, of course. He caught fish on a bare hook with its shank painted red or blue. He also killed fish on Wingless flies with just a dressing on the shank of the hook. In his case, pattern did not matter, he practically ignored it. From his experience a school of anglers became members of this "pattern does not matter" group.

## Changing the Fly

I am a faint-hearted believer in exchanging one pattern for

another all too similar. The substitution of a dark fly for one considerably lighter may well have the effect of attracting fish; and so will the exchange of a fly through the fibres of which light will pass, for an opaque pattern. The latter distinction is often less obvious than would at first appear. If a *Silver Grey* is held up to a strong light, it will be seen to a large extent to be translucent; whereas a *Mar Lodge* similarly viewed allows scarcely any light to penetrate its dense wing-fibres. Yet in the hand, or lying on a table, there will appear little difference in that respect. This distinction in dressing is undoubtedly accidental and not of design.

If I had time to fish a pool twice more, I should try one of these two methods. Change the fly to one of the same size but of opposite colour, that is, dark instead of light or vice versa, and fish straight down; and, if there is no offer from a salmon, replace the original fly and go down again, employing, on this occasion, all the tactics and variations described above. The other plan is to put on a fly, far larger and more brilliant than conditions appear to demand, and fish the pool thoroughly in the hope this will awaken some interest in a salmon or arouse it from its torpor. The function of the large fly is purely provocative; it is intended to put a fish on the *qui vive* and ready to attack the original fly, which should be tied on again after the large one has done its work.

As a last resort, the fly should be changed for one of different pattern; or a large fly used and then replaced by one of a size suitable to the level of the river. The same tactics should be employed of varying the presentation of the fly and of casting it upstream. But if the fish is known to be lying at the edge of a stickle near the head of the pool or close to an area of faster water in the middle of it, an effort ought to be made to hang the fly in the current and at its *cheek*. This can only be done effectually by mending the cast and by holding the rod-point well over the stream and lowering it, so that the fly moves more slowly and swims well below the surface.

## Conclusion

We cannot see into a salmon's mind, we do not know all about his life habits in the sea, except where he goes to when in salt water, and so we cannot really put forward convincing facts about how he should be caught. So what do we really *know*?

We know that, when the water temperature reaches 9° C./ 48° F., the fish will take a small fly fished near the surface, and that the way to keep the fly at that level is to use a floating line. Period.

But while we are fishing with a size 8 to 10 fly another fisher-man has just caught a salmon on a minnow of 1¾ to 2 inches in length, so do we really know what a fish will take or why he takes our lure? I well remember hooking a Ness fish on a No. 1 fly when all the other anglers were using No. 9 or 10, and getting fish on them. The more you fish the more inexplicable becomes the way of a fish with a fly. I killed my first fish very many years ago, and have caught them ever since in all kinds of ways, but have never found the answer to the burning question of why they take what they take. There is no best way to fish a fly?

The best fly is the fly in the water. Does size really matter so much? Does the style of fly dressing matter? So many times have I seen a small fly ignored and a minnow taken, or *vice versa*, that I begin to wonder if all our theories are just theories and nothing more. The older I get the more I come back to Alexander Grant's saying, "let's see it work". And so many things do work, at times. X has a theory which will catch fish, so has Y, but quite frequently these theories fail in practice, in other anglers' hands.

After that the theorists begin to argue. X writes that he cannot hook fish unless he does such and such. Y answers him with equally convincing—on paper—reasons based, he says, on what he has seen. But has he actually seen it, or merely thought that he has seen it? The human eye is easily deceived. It is fatally easy to see what you would like to see. Probably the answer lies in the different way in which each man fishes his fly, so producing a different kind of "take" by the fish. Quite likely X could never hook fish in Y's way, and *vice versa*. And this matter of individual presentation is sometimes overlooked.

There is a tendency amongst those who argue on this matter, to credit the salmon with reasoning powers equal to those possessed by *homo sapiens*. To my mind this is nonsense. So often have I seen theories disproved in practice that I am a sceptic. It seems that salmon do not read books and that he, the supreme arbitor, won't reveal his secret.

## CHAPTER THIRTEEN

# SPINNING FOR SALMON

## Introduction

SINCE the first edition of this book was published, there has been a considerable boom in spinning, and, in consequence, many new rods, reels, lines and baits have appeared on the market. These, in turn, have altered the technique of spinning for salmon, so let us first consider tackle :

## Rods

The materials in use are greenheart, split-cane, glass-fibre, steel. Of these, split-cane is probably the most expensive, but is much loved by those who use it. Spliced split-cane is obtainable and makes a spinning rod with a very sweet action. So also does spliced greenheart. Glass-fibre spinning rods are very light, powerful, and are made in a variety of actions. Steel rods are heavier than glass-fibre, and also are made in varying degrees of speed.

The action chosen depends entirely upon the reel which is to be used. A revolving drum reel (like the Silex) needs a slower rod than a fixed-spool reel which requires a fast rod to get the best out of it. A rod with action coming well down to the upper hand is the best tool to use with the revolving-drum reel.

Where fixed-spool reels are concerned, the bait is flicked off the rod point, so to speak, hence the necessity for a fast rod.

As to length, I feel that the modern tendency towards very short rods is a mistake. A nine-foot rod gives one more control, both of the bait and of a hooked fish. So many people now use seven-foot rods that I am sure they do not realize the difference made by an extra two foot in length. I have used seven-foot rods myself, but prefer the longer rod.

Rings for fixed-spool reel rods are usually of the bridge variety with long legs, so that the rotating coils of line are kept from rubbing against the rod as the cast is made. The butt ring is large so that it will help to break down the coils of line thrown off the end of the reel spool. The other rings decrease in diameter to the rod tip, the top ring being normal size. These rings are usually of hard steel wire. Rings for revolving drum reels are of uniform diameter all up the length of the rod, and are either porcelain, agate, synthetic-agate or stainless-steel lined.

Reel fittings today normally lock the reel securely to the rod by some form of screw-down device. These vary in design, so make sure that the one you buy really does lock the reel solidly to the rod. A reel which falls off while you are playing a fish is calculated to cause a major panic.

## The Reel

There are three types of spinning reel: the Nottingham reel and its variations, the Aerial and Silex; the multiplying reels such as the Pfleuger and Ambassadeur, and the fixed-spool reels such as the Mitchells and Abumatics.

The Nottingham-type reel spins on the point of its axle, hence the term centre-pin reel. Introduced in the 1890s, it can still be obtained in various sizes, and probably four inches in diameter would suit most salmon anglers. The original Nottingham reels had an optional check which was disengaged before casting. Control during the cast was solely by the angler's finger or thumb. Later came the "Aerial" reel which was built with a very light drum, and which also had a screw-on brake to help control during the cast. Then followed various similar type reels with automatic or semi-automatic controls. Their number was legion. They had the merit of simplicity and comparative robustness, but you had to learn how to use them. If the drum was not carefully braked, by fingers or otherwise, the most appalling overrun could take place, and much time lost untangling the line. They could, in the hands of a good caster, put up a very good performance, and many a fish has been killed with their aid.

A typical Nottingham-type reel is an old friend of mine—the "Silex"—shown above. For light spinning the $3\frac{1}{2}$-in. type would be the most suitable, as the drum is lighter than the 4 in. diameter model. It has an adjustable casting brake controlled by a trigger. The amount of brake can be pre-set by a revolving button. As the cast is made, the trigger is pulled, so disengaging the check, and bringing the casting brake into action. When the bait hits

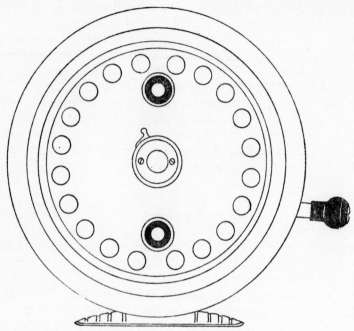

FIG 84  SALMON SPINNING REEL
Nottingham type—the Silex reel

the water, the trigger is released, and the check is re-engaged.
The trick to this reel is to learn how fast to move the trigger.
For best results some experiment is needed, but once the knack is
acquired, the results are excellent.

The multiplier came later. It was developed in America, where
it is called a bait-casting reel, and is in wide use in this country.
The drum is small in diameter and very wide. As line is wound
in it is laid evenly on the drum by a device known as a level
winder. As a help in control during casting there is usually a
screw-on brake and/or a centrifugal brake. Again, you must learn
how to use them. Any revolving drum reel can overrun during
a cast, and cause the most fearful tangle.

The multipliers might be represented by the *Ambassadeur 6000*
—shown opposite. Here is a very well-made and high-class reel
with a level winder; and an adjustable casting brake. Manual
control is by pressing one's thumb on the drum. This reel casts

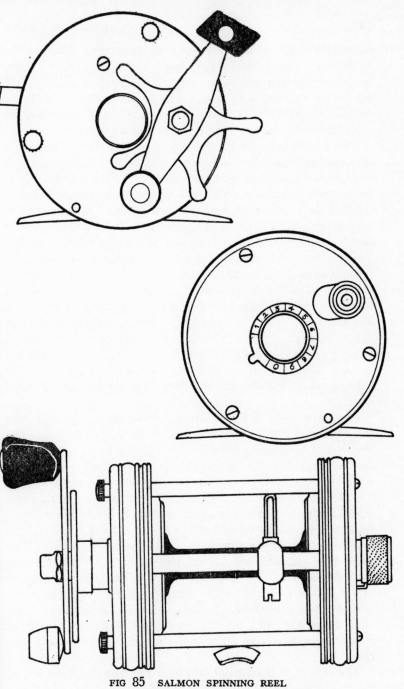

FIG 85   SALMON SPINNING REEL
Multiplying type—Abu's *Ambassadeur 6000*

beautifully, and must have slain its thousands. Due to the Multiplying gear, a heavy fish should be "pumped in", i.e. the rod should be lowered towards the fish and the resulting slack wound in. The rod is then pulled back to the vertical while the drum of the reel is held firmly by thumb pressure, so pulling the fish towards the angler, when the process is repeated.

The fixed-spool reel became popular once the nylon mono-filament line was fully developed, and is now in use—and made —in many European countries and in America—where it is known as a "spinning reel". Its popularity is probably due to the fact that you cannot get an overrun. Once you have learned how to drop the bait on the required spot—a matter of an hour or so's practice—you can fish all day with a minimum of trouble. To my mind, these reels are more difficult to use when actually playing a heavy fish than are the multiplying or Nottingham reels, but some late designs have been improved in that respect. A drawback, too, was the fact that the device which picks up the line and winds it on the reel after a cast was very liable to acci-dental damage. The latest designs have all the works enclosed, and the reel is now unlikely to suffer damage to its more delicate parts. A further problem was the creation of twist while a fish is being played but this has also been eliminated by one talented designer.

For an example of a fixed-spool reel we might, perhaps, take the *Abumatic 280*—shown opposite. This reel will take any line from 4 to 18 lb., and spare drums can be carried in one's pocket, and changed very quickly. All the works are enclosed by a sturdy cover. When a heavy fish runs, the drum itself does not revolve, the pick-up runs backwards and pays out line as if a cast was being made. This eliminates the twisting of line while a fish is being played, which was a fault in early fixed-spool reels. When a fish runs, the angler simply lets go of the reel handle, as if he were using an ordinary fly reel, and when the run ends, can instantly wind in. To cast, one simply presses down a trigger, makes a cast, and releases the trigger at the critical instant.

In fairness it must be said that, when the angler has to cast against a strong wind, the fixed-spool reel is far easier to handle. Revolving reels can be difficult to cast with under those condi-tions.

The user of a fixed-spool reel must see that the spool is cor-

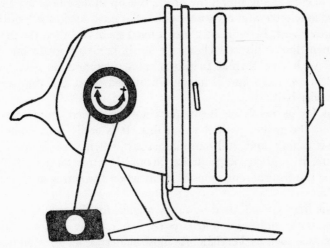

FIG 86   SALMON SPINNING REEL
Fixed-spool type—Abu's *Abumatic 280*

rectly filled. The makers of some reels have engraved on their spools a line showing how far the spool should be filled with line. If the spool is over-filled—right up to the lip—the reel will cast off knots; if too low, the casts will be too short, due to excessive lip friction on the line.

To summarize, the Nottingham-style reel probably would be the choice of an angler hunting forty-pound fish on the heavy Norwegian rivers, while the ordinary salmon fisherman would use today a multiplier or the fixed-spool—especially the latter if casting a light bait. The famous Scottish rivers are, nowadays, being fished more and more with the fixed-spool.

### The Line

There is no doubt that, today, the nylon monofilament line is the popular favourite. It is seen everywhere. It has many virtues and few defects, and it is cheap to buy. It is used on any type of reel. Its chief charms are its great strength for its diameter, its invisibility, the fact that it need not be dried after use, and its lightness. Provided that it is tied to the trace with the tucked half blood knot (see p. 66) it is entirely reliable. At one time these lines were very springy, and caused a good deal of trouble due to coils riding up on the drum, but up-to-date lines are much more amenable and a variety with a flat cross-section is a distinct improvement. If the reader uses a fixed spool reel then the mono-filament line is his best choice. A 12 lb. breaking strain line will cope with any normal British salmon river and its fish. Some anglers use 15 lb. line if heavy fish are expected, but that means a heavier bait.

So far as revolving drum reels are concerned, many anglers favour the white, plaited nylon line. It is easily seen while the bait is fishing, and, still more important, when a fish is on. That, to me, is a great point in its favour. It sometimes is difficult to see the transparent monofilament when the sun is at a certain angle.

Silk lines are still used by many anglers for the revolving drum reels, both undressed and dressed, while others favour newer materials, such as Terylene. As most modern lines are well made, it really becomes a matter of personal preference. But if silk lines are used they must be religiously dried after each day's use, or trouble will follow as surely as night follows day.

Rods, lines and bait weights must harmonize; a light bait cannot pull out a heavy line, and a heavy bait will break a line which is too light. Similarly different types of reel have their limitations.

The Nottingham-style reel will fish baits from $\frac{1}{2}$ oz. upwards with a 12 lb. line, or a 15 lb. for heavy baits. The Multiplier will cast from $\frac{3}{8}$ oz. up to 1 oz. or $1\frac{1}{4}$oz. with lines of from 9 lb. to 15 lb. The fixed-spool will cast $\frac{3}{8}$ oz. upwards with a 9 lb. to 15 lb. line, the latter being used for 1 oz. baits. The fixed-spool's per-formance is entirely controlled by the ratio of bait weight to line size. If, therefore, the bait is light, so also must be the line. For example, a wooden Devon would require a 9 lb. line, a 12 lb. line would result in a shorter—probably too short—cast.

I cannot over-emphasize the importance of this point. The spinner has to balance his gear just as a fly fisherman's rod and line must suit each other. Otherwise, you will never get results which please you.

## Traces

The usual trace today is about one yard in length, and is made of either "Alasticum" single wire of say 9 lb. strength, or

Gaffed! A 23lb fish from the Vosso River, at Bolstad in Norway

27 Conversation piece

28 The traditional ghillie with classic equipment; James Duff on the banks of Loch Tay

of monofilament. I personally prefer the former. A 9 lb. trace has never broken when I was in a fish, and, being so fine, it hardly shows in the water; and it does not glitter.

I simply tie a swivel to the reel line, attach one end of the trace to the swivel and the other end to the bait. As to swivels, the modern ball-bearing box swivel has served me well. A drop or two of oil daily is all it asks, and I never get a twisted line. In the past, swivels were infuriating. They could malinger without warning, and your line became one mass of twists. However, the ball-bearing swivel has changed all that, and we can now fish in peace. The methods of fastening wire to the ring of a swivel are shown in Figures 26 and 27 on p. 67.

After a wire trace has been in use, it will retain a little water within its swivels. I therefore always dry mine before a fire and place it amongst discs of oil-soaked felt, which I keep in an old cast-damper; this prevents oxidation in the delicate moving-parts of the swivel.

## Weights

There are three methods of causing a bait to sink to the required depth. Use a bait that is of itself heavy enough to need

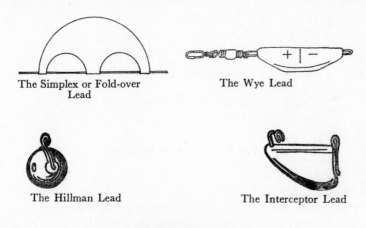

The Simplex or Fold-over Lead

The Wye Lead

The Hillman Lead

The Interceptor Lead

The Jardine Lead

FIG 87   TYPES OF LEAD

no additional weight; place an amount of lead within the bait;
or attach a lead of appropriate weight a yard above the
bait. The effects of the two last on the behaviour of the bait
are quite different. A light bait, held down by a lead at a distance
of a yard or so, possesses a far larger degree of independence
than one in which all the weight is centred in itself. The former
swims more or less horizontally; whereas the heavy bait travels
with its nose well up and, the hooks at its tail being, therefore,
the lowest part of the tackle, it is very likely to run foul of the
many snags that force themselves upon the unlucky angler's
attention. A light bait will swim a little higher than the lead and
often enable the spinner to escape the punishment of spinning
too slowly with, at most, the minor loss of a *pendant* lead.

The question of a heavy bait, such as a solid Devon minnow,
we will leave until the next section and consider the weighting
of a natural bait, minnow, loach or sprat. The most satisfactory
means is to slip into the mouth a little lead wire and close it by
sewing up the lips with a piece of fine copper wire. Another way
is to have a spindle of lead moulded on the central spear that
forms the backbone of many modern flights.

The most practical weight, designed to be attached to the trace,
is the anti-kink type, such as the Hillman lead and others that
may be seen in Fig. 87 on p. 193.

FIG 88   A DEVON MINNOW

Where the weight shall be placed, depends largely upon the
type of water to be fished. If the river is bounded by high banks,
from the tops or sides of which you are going to fish, you will
probably concentrate the weight at a point well up the trace.
This will help the bait to swim on a level keel; but at the same
time will introduce into the act of casting a danger of the bait
curling over, getting behind the lead and being entangled with

the line itself. It is far more difficult to cast with accuracy, when the lead is attached some way up the trace.

If there were no local conditions to modify my views, I should unhesitatingly choose the heavy minnow or spoon and only place enough lead at the head of the trace to ensure the swivel functioning; the weight would take the form of a Hillman lead tied to the ring of the top swivel nearest the line.

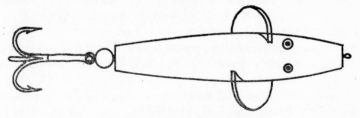

FIG 89    A WOODEN MINNOW

### Artificial baits

There are innumerable varieties of these: minnows, phantoms and imitations of other fish, such as gudgeon, loach, etc.; spoons and wobblers; and wagtails, leather-baits, sand-eel tubes and many other ingenious inventions, all of which at one time and another come up for approval before a much-bewildered salmon!

The typical minnow is the heavy Devon (Fig. 88), which consists of a shell of metal revolving around a central axis, on which the hooks and head-swivel are fastened. This can, for convenience, be called the flight. At the head of the shell are brazed two fins that cause the minnow to rotate round the flight. The best form of flight is that which bears a single treble at the tail and, just above it, a bead to keep the shell from slipping down on to the hooks as shown in Fig. 89. Another way of keeping the shell in place is tying a second treble above the first, so that the lower edge of the minnow rides on the inside of the three bends; this has always appeared to me a waste of a treble and to possess no advantage whatever over the single treble and bead. Devon minnows are made in many different colours and patterns; gold, silver, brass, gold and brown, silver and blue, red (for glacier water), gudgeon-coloured and many others. And very popular now are the light wooden minnows.

There is very little weight in a minnow of this type; some

should, therefore, be introduced in the shape of lead wire wound round the flight. Or a lead can be attached to the head of the trace and the minnow allowed to play as it will.

The spoon relies for its power of attracting fish upon "flash", which is caused by the uncertain vacillating movements of its silver and copper faces. It is essentially a heavy-water bait, although I have taken fish with a one-and-a-quarter-inch spoon at a time when the river was dead-low. Spoons are made in many shapes, kidney, hog-backed, Norwegian and others (Figs. 90, 91 and 92). Most of them require a little lead on the trace to keep them low and to make them function well. There is also a variety of fly-spoons lightly constructed to admit of their being cast and fished with a fly-rod.

I prefer the longer and more slender shape of the Norwegian spoon. One I have which is the deadliest bait I know, either in coloured or clear water, is made of copper. The convex side is left unpolished, and so appears very dull, the concave side is painted dull grey. The mount, with its triangle, is attached to the top ring of the spoon, and is kept in place by fine copper wire passed through a hole in the rear end of the spoon, and once round the flight. This wire easily breaks when a fish takes, and the spoon swings free.

I have also used an all-white spoon, and fish certainly go for

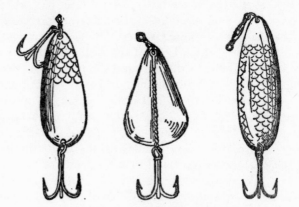

FIG 90    KIDNEY SPOON

FIG 91    HOG-BACKED SPOON

FIG 92    NORWEGIAN SPOON

it; but I still prefer my Norwegian spoon. I feel very strongly
that polished spoons are much too flashy. Something very dull,
with a seductive wobble, is the thing to use.

The Plug bait, which swims instead of revolving, appears to
go into, and out of, favour on different rivers for no apparent
reasons. A number of fish have been killed on the plug, but,
latterly, I never see them used on the rivers I fish. There was
a time when the plug was frequently to be seen. I have a feeling
that the British angler has not taken to it because of its appearance. To his eyes, perhaps, the whole thing looks wrong. The
salmon angler is a conservative person, and not given to using
strange and unusual baits. Plugs will kill fish, but possibly the
wooden Devon has usurped the place they once held, and its
appearance is strictly conventional.

*Natural Baits*

Here is a list of the fish most commonly employed by the
spinner as baits: minnow, loach, colly or collagh, sprat, bleak,
gudgeon, eel, sand-eel and, in the bad old days, parr (the tail
of which was used in much the same fashion as is the spoon).
Minnow is by far the most popular and next to it comes sprat
dyed golden yellow. Of the eel only the tail is used and this needs
careful preparation beforehand.

Small dace, also, are occasionally spun in front of salmon and
in flood-time prove a most successful bait. This fish is a common
bait early in the season on the large Norwegian rivers, such as
the Namsen. Any of the small fish used in pike-fishing are taken
well, when they are spun, and have been known to be snapped
up by salmon, even when the former are being employed as live
bait for pike.

The natural bait is either placed upon a central spear and
the hooks of the flight, known as the *arming*, are grouped round
it and then secured; or it is held in position entirely by the hooks.
If the flight is fitted with a tiny propeller, the body of the bait
will lie quite straight; but, if the curve of the bait is relied on
to produce a wobbling spin, the hooks must be placed, so that
they hold it rigidly in a shape that will cause this movement. If
a natural bait is mounted on a flexible flight and afterwards
bent, in order to make it wobble or spin, it should be examined
after a few runs to see whether it is functioning properly. And

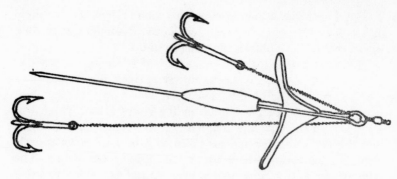

FIG 93    A DEAD BAIT MOUNT

a curve, slightly greater than is usual, is needed to make it rotate efficiently in slack water. I think two small trebles are adequate and that more are a nuisance and are detrimental to sport. One hook of the back-treble ought to be straight; this will help in keeping the arming in position.

A celluloid propeller that can be attached to the top of the trace is an alternative; its function is to make the bait spin as though fins were present on the flight itself. If you adopt this method, which has the undoubted advantage of removing some distance from the bait an unsightly attachment, remember to leave out or jam the swivel at the top of the flight and place a small anti-kink lead at the head of the trace. This will make the double swivel at that point function properly. For spinning a sand-eel there is, of course, a special flight fitted with a corkscrew.

Whatever natural bait you employ, be sure it is tidily put on the tackle and, after a short period of spinning, has no stray ends. Renew it as soon as it shows the slightest sign of falling to pieces, no matter how much trouble this entails. Experienced anglers will bear witness to the value of this precaution; for whatever advantage a natural bait may have over an artificial one, that advantage passes to the latter, if the minnow or sprat is allowed to "go in rags".

As soon as fishing is over for the day, remove from the flight the bait that is still mounted there. Dry and clean thoroughly the whole of it; look over the nylon, wire, or whatever material the spine of the flight is made of; see the hooks shall have keen points in readiness for the next day; and replace any hook the

points of which have been damaged by a rock and cannot successfully be touched up. Then hang the flights and traces from nails
in the wall and strain them with some sea-leads or put the traces
between oiled felts.

## General Principles of Throwing a Bait

The accuracy of a cast depends upon how aim is taken at
the spot where the bait is intended to enter the water. The best
way is to turn the body towards that place before beginning the
back-swing and then to turn the trunk of the body a little, as
the rod is carried back. The rod-point should be held steady,
until the pull of the bait on the tip of the rod tells you that it is
time to start the forward stroke. This latter is a sweep of the rod
that ends with a marked finish to it; and the path of the rod-tip
is lower in the centre than at the beginning and at the end. The
bait thus travels slightly upwards, as it goes out over the river,
and drops more lightly than it would, were it thrown directly at
the water. The most important point of the foregoing is undoubtedly the waiting for the bait to swing right back and give
a tug to the rod-tip; only by doing this can you hope to throw
the bait, especially a light one, with accuracy and dexterity. The
range of the throw depends largely on the amount of kick put
into the finish of the rod, as it propels the bait forward, and
on the delicacy of the control of the drum. If a fixed spool
pattern of reel is being employed, the distance to which the bait
will go depends entirely on the final flick and on the angle at
which the bait begins its journey.

Whatever type of reel you are casting with, the same difficulty
will be encountered in releasing the line at the exact moment, so
that the bait shall go in the direction desired; this will come with
practice, after many upstream throws when the opposite was
intended and after sundry minor accidents, such as catching yourself in the back and getting hitched up in the bushes and other
objects, which at that time will seem to you without number!

## Spinning Tactics

Salmon spinning today is much nearer to fly fishing than it
used to be. When I was a boy, the spinner used huge and heavy
baits, and frequently caught the bottom of the river. Nowadays
the whole outfit is lighter. The invention of the wooden Devon

with a brass tube inside it has demonstrated the fact that, even quite early in the season, salmon will take a mid-water bait, provided that it is fished slowly. Devons are also constructed of plastic, which gives a semi-buoyant effect.

As a general rule in spinning the bait ought to be thrown right across and far beyond the fish, so that it may be working correctly by the time it reaches them. If you notice the bait is about to travel too far and may fall amongst the bushes on the opposite bank, increase very slightly and evenly the pressure on the spool (in all but fixed-spool reels) and the bait will drop before the danger is reached.

In enclosed places, where there is little room for a full swing, the overhead cast will have to be used, and the shorter rods now in common use make this a much easier task than formerly.

Spinning on broad rivers like the Tay or lower and middle reaches of the Wye, is very different from fishing on narrow, or tree-beset, or moorland streams, such as part of the Conway and the Welsh Dee, where extremely accurate throwing is demanded.

When your bait has hit the water fish it exactly as a fly is fished; down and across the lies. I feel that, in the earlier months, one should fish as long a line as possible, well downstream, at an angle of, say 30°. This will ensure that the bait crosses the fish as slowly as possible and according to its weight, the depth and speed of river and the character of the river-bed either allow the bait to swing round with the stream or reel in.

Even in February, fish will take a minnow that fishes well off the bottom so long as it is near the fish, and it moves slowly. If we find that our bait is skimming the surface, due to the river being very fast, the cure can be easy. Take a short length of lead wire, lay it on a level surface and hammer it flat. Then wrap this round the wire mounts of the Devon, making sure that it allows the latter to slide up the trace when a fish is hooked. So long as your wrapped wire is of less diameter than the swivel at the top of the mount all will be well.

Later, one may try the famous Spey trick of casting straight across the river. When the bait lands on the water, give two or three quick turns of the reel handle to take up any slack, and let the bait fish round on its own account. Simply let it do exactly what the river does to it. Do not wind in until the bait is directly below you. This, I am well aware, will offend the cherished beliefs of many fishermen. But it certainly works on a fast, large, and heavy river like the Spey.

Then there is the rather vexed question of casting upstream and bringing the bait down by fairly brisk winding. The reason for the questioning is that it is comparatively easy to foul hook a fish by this method, as the bait runs fairly low in the water.

One of the very best spinners I know tried it out, and his first three fish were all foul hooked. He never tried upstream fishing again. My own experience has been rather different, but I mention the matter here because the novice could find himself the recipient of frosty glares, or even equally frosty words for quite a number of people regard upstream spinning as poaching.

Provided that there is no objection, there is a good deal to be said for upstream fishing. Salmon certainly do take a bait spinning downstream, just as they will take a fly coming down a stream. The best method seems to be to cast upstream at a narrow angle, and pull the bait across the stream and down the cheek of the run. Do not wind too fast; just enough so as to keep the bait spinning and off the bottom of the river.

It is quite surprising at times to see what can be done with modern spinning gear in clear water. Using a wooden Devon with a fixed spool reel and a 9 lb. nylon line, the bait can be cast a long way, and it fishes very nicely. Some anglers may throw up their hands in horror at the idea of playing a fish on a 9 lb. line. Let me assure them that nylon of this size is immensely strong. I have no qualms whatever; and, personally, have never lost a fish while so doing, due to the line breaking. But I never go below 9 lb., because it is fine enough to give long casts with a light bait, and strong enough to handle a fish.

Sometimes, instead of the solid pull of a salmon, you may feel a succession of little tugs at the bait; raise the rod with a good, strong pull, and with luck, you will be into a twenty-pounder. It is curious that big fish sometimes take—especially a spoon—in this way. My biggest-ever on a spoon took it in this manner. At other times they give the normal heavy, solid pull which one expects. Always, and particularly in flood-time, continue winding in right up to the edge of the water. And keep your eyes fixed on the part of the water you know the minnow is traversing. How much of real value is lost to the angler, who does not do it would be hard to say. Personally, I think it is half the art of spinning. The swirl on the surface that indicates the salmon that has missed or turned away at the last moment, the torpedo-wave of the fish that is following cautiously a short distance behind the bait, or the actual glimpse of a following fish is to me the essence of spinning.

On the whole, I think it is better practice to keep the rod-point steady and not to attempt to work the bait through water of moderate pace. The slight addition in attractiveness of the bait, if there is any, is in my opinion, outweighed by the loss of rod-control at the moment a fish takes with a snatch. But the question is a very open one.

In any event, hold the rod well out over the water while the bait is coming round. Many anglers lower the rod-point, so that the latter may be forced down to the level where the fish are lying. The main objection to this is the production of a dangerously taut line. When the bait is below you, lift the point slightly and try to prevent the line and rod being in a straight line. I am sure the fish that takes a minnow well into its mouth has generally hooked itself by the time the tug is felt by the angler. Striking violently will not assist the hooks to catch hold and will only drive home hooks that are favourably placed and probably are already half-way home. If, however, a gentle pull is felt or rather sensed, a withholding of the line, so to speak, a touch, as though a leaf had brushed against the trace, do not hesitate a moment. Lift the rod evenly and tighten; salmon that take this way are thinking of letting go, before they have yet laid hold. I have assumed in this paragraph that the minnow or spoon is armed with not more than two trebles, the points of which are of the keenest. Many a fish has been allowed to go free, because the angler has not observed the flash, as a salmon turned away with minnow in its mouth or swerved from a minnow it would have taken, had the bait been presented a second time and in a different manner. These salmon have seized the bait and have gone forward with it, which is equivalent to their having taken it on a slack line.

Even with all the attractive modern spinning gear at one's disposal, and the pleasure in using it, however, I feel that spinning is overdone. Look through a modern tackle catalogue and see how much space is devoted to spinning gear, as compared with fly tackle. That, in itself, is a fair guide to the present market. Then go to a famous river and count the spinners and fly fishers. When I was young, spinning was not really respectable, so I, perforce, became a fly fisher. I still like it best of all the methods in use today.

## CHAPTER FOURTEEN

# PRAWN, SHRIMP, AND WORM

## Fishing the Prawn

WHETHER salmon on seeing a prawn in fresh-water recognize it as part of their staple diet or of their occasional food it is hard to say; but they eagerly take it boiled, as freely, I imagine, as in its natural state. That they prefer a prawn to which the *ova* are still adhering is certain; and in putting the bait on the flight care should be taken to ensure these being left undisturbed on the belly of the prawn. The whiskers, the legs and the scales ought to be most tenderly treated and the treble hooks, if they form part of the flight, should be hidden among the two first-named parts; but the two flukes of the tail I break off, as I find they impede me in my task of mounting the bait. When the prawn is to be spun, the head ought to look towards the tail-hook, so that the water-pressure shall not lift and strip the scaly covering of the body. Most prawn-fishers prevent this from happening by binding the body with fine copper wire. An ingenious development of this is to take a ten-inch length of red elastic thread. To one end tie a small hook and fasten the other to the lower ring of the swivel at the head of the flight. As soon as the prawn is in position, the silk is taken round the entire length of the body and back again, until all is firm, when the hook is pushed gently into some secure hold. In this way, all tying and untying with its inevitable messing of the fingers is dispensed with.

There are three methods of fishing the mounted prawn: spinning, floating, and sink-and-draw. Also the bait can be thrown out as in spinning and allowed to come round before being wound in. In this instance the bait is not revolving but is swimming round slowly with the current and is unencumbered by any but the smallest leads.

Spinning is better adapted to the broad, evenly-running stretches of a river flow. Whereas sink-and-draw is the only

practical way of fishing the throat of a pool (close into the rough),
the neck, where the river is constricted and pours over a sort of
step in its bed, in very deep "pots", in places where shoal water
drops down into a deep and also in holes and backwaters, where
salmon often rest during the midday heat. These conditions are
ideal for the employment of the sink-and-draw method of prawn-
fishing.

*Prawn Tackle*

The simplest form is that which consists of a single hook; this
should be tapered shank, round-bent, of the finest quality and
the point must be very keen. The hook is whipped very neatly
to a length of nylon in the other end of which a loop has been
tied. The methods of fixing the prawn on the tackle are impaling
it on the hook, by passing the point through the body, or by
threading it on the shank by using a baiting-needle, a far better
way. The single-hook tackle is far from satisfactory, as nine times
out of ten it spoils the bait. I have attached the prawn to the
single hook by means of copper wire alone and have found it
quite firm enough, but I prefer to use a tackle with a single treble
or back-to-back double at the head and a double on the back or
underneath, guarding the *ova*.

Many flights have been constructed for spinning the prawn
and one method is to mount the prawn on an ordinary tackle
that gives no kink to the prawn and bears no fins and put a
celluloid propeller below the first swivel at least twenty-four
inches from the bait, and a small Hillman lead (Fig. 87) in the
upper ring of the swivel. It is important that wire, *not* nylon be
used between the flight and the propeller. Figs. 94 and 95
illustrate flights in use today and give a better idea of their special
functions than could a verbal description.

One of the main principles in designing a tackle is to use the
minimum number of hook-points consistent with adequate ability
to hook and hold. Another is to hide the points and yet not to
blind them, so that when the salmon closes its mouth on the
bait, no part of the prawn shall guard the points and prevent
them entering the flesh of the fish. If weight is attached to the
tackle, pains should be taken to see it shows as little as possible;
it had better take the form of coils of lead-wire wrapped closely
and evenly round the central wire or gut of the flight. The best

method of attaching lead-wire is to place a needle alongside the
gut and wrap the lead around both; withdraw the needle and
tighten the lead by rolling it.

Here is one method of forestalling a salmon in its attempts to
take a bite out of the back or to suck the eggs from under the
belly, two frequent tricks it plays on the unsuspecting fisherman
and it usually gets away unscathed. A needle, sliding on a loop,

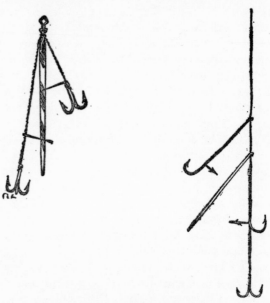

FIGS 94 & 95   PRAWN MOUNTS

to hold the prawn out straight; a lightly-leaded flight, consisting
of a single hook at the belly and a back-to-back double or a
treble at the head; a single or back-to-back double on the
angle of the back of the bait (Fig. 95). The single hook should
have whipped at its back a piece of stout copper wire, which
will pierce the body and keep the hook projecting in the right
direction; the wire, however, should not be so long that the end
of it has to be turned round the prawn; this breaks the bait.
The main and the subsidiary flights are kept in place with a
binding of copper wire or of nylon to which the small eyed hook,
recommended on page 204, has been fastened. The belly-hook is

to be set in the vertical plane and the double at the head in the horizontal.

It always pays to look after prawning tackle, to remove the bait at the end of the day and clean the flight scrupulously, so that the metal parts shall not rust. Look at the points of the hooks and, if they are dulled or turned, sharpen them again in readiness for the morrow.

A rod, reel and line suitable for spinning will serve equally well for prawning. The trace is usually of some form of strong single wire, such as Alasticum or of nylon. The former has the advantage of not snapping in the air, while travelling forward during the act of casting, if there should form in it the smallest kink. Prawn-tackles are easily lost through catching snags on the river-bed; nylon here fills the bill on account of its cheapness and also because leads can be attached without causing the damage to it that is done by them to wire.

The usual length of a trace for prawning is about three feet; a swivel is usually fitted at the head of the flight and a double swivel is fastened at the top of the nylon or wire. If the prawn is destined for spinning and an independent propeller is to be employed to impart torque to the bait, a fan of celluloid is placed up the trace, so that it controls the lower ring or the lower swivel and thus causes the bait to rotate.

For the sink-and-draw method in deep holes there are two points in the tackle where the weight can be fastened: a large lead, threaded on a fine strand of nylon, is suspended below the bait and acts as a leger; the same type of lead can be tied to a swivel or ring specially introduced into the trace at a distance of two feet or so above the flight. The advantage of the latter way is that the prawn floats round independently and almost on a horizontal keel; also, instead of being rigid, it moves attractively in obedience to any current in the vicinity. Except in the method of sink-and-draw, fish as light as you can and always fish slowly. It gives the fish a good chance to see the bait, allows the bait to sink and provides the current with an opportunity of endowing the dead prawn with the semblance of life. Further, the salmon receives ample time to get a fair hold on it, instead of the tug on its mouth, caused by the weight of the stream on a taut line, giving a clear warning that it is high time to let go.

Whether a salmon that has taken a prawn should be *struck*

at once, or allowed to pouch the bait and then *struck*, or should be permitted to hook itself, is a thorny question. The most rational solution appears to me to allow the salmon to get a proper hold of the prawn and then to assist the hooks to penetrate.

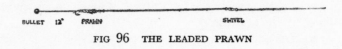

BULLET   12°   PRAWN                              SWIVEL

FIG 96   THE LEADED PRAWN

Some anglers drop the rod on feeling a fish take. An Irishman and an exceedingly-fine fisherman, whom I met on the Chester Dee and on the Spey, lowers the point of the rod and gives out slack line, a coil of which he always held in his hand, while the prawn was swimming round. He then tightened rather strongly. When he was reeling in, he kept the rod-point high in readiness to give slack line; also an elevated rod made it possible to draw in the bait very deliberately without fear of it getting foul of the bottom.

### Preserving Prawns

Most anglers do not care to concern themselves with this matter and buy their prawns ready bottled for them. This habit is expensive. If you are expecting to use some scores of these baits during the season, it is far more economical to prepare them yourself. Buy from the man who catches or who boils prawns (the former will naturally charge less) the number you need and, if possible, get them in sizes by the dozen; this will save sorting them later and ensure you possessing an adequate supply of the rarer and most frequently needed small size. Salted prawns are very poor substitutes, but the stale kind, on sale at the shops of inland towns, are very soft and soon fall to bits.

Insert straight pieces of wire of hairpin gauge in the prawns. The baits will thus remain straight and have in them a hole, into which the pin of the flight will fit. Place them in a jar containing a solution of glycerine and water in equal quantities, to which a little formalin (forty per cent aqueous solution of formaldehyde) has been added, and cover them over with a tightly fitting lid. Another preserving-fluid is a solution of equal quantities by weight of sugar and water. I have tried the effect of this treatment on boiled prawns alone and have no idea whether the same preservative would be successful when they are unboiled; nor have I tried the effect on salmon of prawns presented in their natural state. Dyed prawns I have used with good results. I dipped some that had lost their colour in a cold solution of aniline magenta; and they were readily seized by a brace of salmon that had made a temporary home of a large deep back-water. Fish in that hole were usually the despair of every angler throughout the season. Hooking a fish there and playing it might be accomplished: landing it was quite another story! I have never, however, had any success with the plastic prawns sold in fishing-tackle shops.

## Prawning

Spinning the prawn is to a very large extent covered by the rules of spinning with a minnow or spoon. The difference lies in the speed at which the bait should be wound in; in prawn-ing, it can hardly be brought in too deliberately, consistently with the rate at which the water is flowing. In a very slack stream, there is a danger of the hook catching in some snag or obstruction on the bed of the river; the rod-point should be raised a little, or, alternately, the line recovered somewhat faster. In a back-water, the set of the current varies from place to place and ought to be studied closely, if you are to make the most of it in prawn-fishing. A whirlpool is quite able to suck down or hold the line; and the bait will sink down amongst the very rocks you think it is clearing by a good margin. The whole procedure is a com-paratively simple mode of salmon-fishing and needs little more said about it.

The sink-and-draw way of using the prawn requires an intimate knowledge of the river-bed at certain spots favoured by salmon and experience enough to recognize the pull of a salmon, when a novice would think the bait had got foul of rock, weed, or sunken bough; and that experience is dearly purchased and never infallible in practice.

The throat of a pool in low water is well adapted to the use of the prawn. The rod is held over the rough water and the line is paid out in jerks, so that the prawn appears to be moving by those characteristic backward jumps, which it achieves in life by flicks of its powerful tail. Let the bait go down as far as you think necessary to cover all the lies; this may well exhaust sixty yards of spinning-line and even more. Then swing the rod-point over and reel up slowly, so that the bait explores the slack edge of the current and gives a second chance to salmon that were too slow or lazy to come, when they saw the bait the first time, or that saw it at the wrong angle. It is generally accepted that a prawn is most likely to be taken by a salmon, when it is first seen. Work the bait in different parts of the rough water, always allowing it to go with the current and never against it, otherwise the scales of the body will be disturbed; and no fish can be expected to look at an untidy prawn. This way of fishing the prawn can be done equally successfully with a rod, reel and line constructed for fly-fishing, as it is quite a simple matter to draw line off a fly-reel and to pay it out; and often the additional reach afforded by a long rod makes all the difference in being able to let down the prawn on the far edge of a stickle. If a shorter rod had been used, the point would have projected only as far as the stream and the bait would have been washed round.

The length of rod in prawn-fishing is sometimes a vital matter when you are fishing a "pot" in a river with a rock-cut channel. There is such a place on the Dart : a narrow neck of rock through which the water enters and spreads over the surface of a very

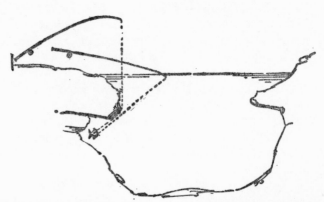

FIG 97  Unless the point of the rod is thrust out across and into the water there is danger of the line being cut by the rock-edge, as the salmon runs upstream

deep hole. Centuries of wear have undercut the rock at the neck
and the line attached to a salmon when it runs upstream, is taken
beneath this sharp ledge and infallibly cut, as though by a razor
(Fig. 97). Fortunately, I received warning of this, used a sixteen-
foot rod and, on hooking a fish, reached out with the point as
far as I could and dipped it under the surface. The line tightened
up free of the obstruction, but was so badly drowned that, when
the salmon leaped from the water, it was some twenty-five yards
above the point where the line entered the water. For a moment
I doubted whether that could have been the fish I was playing,
until I noticed the line it was dragging after it. I was lucky to
get that fish! It was in apple-blossom time and there were sea-
lice on it.

You can never be sure how a salmon will come at a prawn.
One day you will feel a gentle touch, as the bait is delicately
picked up; the next the fish will take it boldly, so that you feel
a snatch, a sensation of the bait being shaken and, I hope, a
steady pull, as line is torn off the reel. Only too often the snatch
is followed by a straightened rod and a limp line, for the losses
in this mode of fishing are exceedingly heavy, and they are without doubt due to the attempt to fix in a salmon's mouth an absurd
array of rather dull-pointed hooks.

The other kind of place where the sink-and-draw game often
pays is a broad pool, across which you throw the prawn and then
recover line in short jerks that give a most attractive motion
to the bait. This way has now largely been superseded by
straightforward spinning.

There is, lastly, a special way of dibbing with a prawn in the
deep holes and backwaters that are common features of rivers
flowing through rocky beds. The disadvantage of using either
prawn or worm in the manner about to be described is the ease
with which salmon can thereby be snatched, especially if a large
lead is employed as a sinker; but the backwater, in which I have
most often practised this form of prawn-fishing, does not lend
itself to snatching, because there are far too many sunken snags
and too few salmon. A tree thrusts itself almost horizontally over
the backwater. Along this I used to climb, until I could poke
the rod-point through the branches and, by releasing the small
coil of line held in my hand, let the prawn gently down into the
depths, that is, with the water at normal summer-level, about

ten feet. As soon as I felt the bait touch bottom, I started, by pulling line through the rings, to lift it very deliberately to the surface and then allowed it to sink again at the same pace. If there was no reply in the first area, I went on to another and thus covered all the backwater within reach of an eleven-foot spinning-rod. It was not very easy to tighten on a fish that came up for the prawn; it was the most awkward place I ever knew in which to play and gaff a fish; yet the sight of a great salmon ascending through several feet of clear sunlit water to grab the prawn and go off with it across its jaws was well worth all the trouble and the loss of far more than were landed. One day, I made the experiment of not striking when the salmon took the prawn. The line was quite slack, but, after half a minute or so, the fish spat the bait with considerable force from its mouth and smacked it very savagely with its tail. After that, I decided the hooks should be pulled in as soon as a pluck was felt. A remarkable thing about this prawning was the way fish took old and bleached baits dipped in magenta aniline dye; they appeared quite indifferent to the colour of the bait. For prawning in this manner, use a trace of nylon, a *very keen* single round-bend hook and a lead attached below the hook by a foot of fine nylon.

In some rivers it is possible to spot a salmon and guide the prawn to it. I know a rocky ledge with clear and shallow water flowing over it that is a chosen lodge, where salmon rest in the month of May. You must creep up gradually from the upstream side (for it is a backwater), until you can see over the edge, and you are almost sure to find a fish in possession. Dib a prawn above and allow it to come round with the eddy in front of the fish. It may not be taken at once; it will, perhaps, swing in the current for a minute or more, before it arouses any interest; it may not be taken at all. But if you do it skilfully, the odds are in your favour.

*Shrimp Fishing*

The shrimp used in this mode of angling is a baby prawn, which when straightened out and trimmed, is no longer than one and five-eighths of an inch, from tail to beak. It comes from the Galway coast and is also found off Dorsetshire. Fortunately, it can now be obtained bottled and preserved, of the right shade of red and already straightened; but, if this particular variety of prawn is unobtainable, ordinary shrimps should be got from a fishmonger, freshly boiled and plunged into salt-water, in order to toughen and redden them, in so far as this treatment can produce this effect.

A shrimp can be presented in several ways, but the most effective, in my opinion, is spinning it. If you decide not to spin the bait, you can fish it with a fairly-long, two-handed and light fly-rod, and you have the choice of single-hook and double-hook mountings.

In mounting a shrimp on a single-hook tackle, you are less likely to damage it, if you use a baiting-needle, inserted below the feelers, to pull the hook-to-nylon through, than if you insert the hook-point in the bait and attempt to work the shrimp over the bend. After the baiting-needle has been disengaged from the nylon-loop and the shrimp adjusted on the shank, a short length of wire must be used to hold all in position. The trace should be of nylon with a short piece of lead wire coiled round it, to sink the bait.

As a shrimp fished in this manner is not spun, a float may be needed to keep it off the bottom, as it is going down the smooth dubs of slack pools. But with this type of tackle, the shrimp can often be dropped into broken water behind boulders and worked on the *sink-and-draw* principle. And where you can command the deep side of a run under an overhanging bank, you can lob the bait upstream, follow it down and pay out line as the un-leaded shrimp wends its way downstream and always in advance of the lead, which comes behind it bumping along the river-bed. The weak point about this method is the short distance to which it can be fished; it is only adapted to the places where there is a long *gutter*, down which the fisherman, by paying out line, can let down the bait. Still, it is a fairly-effective method of taking fish on a long, light rod for which two hands are necessary and is a change from fly-fishing.

If you feel a holding of the bait, as though it had got foul of some snag, tighten at once. Do not allow a fish to go off to pouch the bait, as you would do, were you using a worm.

Shrimp-fishing is far more effective, if the distance to which the shrimp can be thrown is much extended by using a light spinning-rod with a light line of 8–10 lb. B.S. and adding a little weight to the trace. A shrimp or small prawn weighs about one-twelfth of an ounce. In most instances, a lead, heavier than one-eighth of an ounce, would be quite useless for fishing a river of the type I have in mind during a period when it is running at summer-level.

*Equipment*

The tackle I have found best is that which consists of a celluloid flange and a swivel fitted to a single-pin mounting; the flight is one small treble whipped to a length of nylon and the shrimp is bound to the tackle by red elastic thread.

FIG 98   THE MOUNTED SHRIMP
Single treble-hook mounting of a shrimp, which is kept in position
with red elastic

The best rod for the purpose is either a light one-handed spinning-rod or one that is nine and a half feet in length and weighs about ten ounces; the latter I find more practical for fishing among bushes and it suits my own method of fishing out a cast.

*Spinning the Shrimp*

Fish the shrimp as though it were a sunk fly. Always cast it beyond the lie of the salmon and present it, so that it passes, as far as you can judge, a few inches upstream of the fish and practically at the depth at which it is lying. The factors governing the depth at which the shrimp will fish are the speed of the current, considered in relation to the size and pitch of the propeller at the head of the tackle, the position of the rod-point and the weight of the sinker. You can control the depth by the rate at which you wind in, or by not winding in at all, and by altering the pitch of the celluloid fans. All these things are of the utmost importance, because I am practically certain that many fish take the shrimp, having hardly moved from where they are lying.

The stream is best searched by casting at a steep downstream angle, so that the bait comes across to your own bank as slowly as possible and at a depth that makes it easy for the fish to take. Fish in good lies—at any rate in summer—will not leave them if they can help it; you ought to try, therefore, to put the bait very close to them. Progress down the pool consists of the usual number of casts of similar length delivered at a constant angle across the water, though as soon as I have worked off the broken water into smooth runs, I make a practice of casting alternately downstream, as described above, and of fishing the cast slowly across a known lie and then making a straight throw across, or even upstream, from where I am standing and then wind in fairly rapidly. This will sometimes arouse the exceptional fish that will run, in summer-time, at a quickly-moving object.

Fishing a pool from the shallow side, I prefer to fish out the cast, so that the bait would bump the bottom, if I did not begin to wind in as soon as the line straightens below me. I am thinking, at the moment, of wading to a depth of about three feet six inches in a pool that is deeper beyond me, but shallower inshore. If a cast straightens out without an offer from a fish, I wind up quickly, while the bait is passing over the shallows, because I do not like a fish to follow or attempt to take in this part of the pool.

If you are fishing the pool on the deep side, cast much flatter and across the stream and, after winding a few turns to get contact with the bait, stop winding, because the bait is already half-way across. For the last part of the journey across, let the bait actually take out a little line and sink downstream, but not so fast as the current, or else the bait will cease to spin. When the line is right under your own bank, wind it in very slowly, with the point of the rod held almost in the water.

I believe a shrimp is an effective bait at most times and in all seasons, if it is fished with regard to the conditions then obtaining. If fish are in the pools, the variable conditions to be studied are the height, temperature and colour of the water.

*Water height.* Using a shrimp weighted with an ounce and a half of lead, I have been able to catch fish in spate-water. On the other hand, I have taken fish in water hardly deep enough to cover a fish at all. But the ideal conditions are those of low summer-level, which indicate the use of a fly of size 9 and smaller.

*Water colour.* I like it gin-clear. The more colour there is in the water, the less salmon take the shrimp. If you cannot see your boots when you are wading knee-deep, do not expect this bait to be of any use at all.

In so far as *atmosphere* is concerned, a bright day and a clear sky, or a fresh wind with cloud is the best. When there is continuous rain, a cold wind from the sea, mist, fog, or on an afternoon that is heavy with thunder-heat, you are unlikely to do much good with a shrimp.

I find an afternoon-sun shining down a pool is hopeless; it pays to wait until the sun has gone below a hill before attempting to fish in the evening. As soon as the glow disappears, exchange the shrimp for a big fly. If you can see the shape of a shrimp, but not its colour, you can be sure it is too late in the evening for this mode of fishing.

By far and away the most important feature, providing water-height is reasonably favourable, is *water-temperature*; and this is a condition that can be met by the angler by choosing the time to fish. My own records show that certain times of the day are effective for the months in which shrimp-fishing is practicable:

| | |
|---|---|
| *May:* | *Between 11 a.m. and 3 p.m.* |
| *June:* | *Between 9 a.m. and 1 p.m., and 8 p.m. and 9 p.m.* |
| *July:* | *Between 5 and 7 a.m., and 9 and 11 p.m.* |
| *August:* | *Between 8 and 11 a.m., and 7 and 8 p.m.* |
| *September:* | *Between 9 and 12 noon, and 7 and 8 p.m.* |
| *October:* | *Any time up to about 2 p.m.; but, although fish take freely in this month, they are hardly worth catching.* |

Wind is a nuisance with such a light bait, from the casting point of view, but a downstream wind, if one can wade out far enough and fish further downstream than usual, is an advantage, because it increases the fishing-area and makes it possible to fish water that without wind would be dead. You can use the wind-ruffle to spin the bait. Many fish will come on the take under the influence of a ruffling wind—conditions which make fly-fishing very unpleasant.

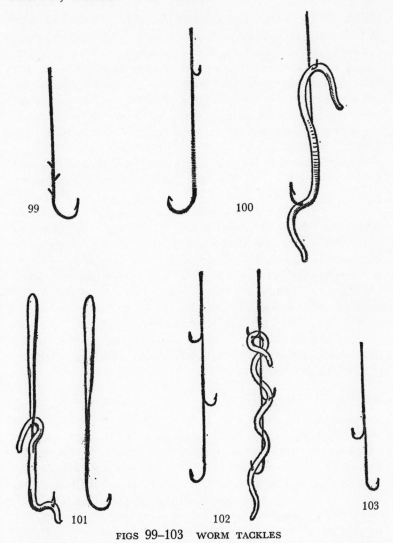

FIGS 99–103  WORM TACKLES

Strike hard and to ensure success, fish with as little belly as possible and also keep the hook-points keen by the use of a carborundum-stone. Keep a *tight* line from the moment you feel a fish is on.

Playing the fish is probably the greatest excitement that

shrimp-fishing has to offer, owing to the lightness of the line used. A little thought will reveal the fact that a light line definitely precludes anything in the way of pulling a fish upstream to land him. I have lost so many fish experimenting with light lines, that I am able to say these light lines force you to keep below the fish all the time. If you are fishing from the shallow side of the pool, you can so work on a fish from below, that it beaches itself above you. Do not reel up. Walk inland. Of course, if you are fishing off the bank on the deep side, you can only land a fish with the assistance of a gaff, and even then you should keep below and let the fish fight its way in the stream above you.

I realize this does not attempt to survey all phases of shrimp-fishing, or light-tackle methods, but I think the shrimp is one of the few, if not the only bait, which, if selected small enough, can be fished alongside, behind, or even in front of a fly, without detriment to the fly's prospects. During August of one year, when the water was low, one pool yielded us fifty fish, of which half came to a No. 11 size fly and half to an inch-long shrimp. It does not appear from this example that shrimp-fishing spoilt the pool for fly-fishing. I hardly think the same thing would have occurred had we mixed fly-fishing with prawning, worming, or spinning an artificial bait.

## Worming for Salmon

I know of only five species of tackle that are of practical value in this kind of worm-fishing: the single round-bend hook, to which several bristles have been whipped, in order to support the bait and keep it in position (Fig. 99); the same type of hook and a small hook whipped an inch above the end of the larger one, to which the head of the worm can be attached (Fig. 100); the round-bend hook whipped to a loop of nylon within which the head of the topmost worm can be slipped, so that the whole bait is extended in an attractive manner (Fig. 101); the Stewart tackle (Fig. 102); and that invented by Cholmondeley-Pennell (Fig. 103). The two last-named are not particularly efficient in hooking, as the small hooks, three in the first instance and two in the other, do not project enough to go home easily and with despatch. Of the three single-hook tackles the third is my favourite; it was given to me by a friendly fisherman I met on Speyside and I have

not come across it since then. The method of baiting these tackles
will be seen by referring to the figures.

The weighting of a worm-tackle is done either by tying with
a length of fine nylon a small lead below the worm, so that it
will function as a leger and allow the bait to be fished at a
constant distance from the bottom and also save the tackle,
because the lead, being round, will roll over many obstacles that
would afford a fatal attachment for the hooks; and if a snag
holds the weight so tightly, that it cannot be retrieved, there is
no more damage caused than the loss of the lead and nylon. The
placing of the lead in this position is well enough in coloured
water; for use in a low, clear stream, the lead ought to be far
less obvious and the mode of fishing somewhat different.

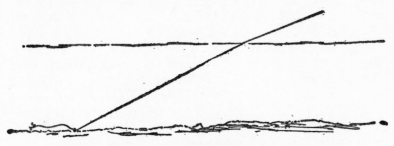

FIG 104   The worm tackle weighted above the worm

The trace to which the worm-tackle is fastened should be a
length of nylon, in each end of which a loop has been whipped.
For clear water, take a thin trace and fasten half-way up it a
lead, making the attachment with fine nylon or with tying-silk;
or the lead may be run on to the trace and held from descending
as far as the worm by the presence of a tiny split shot nipped on
the nylon. This form of tackle is adapted to running and by its
aid a worm can be thrown across a sandy pool and allowed to
swing round under the influence of the stream. The lead will
roll along the bed of the river and the worm will precede it
slightly raised above the sand. You will sense many obstructions
and feel frequent checks in the journey of the worm across to
your own bank. Every time you must make certain it is a snag
and not a fish that is the true cause of the tightening of the line,
until you learn to know almost by intuition how to distinguish

220 SALMON FISHING

between them. As often as not the salmon moves off with the
bait and this should be hint enough to let out line, if the current
allows, until the fish has ceased running. You may then reel up
cautiously, until you can feel a weight, and tighten. A small pull
will usually fix the hook, which by that time will probably have
been taken well down.

Worming for salmon in thick water is like worming for trout.
The line should be kept as taut as possible and the bait held
up off the bottom. Whether it is better to tighten at the instant
the pull of a salmon is felt or give line for the worm to be gorged
I do not know. In fast water, you will often have to throw the
worm upstream, in order to get it to the required depth; this is
about the most promising way of losing tackle through getting
soundly fixed amongst the boulders! But the risk will have to be
taken, or another spot must be found. This is probably the occasion when the otter might be a godsend.

The deadliest time for worm-fishing is, in my experience,
during a low-water spate. Some years ago, I was trying for some
fish that I knew were lying within a rather restricted area and
had taken out fine tackle and a long trout-rod. There was a
sudden thunderstorm a short distance upstream and the river,
without rising more than an inch or two, came down thick yellow
with road-washings. I luckily had some worm-tackle in my wallet
and a lead I had previously been using on the Dart. Under the
stones there were a few large worms, squirrel-tails, to be had and
by the time the rain had ceased I was ready to test conditions
Chaytor had found so favourable for the use of the worm. I
failed to hook the first fish that took the worm, partly through
my haste in tightening and partly, because I had forgotten the
rod I was using would yield too easily and could not be expected
to pull home the large hooks. But the result of my fishing fully
justified what Chaytor had written of worming in a low-water
spate.

*Worms*

Fresh worms are never as tough or as lasting as those which
have been prepared. Get some large lob or dew worms; place
them in a tin with plenty of dry moss and leave them there for
a few days, a week if possible; they will then be scoured and
free from the slime that makes them slippery to handle. When

you take out your quota for the day, remember to slip into your pocket a small tin of grit and dip the worms in this before attempting to thread them on the hook. The grit that adheres to the worm will provide an excellent grip and make the labour of putting a worm on a hook an easy task.

CHAPTER FIFTEEN

# HOOKING, PLAYING AND LANDING

*Hooking*

HOW many fishermen really know the way a salmon comes to the fly? Its way is not that of a trout which takes on the surface or after it has turned down; for when a salmon makes up its mind to take a fly it slants upwards very gently and sets a course to intercept the fly immediately upstream of its lie. It has no intention of spending any unnecessary energy in achieving this object. Provided it has correctly worked out its own speed and that of its quarry, it will take the fly just as its own speed drops to zero. It will not seize the fly in its jaws but as it swims towards the fly it will open its mouth and suck it in. The latter is then drawn in together with a gulp of water which in the ordinary course of events would have been "inhaled". Having taken the fly the fish will then sink backwards and downwards to its lie, that is, it allows the current to carry it back and merely increases its own depth. From this it will be realized that the fish that makes the "perfect take" is a very difficult fish to hook. Inexperienced fishermen, unaware the fly has actually been taken, often accuse the fish of *coming short*.

For years I thought in terms of "head-and-tail" rise. I now know that to get a salmon to show like that is tantamount to saying the fly is being fished incorrectly, probably too fast, so that the fish has to turn, rise and grab. Whenever an angler tells me that "it took with a perfect head-and-tail rise", I know instinctively his next words will be "and I rose two others and pulled yet another". As I said, a salmon does not rise and go down with the fly as a trout does. He sees it in front and to one side and swims forward to intercept it when directly ahead. He tries to remain on an even keel all the time. All seen rises are caused by fishing either too fast or with drag. Thus the fly is being pulled towards the surface, which occasions the head-and-tail rise.

It is my guess that something like 70 per cent of all the fish hooked on the fly are either those who have miscalculated the speed of the fly or who have been chasing a fly dragged by the angler. In each case the fish is determined to get the fly, turns slightly, grabs it and then turns back. In the former case the angler feels a pull and the fish is hooked. Again, a fisherman may *mend* the line just before the fly gets to the fish, thereby decreasing the speed of the fly. In this case, the fish turns to take the fly, the angler feels a gentle pull and exclaims, "Trout". He is wrong; it was a salmon.

When a salmon takes a fly confidently, the latter will often be found stuck far back in the throat. I have known one instance of the fly having been drawn into the mouth with such force, that it was carried out through the gills in company with the water expelled in the ordinary course of breathing. The bend of the hook had caught the edge of the gill cover and, without actually having been hooked, the fish was held firmly enough to be played and successfully landed.

A salmon hooked in the back of the tongue hardly makes a fight for it, but comes meekly to the gaff. The only explanation for this I can suggest is the proximity of the heart and of a main artery to this region. The tongue in the salmon is fixed, not free as in the land animals. Nevertheless, it is possible to hook a salmon in the tip of the tongue and for the hook to tear through the tender flesh of which it consists and for the salmon, in consequence, to go free.

The most secure hold on a salmon is undoubtedly in the corner of the jaw, for there deepest penetration can be obtained. A hook fast in any part of the edge of the mouth, either in the top or in the bottom mandible, is usually to be depended on to hold; but even there small hard bony regions exist into which a hook-point can only be made to enter if considerable force is exerted. When a salmon has been hooked in the point of either the upper or lower jaw, I imagine it followed the fly for some distance and then took it directly from behind. When a hook is stuck fast in the corner of the jaws, it is quite clear that the fish has come across at the fly or has swum up stream with it in its mouth and has turned its head down, before the angler tightened.

*Pricking a Salmon*

Upon the question of whether a salmon will come again that has taken a lure into its mouth, has felt the sharpness of the hook and has succeeded, before the barb has been pulled home, in ejecting the hook I prefer to keep an open mind. If a fisherman *pricks* a salmon and shortly afterwards and in the same place hooks one, it is rarely possible to be quite sure whether the latter is or is not identical with the fish he missed a few minutes earlier. Only once have I been in a position to say with certainty a fish I had pricked cared so little for the pain of being pricked or the sensation of having the fly torn from its grip, that it returned again and again to the assault, until it happened to leave things too late, failed to eject the fly in time and was soundly hooked. Inside its mouth were numerous tears and gashes, which were still bleeding from the scratching of the hook-point. Looking at the position of the wounds in the mouth, I could not conceive how this salmon had been able to postpone being caught until the fifth time of taking the fly.

A salmon that is thought to have been pricked often acts in much the same way as one lightly hooked. It *shows* almost immediately afterwards and sometimes gives a spirited gymnastic display, by making a series of flat jumps or *ricochets* across the surface of the pool, reminding one of the stones thrown, as in "ducks and drakes", to skim along the top of the water. Fright also will very often be the cause of a salmon rising straight-away and leaping from the water, chiefly I imagine due to having been touched by the line or having been pricked externally by the hook-point, or through having had the fly snatched away, before it could close its jaws upon it. Evidence that a salmon has been pricked on the outside is sometimes supplied by a scale being found transfixed by the point of the hook, when the fly has been brought in for examination. The fish has thus clearly escaped being foul-hooked by a very narrow margin. Foul-hooking is the penetration of the hook-point in any part other than in the interior of the mouth. The fish has for some reason or other failed to get the fly into its mouth or has not closed soon enough upon the fly when it was there. Instead, the salmon has run up against or has rolled over on the cast, the fisherman has felt a tug on the line and has tightened, only to find he has pulled the barb into

29 & 30 Artificial aids; *above*, the Salmon Pass, Llangollen Weir, on the River Dee, Denbighshire; *below*, the Salmon Ladder at the Pitlochry Dam, Loch Faskally

31 Breeding new species of salmon; catching grilse in an upstream trap
near Newport, Co Mayo

the flank, the belly, a fin, the tail, or some other part of its body. Pricking a salmon on the outside and foul-hooking occur so frequently, that I attribute to them some of the losses usually put down to pricking a salmon in the mouth, or to the hook having torn through a very slight hold. Sometimes the angler is to blame.

## Playing a Salmon

Once I hooked a salmon that made off on its first rush with such speed, that it beached itself on the shore opposite, where it lay writhing and kicking until I cautiously drew it back into the water. It thereupon landed itself on the bank from which I was fishing, but did so at a place I could not reach, owing to intervening bushes and an awkward wire fence. Again I pulled it gently back into the river; and the contest followed a normal course. But sometimes you will see a salmon, after a moment's hesitation, get off the mark with such speed that, before you realize what is happening, it is running up the shallows in the tail of the pool; or it is showing its back, as it makes its way with snake-like motions through the thin water. Take advantage of the second's grace, given you by a salmon as soon as it is hooked, to take stock of the situation, if you have not done it before. Note the easiest way out of the pool and think out the best manner of dealing with any emergency that might arise. Look at the time, so that you may, later on, be able to gauge the most likely taking-periods for that season of the year.

You will probably be obliged, on first hooking a fish, to let it go wherever it may be urged by the sensation of restraint imposed by a taut line. But do all within your power to guide a running fish away from snags and from a strong central run, if there be one in the pool; by entering this it may put a bight in the line, so that the latter is drowned, and thus dislodge the hook or straighten it against the resistance, offered by the slack line to the water. The only method of saving yourself from this indignity is to keep the line as taut as you can and to lift the rod-point high, especially if there are rocks ahead.

There is, however, an exception to this. If you are standing on a bank to play a fish, get opposite to the latter and carry the rod-point almost horizontally downstream and a little inland. The result of this is to put side-strain on the fish with the minimum

P

length of line through the rings, so that the line is kept taut
and there is little danger of it being drowned, and the factor of
elasticity in the line is preserved. This needs some explanation.
If the angler on the bank lifts the rod-point, the line is stretched
taut and leaves the water close to the fish. Every kick and
struggle, therefore, is felt directly by the tackle, whereas the
water acts as a shock-absorber.

As soon as you feel that a salmon has come to the end of
its run, gather in line as expeditiously as possible; a slack line
is an invitation to a fish to take it round some snag or sub-

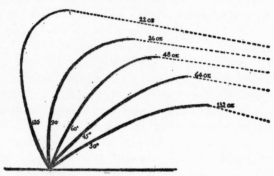

FIG 105    This shows the strains that can be exerted by a rod
and makes it clear that "butting" (120° or so) is the worst possible
way of putting additional pressure on a fish

merged stone, through which it is either jammed or chafed and,
perhaps, cut. At times a salmon will come back so quickly, that
you will wish your reel was of the multiplying pattern; but the
pressure of the water against the line will generally be enough to
hold the hook securely in position, until the rod resumes the
strain. If the bank is clear of bush and fence, walk backwards
inland while you are reeling in.

Above all, keep the point of the rod up. The more the rod is
bent, the safer is the cast from being broken by a sudden strain
and the less is the leverage upon the fish. This is rather different
from the effect that anglers of the last century thought they were
achieving by "giving a fish the butt". The main deduction one
draws from the diagram above is that, to put more strain on a
fish, the rod should be lowered, so that the pull is straighter. It

is, therefore, clear that until the moment has arrived for dealing
more severely with the fish, i.e. in the closing stages or to prevent
him reaching some snag, the rod-point ought to be kept well up,
especially when very fine tackle is being used.

How a salmon will sometimes appear cunningly to make use
of the current, in order to get a rest during the course of the
struggle, was most ably demonstrated to me by one that, after a
round of five minutes or so, made a point of swinging under my
own bank, in an area of slack water, sheltered by a group of
stones below where I was standing. There it lay recovering its
strength, nor could I move it. Eventually it swam out again into
the main stream. This procedure went on for three-quarters of an
hour, reasonable enough if the fish should turn out to weigh forty
pounds or more, but something more than generous to the fifteen
pounder it proved to be. At length, I got that salmon by holding
it very lightly and so persuading it to go above me; I then put
on all the pressure I dare and, using side-strain, brought the fish
into a convenient bay, higher up than where I was standing. The
rest was easy. I do not offer this example as evidence that a
salmon has intelligence enough to ally itself to the current with
the purpose of beating the angler in one way or another. The
incident happened through the configuration of the river-bed and
the flow of the current adding to the difficulties I had created
for myself by handling the fish badly.

Two other manœuvres that a salmon frequently employs are
"boring" and "jigging"; and how many anxious moments these
have caused. Boring gives me the impression that the salmon is
straining, as a horse strains at the bit; but jigging feels as though
the gut were being pulled in little jerks, as a horse will pull and
get its head down, when it is trying to throw the bit forward and
get it between the teeth. Of the two jigging is the more alarming,
but a hook, once well home, is rarely dislodged thereby. Yet every
moment I expect the hook to be worked free.

Boring is little to be feared, except when it means the searching
of the sides and sharp edges of the rocks in the pool. It then
becomes perilous, from the fisherman's point of view, because the
cast may be chafed and even rubbed right through. When a
salmon is doing all it can to rid itself of the pull of the line, it
strains against the latter with its head down, sometimes at an
angle as great as forty-five degrees from the horizontal; you will

often notice this when, in the course of the struggle, it comes near to you, provided that the water is limpid enough for you to see what is taking place. This familiar attitude is clearly adopted by the salmon, because it can in that way get a greater purchase on the water than in any other. When you have forced a salmon to lift its head, you may take it as a sign the struggle is all but over; also you will understand, what the ghillie means, when he tells you that "its head is still down", or that "it is coming up".

Walking a fish up is a simple trick by means of which it can be persuaded to move upstream out of the vicinity of a snag or from the draw of pool. The rod-point is lowered, the line held and the angler walks gently upstream dragging the fish after him; but the line should be held delicately, so that it can be released if the fish should start to run. The whole manœuvre should be carried out boldly and it is essential that the tension of the line be even.

Handlining is a desperate remedy to bring in a salmon that you have allowed to "anchor" itself in a stream by lying at an angle to the flow, and which cannot be moved by side strain with the rod, or is half played-out and is floating down to the tail of the pool. Drop the rod-point, pull on the line alone and you will be surprised what a purchase is thereby placed on the fish. Hold the rod quite loosely; you want to get rid of its pliancy for the moment. Pull firmly on the line alone, but always exercise your sense of "touch", so that the line shall not be strained beyond its tensile strength. In a general way, I believe few fish can resist this direct pull; they are bound to come in.

If you are fishing on a bank and the salmon you are playing runs in towards you at a speed that allows no time to recover line, walk inland and take up line in that way, until you are able to reel up and walk forward again. If the fish is still fresh, it is better not to reel up short, but to play it from the place to which you have retreated and preserve the elasticity of a longish line. As soon as the salmon goes out again, you can follow it to the bank and resume playing it in the usual manner. Occasionally a very tired fish beaches itself. If it should have chosen to run up your bank and a ghillie is with you, walk back inland and keep the same length of line out rather than run the risk of being broken through the line being reeled in short. If, however, you are alone, reel up steadily and keep the rod-point vertical, until you are able to reach the salmon and gaff it.

A fish that jumps frequently in its efforts to get rid of the fly or bait which holds it, or rushes about the pool, soon comes to the gaff; so far from trying to control a lively fish, an experienced angler will, in most circumstances, allow it to play itself out, although there will be anxious moments when the leaping is going on. But, if the point of the rod is dropped when the fish leaves the water and the line is tightened up directly it returns, there is little cause to fear the loss of a well-hooked fish. There appears to be some kind of resistance in a taut line that helps a fish to twist out the hook and seatrout are even more expert than salmon in freeing themselves when they are in the air.

While a salmon is running, the hand should be kept quite clear of the reel, for a finger or a coat-sleeve, incautiously allowed to get foul of the handle, is almost sure to put a dangerous check on the fish; and that generally entails a broken cast or a fly torn from its hold. If the spring controlling the pawl of the check is too weak to prevent the line from over-running when a salmon is taking it out, the same spring should, if possible, be adjusted or replaced by a stronger one, as soon as you can obtain one.

All fishermen and many others as well must surely have heard or read of salmon that take a fly—no, snatch is the correct word —and rush madly off with eighty or one hundred yards of line (strip it off the screaming and protesting reel is the true phraseology!). As far as my experience goes, this is not typical of a salmon's tactics, unless it has been hooked in a sea-pool, is foul-hooked in the tail, or has a heavy current as its ally. The story of these energetic fish is often made to end happily; but in real life a salmon that has taken such a length of line off the reel has passed so far beyond the fisherman's control, that there is little likelihood of his regaining it. At the other extreme, there are fish of quite different mentality, whose idea of fighting for life consists in attempting to embrace the fisherman's feet, a most uncomfortable procedure. Salmon that adopt these tactics are very difficult to play; they will neither run nor stay out in the middle, breasting the current, and they refuse to come near enough to be within gaffing distance. The best plan is, first of all, to play them on a very light line, then to treat them as roughly as you dare and, in short, to do everything and anything that

will possibly encourage them to go off into midstream. Half the
secret of playing any salmon is to follow a middle course between
holding it so tightly, that it cannot run and tire itself out, and
being so lenient, that it either will "sulk" or will take the cast
round a stone. Side-strain from below, exerted by a rod held
almost horizontally, pointing downstream and swung in towards
the angler's own bank, is the other half. Too much law can
easily be given and must be avoided. A fish on the bank is the
only one that counts.

"Sulking" is probably a manifestation of extreme fear and is
likely to happen, if the fisherman has been unwise enough to play
a salmon with so light a hand, that it has had the opportunity
to change its flesh into lead and to anchor itself securely to the
bed of the river!

*Side Strain*

The method of applying side-strain is to lower the rod in the
direction in which the river is flowing until it is almost horizontal,
bushes and guard-rails permitting. A strain can then be put
on that is very difficult for the fish to resist, because it swims with
an undulating movement of the whole body. The effect of a side-
pull is to make it far easier for the fish to turn in the direction
one desires and doubly difficult for it to bend its head in the
other; there is a sort of bias placed upon it (Fig. 106). How
different this is from the ordinary vertical tension, by which one
attempts to achieve the impossible, namely, to lift the fish bodily
out of the water. Side-strain with a lowered rod-point is peculiarly
useful when you are standing on a high bank to play a fish,
because the line is made to enter the water at the same angle as
it would, were you wading. Thus the pull on the fish is no
longer direct, that is to say, it passes for a short distance through
the water, which functions as an intermediary between the cast
and the fish. On the other hand, the rod-point ought to be kept
high if the fish is travelling through a rock-strewn part of the
river, or through rapids, and whenever there is a danger of the
line being drowned in heavy solid water. The diagram below
illustrates this.

Sometimes a salmon gets beyond the fisherman's control,
because either he has applied side-strain too late or its effect has
been neutralized by the influence of an intervening current, so

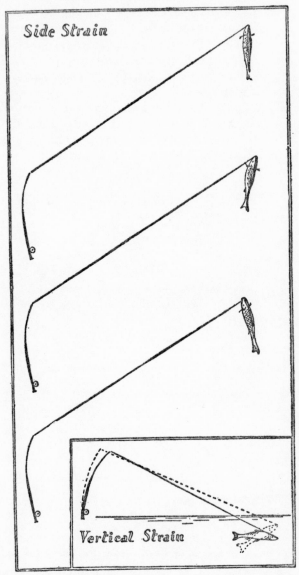

FIG 106 This illustrates the points of side-strain as discussed in the text

that the fish sets off with determination for the pool below and
has, perhaps, already reached the *draw* of the pool in which it
is being played. There are only two things left to do. Slacken off
the line, point the rod at the fish, take your fingers off the handle
of the reel and, in order to relieve the fish of all check, let line
be stripped from the spool.

It usually happens that a fish turns upstream as soon as it no
longer feels any strain from above. If it should do this, slack
line will be carried past it by the current, which will make it
think the danger is now below and will encourage it to continue

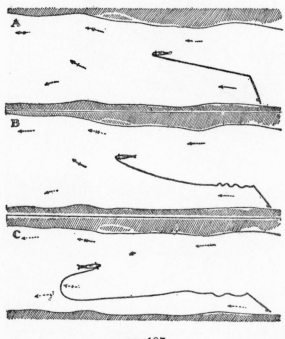

FIG 107

A.   A salmon is making off downstream and out of the pool

B.   The rod is pointed at the fish and line torn off reel as quickly
as possible

C.   Should the fish hesitate and turn upstream, the line will float
below, pull its mouth from that direction and encourage it to come
up again

moving up (Fig. 107). When you are satisfied it is really coming upstream, recover line and lead the fish back into the main part of the pool. The manœuvre of slacking off is designed when the current, not the strength of the salmon, is your adversary. Try and compel the fish to join you in fighting the stream. The other and final method of saving a salmon from going down into danger or to a place from which you cannot recover it is that of handlining (see p. 228).

Always land a salmon as expeditiously as possible without using brute force, if only for the reason that the period in which the hook can come away is shortened. There rarely is reason to have taken as much as a minute a pound in weight of a salmon, except when you have to deal with a salmon that has been foul-hooked or with a lively grilse. I refer here to fishing with tackle of stoutness appropriate to ordinary wet-fly methods.

## Landing a Fish

If you have never seen a salmon landed, you will want to know the signs of when it is tired and ready to bring to the gaff. First, its head comes up as I have described on an earlier page; then the salmon will, if it is allowed, thrash on top of the water in a last effort to get free and sometimes it meets with success; lastly, when it is thoroughly played out, it turns over on its side and very often surrenders itself to the current. It is too early to gaff a salmon that is only in the first stage of exhaustion, because you will thereby run a grave risk of losing it by gaffing the line or the fly instead of the fish.

When a salmon begins to thrash, it is high time that you slackened off a little and raised the point of the rod, because it has evidently far more liveliness in it than you have allowed it to demonstrate. This is due to your having brought it by main force almost within range of the gaff and thus made it appear more exhausted than it really is. Hold the fish less tightly and let it tire itself out more completely before attempting to bring it close in. Sometimes a salmon thus given a little more law will go off for a short run into the middle of the pool; but, when next brought in, it will come easily up to the gaff. The most favourable moment at which to gaff a salmon is before the last stage is reached, for, unless you are intending to tail a fish yourself or to beach it, there is small need to tire it out completely. Conversely, a ghillie will be able with safety to gaff a fish some minutes earlier than you could have done it yourself. I used the word "safety", because, by taking risks that have in them the makings of a first-class nightmare, a ghillie or another angler can, and sometimes does, land a fish with many minutes of resistance still left in it; but I can imagine when and where this would be the correct and only thing to do.

Only on the rarest occasions attempt to gaff a fish that is running at some depth below the surface, because the refractive power of the water is alone capable of so distorting the true line of aim, that the blow will miss the flesh, may by ill-luck strike the line and dislodge the fly from its hold. And a snatch with a gaff generally tears and disfigures a salmon, the last thing a lover of angling would wish to witness, let alone be responsible for. But, if the fish is heading straight for danger you must take what is possibly your last chance of securing it.

A tired fish will sometimes try to get away by surrendering itself broadside on to the current and a most difficult fish it is to bring to the gaff.

When you are drawing a fish towards the gaff, be on your guard for the frantic dash for freedom that is sure to follow the first sight it gets of you. This is where a well-oiled reel, carefully adjusted variable check and a smooth joint between line and cast will give you the confidence to reel up short, because you know you can instantly give further licence to a salmon, if it should dart off once more into the middle of the pool. After a time, however, it becomes exhausted, so that it can safely be gaffed and lifted on to the bank.

Exhaustion is due to interference by an angler with the rhythm of the mouth/gill mechanism, which controls the intake of dissolved oxygen and the excretion through the gill-rays of noxious substances in the blood-stream. Usually a gravid fish or a kelt returned to the water will soon recover from its experience of having been played to a standstill and of having been removed from its own element by tailing.

## Gaffing

When fishing on the left bank of the river, you will find it more convenient to change the rod to the right hand, as soon as you begin to draw a salmon close enough to gaff it. The line is first reeled in until the top of the cast is still two yards away from the top ring. The rod is then swung back over the right shoulder and well inland, so that the salmon may be brought as close as the length of line will permit. Unfortunately this, the only sound, method by which you can draw the fish up to the gaff you are wielding bends the rod in a way that robs it of most of its power; but on the other hand increases enormously its compensation-factor, if the fish should kick or suddenly bolt out into the middle of the pool.

This handicap is not imposed when the angler is accompanied by a ghillie, who can approach the fish without the line having to be reeled in short; this in its turn means the rod can be lowered a little and additional tension exerted that will bring the salmon speedily within reach of the gaff. Press the butt of the rod against the top of the left thigh, and have the right arm well extended, so that the reach of the gaff may be as full as possible and the weight of the body is for the most part thrown on to the left or inside foot. Make the most of the reach of the right hand and keep the flexed rod-point as far as possible away from the riverside. It is undoubtedly far easier to gaff a salmon that is being played on a short fly-rod or on a spinning-rod than on one of fourteen feet or over.

It is a great mistake to lift out of the water the head of the salmon you are about to gaff; it puts far too much strain on the cast and there is no proof that it serves any good purpose, although I have heard some fishermen say a salmon is thereby rendered temporarily blind in the eye that is exposed to the air! Another thing scrupulously to be avoided is attempting to gaff a kicking salmon, whether you are landing it for yourself or are rendering another angler the service you should be glad to give, provided it is asked. Accede to a request for help and put your whole heart and skill into the work you are doing for another, but be very chary of offering to land another man's fish. Further, if you are in any way doubtful of your ability to gaff it at the first offering, hold back and refuse to take the risk. Tell the other man why you have done this and wait until he brings the fish round again, and presents you with a more favourable chance. There is only one exception to this rule that you should allow yourself. If you can see the hook in the jaw of the salmon and

have reason to suspect the hold is slight and likely to give way
at any moment, take the first possible opportunity of gaffing that
is offered.

Nine times out of ten gaffing a salmon is the easiest thing in
the world. The hook is calmly placed over the back of the fish
and opposite the front of the back or dorsal fin; the point is
inserted by drawing the fish towards you across the water, so
that it is impaled on the hook by its own weight. The point of the
gaff, therefore, should be kept needle-sharp. There is no need
whatever to snatch at the fish or to try and drive the point well
home. Place the gape over the middle of the back, press the gaff
down against the back, so that a deep bite shall be taken, and
draw the gaff towards you. At the moment the point of the
gaff enters, allow the line to go slack and only lift the fish up
when it has reached the edge of the bank. I have assumed that
most men are now agreed it is better to gaff a salmon over its
back and only to gaff from underneath a very small salmon or
seatrout, fish below a limit of four pounds. Wipe away with a
handful of grass any drops of blood, wash the fish, cover it in
the cloth and then place it in a cool spot deep among the ferns
or undergrowth.

Before the salmon is put aside in a safe place there is one more
rite to be performed. Look the fish over; see if there are any
parasites in the gills and what colour the latter are; see whether
any sea-lice are present (you may expect to find them if the sea
is within ten or twenty miles; note the sex and condition; look
carefully for any peculiar marks and, if you have a spring-balance
with you, weigh the salmon. Above all, do not trust to your
memory, but write these details down so that, later on, they can
be entered in the fishing-log.

If you are going on to another pool and are leaving the salmon
behind until you return, find some safe place for it that is out
of reach of otters and hidden from passers-by. If a fish has been
bled, it should be wrapped round with a strip of cheese cloth,
hung from a high bough of a tree and covered with some small
leafy branches. A salmon that has not been bled is best tied head
and tail to a stout stick and laid horizontally across forked
branches.

*Other Ways of Landing Salmon*

On many rivers it is the custom during the springtime fishing, when the kelts are still coming down, to forbid the use of the gaff, so that the fishermen on those waters are compelled to adopt other means of landing salmon. Very often a wide and deep net is employed, a sound enough device when there is a ghillie at hand to give his undivided attention to its manipulation. He can easily hold it, even against a considerable stream, while the fish is drawn down into it, head first. But my efforts to net my own fish were so ridiculously ineffective, that I gave up any more attempts and resolved to land, by the method of tailing, the fish I was legally forbidden to gaff.

FIG 108   THE PROPER WAY TO TAIL A FISH
Note carefully how the hand is placed, so that the fish is lifted
without any feeling of awkwardness on the angler's part

Tailing a fish is quite easy. You ought, however, to be sure, before you try to grip its tail, that it is thoroughly played out and will offer little resistance when it feels the grip of your hand. You should also make certain of gripping the tail just above the two knobs on each side of the base of the tail-fin, so that the little finger is nearest to the head of the fish, otherwise the salmon will slip out of your grasp. Thus a salmon should be tailed with the left hand, when you are fishing from the left bank, and with the right, when you are on the right bank. The grip of the hand would be just as firm, if you reversed it; but you would find it very awkward to lift the fish in this way high enough above the water to prevent it kicking and also much heavier to carry. A useful tip, too, is to first cool your hand in the water.

The tails of grilse and seatrout are unprovided with these con-

venient knobs and therefore it is best to net them or beach them.
If the fisherman is very skilful at tailing and has a blacksmith's
grip, he may be able to carry a grilse by the tail long enough to
enable him to reach the shore, but a large seatrout is a far more
difficult fish to land without either net or gaff. It is sometimes
possible to land a small seatrout by gripping it tightly around the
middle and lifting it out. But for those without the courage to
tail their fish by hand there is the mechanical tailer described
on p. 53.

If the river's edge shelves conveniently, you can safely beach
the fish you are forbidden to gaff or are unable to tail by running
it gently up the shingle and cutting off its retreat by standing
between it and the river.

When the salmon you have just caught has been faithfully
dealt with in every detail and before you enter the water again
to resume fishing, examine the fly carefully and cut it off. Look
over the cast for any signs of weakness, fraying or knots made by
the wind. Before resuming, look at the hook and re-tie the fly.
Then examine the line and make sure the coils are tightly wound
on the spool. In recovering line after a salmon has turned and
is running towards you, there is often no time to wind it in
properly. The loosely-wound line takes up so much room, that
the spool runs jerkily and sometimes the line binds altogether.

## CHAPTER SIXTEEN

# SALMON SCALES

BY W. J. M. MENZIES

SCALES of fish are, in some respects, not unlike hair in the case of the human being. Formed in the skin their usefulness is partly protective and partly indeterminate. In fish it is true they may represent the highest form of development and in the human, if our accepted ideas of progress be correct, they may be but the degenerate remains of an earlier and more ample covering. In both cases they are developments which take their origin in the true skin and are very obvious externally.

The resemblance, however, is not much more than superficial, and although both scales and hair are highly specialized parts of the anatomy their origin and subsequent growth are very dissimilar.

The small fish is not hatched from the egg with a covering of scales or even with a partial covering. At the time of emergence it is entirely without them even in the most rudimentary form. Its skin, completely naked from head to tail, is smooth and unbroken and has yet to form the pockets in which the scales will appear and grow. The actual mode of scale development and growth is perhaps a subject for the physiologist rather than the general reader, and, indeed, it is a subject that until quite recently has not received the detailed investigation which it requires. Even at the present day our knowledge, and especially that part of it which concerns the ultimate degeneration of the scale at the time of the maturity of the fish, is by no means complete.

Paget in *The Scales of Some Teleostean Fish* (1920) showed in detail how the growth starts in the young fish and the manner in which it proceeds in after-life, and subsequent research has tended to confirm his original findings. As I have just stated, the salmon when hatched, the alevin as it is then called, has no scales, but it is not long, some four to six weeks or so, before the first rudimentary beginnings in the skin may be found by means of microscopical examination. Minute as are these beginnings, they are by no means uniformly distributed throughout the length and breadth of the fish but, at first, are confined to a comparatively limited area. This area, situated below the dorsal fin and along the lateral line, is fairly rapidly extended towards head and tail and second and third rows of scales immediately above and below the first quickly follow. The commencement of growth depends more upon the length of the fish—about one and one-quarter inches—than upon date. It is to be observed in early spring and in the course of the summer the fingerling has completed its coating.

The actual development of each individual scale is a complicated process which takes place within the skin itself. Growth commences in the form of a minute platelet in the dermis, that is, in the true skin which in turn is covered by the softer external covering of the epidermis. As this platelet develops it pushes and elbows its way, as it were, until finally it almost breaks through the dermis and stretches the tougher outer layer into the epidermis. At the same time it enlarges the space which it occupies in the skin in the other direction and forms for itself a complete pocket. One end of the pocket is based near the inner side of the dermis and close to the muscle while the other in later life extends far into the epidermis and the protruding part of the scale is enclosed in a more or less elastic close-fitting covering. It is this last stretching process of the exceedingly thin membrane which in the larger fish gives the false appearance of the exterior portion of the scale being free and exposed. Such appearance is illusory, however, as will be very easily discovered if a careful examination be made of the skin of a fish with a needle, the point of the blade of a knife, or some such instrument. It will then be found that the apparently free portion is in reality by no means free but is entirely surrounded both back and front by a cutaneous covering which emerges bulbous-like from the original smooth covering of the outer surface of the fish.

The scales themselves are relatively thin, flexible, almost colourless plates, which by reflected light have a somewhat dull appearance and by transmitted light show a series of what appear to be concentric lines of which many are incomplete and only a few form an ellipse.

32 The upper reaches of a typical Canadian river; Otter Falls on the Alaskan Highway

33 Playing a salmon on the River Hrutafiardara in Iceland

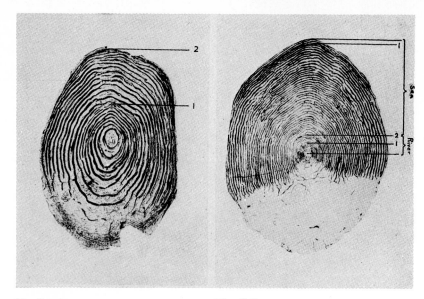

34 Smolt.
   5in. long; Aberdeen Dee

35 Grilse.
   2¾lb.; 5·25 cm.; Aberdeen
   Coast; 18 April

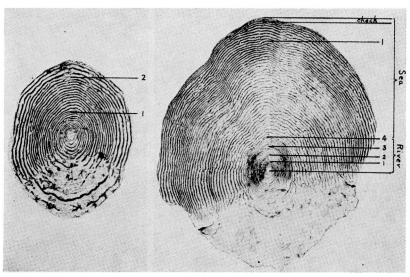

36 Hatchery Smolt.

37 Grilse.
   6lb.; 24·5in.; Grimersta; 16 July

Section cutting and microscopic examination has shown that the scale is not a homogeneous whole but that it consists of two layers. The one, and the lower, layer when the scale is in position on the fish is of a fibrous nature and, if viewed under the microscope, is seen to consist of a series of layers of fibres or rods not arranged in any one direction or laid down in any series of rectangles in regular interlacing but running across and through each other in many directions. Nature in her wisdom has arranged them as seemed best and, as is usually the case, has made the work uncommonly perfect so that a maximum of flexibility with a minimum of liability to crack or break is obtained. The upper, or outer, layer of the scale is of very different material and consists of a substance, hyalo-dentine, much harder and even to some extent, especially when dry, brittle. Allied, as its name implies, to the ordinary dentine of teeth, hyalo-dentine alone, unless in relatively thick and cumbersome plates, would be very liable to crack and break up. If sufficiently thick to withstand the ordinary risks of damage it would be so strong and unyielding as not to conform with the movements and flexions of the muscles and body of the fish. Closely combined, however, with the comparatively soft, admirably flexible and relatively tough layer behind, the dentine portion of the scale can still give the necessary stiffness to the whole without in itself being either too heavy, too unyielding, or unduly liable to fracture and destruction.

At the time of the completion of the scale coating when the little fish is some three or four months old a certain and well-defined number of platelets are required to cover the whole body. To maintain this entire investment as the fish grows and as the surface area of the body increases the scales must either become more numerous or each of those already in position must be enlarged individually. Fortunately, as I shall show later, nature has arranged that the latter, and not the former, method is adopted and the increased area to be covered is met by an increase in individual scale size. The number of scales, unless by reason of accidental injury, remains constant but the total area covered by them and the area of each scale by itself is greater.

In the normal scale the enlargement is not uniform in all directions. This is partly owing to the shape of the scale itself and of the fish and partly, apparently, is in some measure due to the fact that a portion, the front or anterior portion in practice, is comparatively deep-seated in the softer tissues of the skin and that the other portion, the hinder or posterior part, is more exposed, practically on the surface and covered only with the very thin layer of dermis and epidermis.

A typical scale from the side of a salmon is oval in outline and, while not in any way comparable with the large scales of some of the carp family, for instance, is not a small object. The size and shape of the scales, however, vary considerably with the position which they occupy on the body of the fish. Along the sides the largest specimens are to be found immediately above and below the lateral line and in the middle region of the body; those farther removed from the lateral line, both towards the back and towards the belly, become gradually smaller as do also the scales which grow nearer to the head and the tail than to the centre of the body. In fact, nature has so adapted their form and shape as to fit most conveniently and comfortably into the curves of the fish at the point where they are situated and to yield most readily to the flexions of the whole body and the movements of the muscles underneath the skin during the motions of swimming. On the actual ridges, as it were, of the body, the dorsal and ventral contours, and immediately on each side of them and again right in the front of the body, just before the head is reached, as well as in the caudal region the scales are minute and are quite irregular in shape as the exigencies of these situations necessitate. Similarly very small scales of quite strange and unusual outline are to be found arranged round the nooks and corners of the fin bases.

As I have previously stated each individual scale increases in size as the fish becomes larger. The point of origin, consisting of the two layers of hyalo-dentine and of fibrous matter, takes the form in surface view of a plain platelet of minute size. From this platelet the fibrous layer is gradually pushed out equally in all directions and on it the specialized cells which are devoted to the formation of this part of the organism deposit the dentine layer, not, however, in the same flat plain as the dentine of the nucleus nor in the amorphous manner of the softer stratum, but on a very definite plan. In a section cut right through the scale the dentine is seen to be laid down after the manner of the ridge and furrow which is so well exemplified in the orderly arrangement of heights and hollows in a newly ploughed field. When viewed by transmitted light the hollows are naturally the more transparent and pass the greater quantity of light; the heights, being thicker and consisting of a greater amount of material, are more dense and seem to be dark in comparison with the more translucent hollows. In fact, unless one were acquainted with the actual structure of the scale the ridges might be taken for lines on a plain lighter ground.

The original platelet laid down in the young stages is roughly circular and at first the scale growth is in this shape. The ridges are practically continuous and are set as the complete circumference of the figure. As both the scales and the fish become larger, however, the increase in length of the animal, rather than the vertical height from ventral to dorsal contour, becomes the dominant fact and to this the scales have to conform in their endeavour to accommodate themselves most advantageously in the general economy. They therefore become laterally somewhat compressed and gradually assume an oval instead of a circular outline.

From the beginning of the scale origins, dotted about as minute points scattered evenly throughout the skin, the growing scales gradually pass through the circular shape to the final oval form reached when they make a complete scaly covering overlapping each other and entirely enveloping the soft tissues. As growth progresses and each scale begins to trespass on the ground of the neighbouring scales so is the front edge depressed deeper into the skin pocket and the hinder, or so-called free or exposed, edge elevated more and more above the original level of the skin surface. Finally the arrangement closely resembles that of the tiles on the roof of a house, but instead of the general layout being from the ridge, or the top of the back, downwards it is from the head to the tail. Were it otherwise the water during the progress of the fish would not flow evenly over the surface of the body but would necessarily get in under the outer parts of the scales and "ruffle" them.

Whatever may be the primary purpose of scale ridges, and it would seem that the mechanical strength and efficiency of such an arrangement must be much greater than a similar area constructed of the same material with a plain surface, a secondary result is that man has been able to turn their arrangement to his own needs after centuries of indifference followed by many years of study and experiment.

Even a cursory glance at the scale of an adult salmon when held up and viewed by the naked eye reveals that the ridges are not uniformly distributed throughout the whole of the scale, but that they are alternately set closer together and wider apart so that an illusion of light and dark bands on the scales is produced.

It is unnecessary to trace, in detail, the history of the discovery and elucidation of the meaning of these bands. Sufficient, perhaps, it may be to say that the credit of the original discovery seems to belong to one Leuwenhoek, a Dutchman who lived towards the end of the seventeenth century, and who found the conditions to exist not in the scales of salmon or of a purely marine fish but in those of the common carp. Eels were the next choice of a further investigator (E. Baudelot, 1873) and a most unfortunate choice it was. The scales of the eel are not only exceptionally difficult to extract from the skin of the fish, but, when found, are not by any manner of means easy to read. Also, even when the clue has been discovered, a number of corrections have to be made. The age of this fish when the first scale is laid down is about three years and there is a very great difference in the time of their formation in different parts of the body.

Modern scale reading as an exact science may be said, however, to have been started in 1904, when Stuart Thomson undertook the task of interpreting the markings on the scales of cod. He found that they responded to certain laws and that the age of the fish could be read with a deal of facility and accuracy.

Henry W. Johnston applied the same method to the scales of salmon and found an equal response in them, though, owing to the dual life of this fish in fresh and salt water, there were complications which at first were not easy of interpretation. Marking work helped to elucidate the obscure points and to prove up to the hilt the original suggestions, and in course of time a complete basis of fact and proof of theory was established.

As we have seen, fry start their scales at a length of about an inch and a quarter in the form of a simple flat plate which in after-life is commonly referred to as the scale nucleus. Subsequent scale growth takes the form of ridge and furrow, at first roughly circular, complete and concentric with the nucleus. Later the ridges, confined to the anterior part of the scale, are incomplete and oval instead of circular, but are still arranged symmetrically about the point of origin and the earlier circular ridges. Once started, scale growth is continuous so long as the fish continues to feed and its body to grow but, once feeding ceases and growth for the time being is finished, the scales also cease to add new material to their structure. Indeed, they may then reverse the former process and return certain of their constituents to help to maintain the general bodily needs and energy.

If the scale of an adult salmon be held up and examined by the naked eye, by transmitted light, various bands may be discerned and an expert may even be able to say roughly the age and whether it has spawned or not. A small pocket lens is an aid in revealing more detail, although personally I have not found its use entirely satisfactory. There are difficulties in getting the light exactly right and I find accurate focusing is not easily effected.

But if it is desired to ascertain the age of a number of fish at leisure the most satisfactory way to collect the scales is to scrape off a number with a rather blunt knife from the shoulder of the fish, i.e. just above the lateral line and slightly in front of the dorsal fin, and place them in an envelope. It is sufficient merely to wipe them off the knife on to the sides of the envelope and allow them to adhere to the paper.

As we have seen earlier in this present chapter, the scale growth starts in the form of a simple plate to which are added a series of ridges and furrows at first concentric and later, although still growing in the same orderly arrangement, in the form of an incomplete ring. If we examine the scale of a smolt (pl. 34), we find that these ridges and furrows, which appear in the form of alternate dark lines and spaces when viewed under the microscope, are not at all evenly spaced out, but that there are certain groupings. Bold and distinctly constructed, at first the ridges are clearly distinguishable the one from the other while the furrows are comparatively wide. After a time, however, each ridge is quite evidently not so far from its neighbour as in earlier life, and the ridges also are not quite so strongly depicted. There is first the zone, or band, of widely spaced, clearly differentiated ridges, and afterwards a narrow and much more closely spaced band forming a dark mark on the scale.

The significance of these variations in the growth and appearance of the scale is not on the surface evident, but by means of much painstaking research and work in laboratory, at the river-side and on the sea, extending over very many years it has been elucidated and is now very well understood.

The whole of the changes shown, and the entire success of scale-reading as a means of tracing and determining the life history of salmon, and of other fish, hinges on the fact that scale growth is correlated to the body growth of the fish and responds directly to the stimulus of favourable and unfavourable places and seasons, so that it is a complete and indelible index of the bodily happenings.

During the course of late spring, summer and early autumn conditions for growth are good. Temperature is genial, all water life from the smallest forms upwards is abundant, the larder is consequently well stocked, and the activities of the fish respond very markedly to the temperature. The fish feed greedily on the store provided for them, the body reacts correspondingly and at the same time the scales, to compete with the rapid expansion of the surface which they have to cover, grow rapidly also.

The scale fortunately when under the necessity of increasing in size quickly does so not merely by increasing the number of ridges and furrows which are laid down but also by an increased width between each ridge. It is as if the cells which form the scales were using their greatest endeavours and were distended in their efforts to cope with the situation. In consequence of the relatively considerable width between the ridges a comparatively large amount of light is passed freely and with little or no obstruction. The aggregate effect is that of a comparatively light band round the anterior portion of the scale. In early life during residence in the river the ridges may be completely, or partially, continuous round the posterior, or exposed, portion of the scale also, but even at this period the effect of light and shade is not so clearly shown on this part. In later life no ridges are formed on the posterior portion and, in consequence, it is entirely valueless for the purposes of age determination.

As autumn merges into winter so does the fresh-water food supply dwindle until finally it either dies out or retires into winter quarters until once again stirred to activity by the rising warmth of the coming spring. Temperature alone would also appear to play some part in the feeding habits of young salmon, and, while on the warmer days of winter they may feed as opportunity offers for a short time about noon, on other occasions when thermal conditions are less favourable they may refrain from food entirely.

As the grosser feeding habit of summer gradually tapers off to the less ample meals of winter so does the rate of growth decrease in corresponding proportion. During the depths of the winter the food taken may well be not enough, or at the best not more than enough, to repair the wastage inevitable in maintaining life and such limited activity as may then be indulged in. Active growth is replaced by a passive state in which weight may actually be lost although length of necessity must remain constant. At the end of the coldest period, when the first feeble effects of the returning warmth are felt, feeding slowly increases and growth may again start and continue as a sort of inverted reflection of the decelerating process of the early winter. It is gradually speeded up until finally it once again attains its fullest activity.

During the slowing down and speeding up of the feeding habits scale growth corresponds and with the more restricted area to be covered produces a more restricted result. The ridges and furrows instead of being widely spaced and bold in outline become thinner and closer. The band, or zone, which they form, the so-called winter band in contradistinction to the summer band as the widely spaced zone is named, when viewed under the microscope appears dark and narrow and in marked contrast to the wide and light appearance of the other part of the year's scale growth.

Throughout life, therefore, or during the part of life in which body growth is made, the scale growth registers this alternation of rapid and slow increase, of light and dark zones, of summer and winter bands. In plate 34, a photograph of the scale of a two-year-old smolt just at the end of its second slow growth period, I have marked the points which are essential to its correct interpretation. At first we have the original platelet, or nucleus, and then the zone of rapid growth, which terminates somewhat abruptly, as if no winter feeding had been indulged in, and completes the first year of life. Thereafter follows a similar light zone and a dark band of finer ridges, indicating the end of a second year. At the stage when the scale was taken there is no means of determining whether the fish was a parr or a smolt. The assumption of the silvery dress, and the outward manifestation of the preparation for sea-life, has no reflection in the scale growth or the scale form. The silvery coat has its origin solely in the skin and depends for its effect on the deposition of a certain substance, called guanin, in such a way that light is reflected and the underlying spots and colours of the parr stage are masked and hidden.

Should a scale be taken and examined from a salmon at a stage later than that of a smolt, however, there can be no doubt as to the age at which the smolt dress was assumed and the migration to the sea begun. And for this reason : the food supplies available in the fresh waters are infinitely less plentiful than are those available in the seas and oceans, and salmon are essentially opportunists ready and willing to consume all that comes their way which is within the compass of their capacity.

Brought up, as it were, during their youngest stages on the comparatively limited diet of the fresh-water their growth is slow indeed in comparison with that which is made once the ocean feeding grounds are attained. The faster the body growth the bolder are the scale ridges, and the transition from the one environment to the other is as clearly registered on the scale as if it were recorded in a diary. There appears to be little or no intermediate stage nor, so far as experimental evidence goes, is this to be expected. The salmon smolts once they have left their temporary gathering ground either just above, or a short distance within, tidal limits do not tarry in their journey down to salt-water. They press on with the ebb tide right through even a long estuary such as that of the Tay, up which the tide runs for a distance of approximately forty miles. They are evidently prepared for the change externally, and one cannot but suspect that there must be some internal preparation also for the very violent alteration of the salinity of the water in which they live. Once prepared they make the change without delay, and the change in feeding habits and in food supplies is necessarily equally abrupt and is shown on the scale in a corresponding manner.

The scale ridges formed during the fresh-water life although differing in appearance between summer and winter also differ markedly from those formed in the sea. At all periods of the year the marine portion of the scale carries much stronger ridges and much wider furrows than does the part formed during the parr

38   Very large Spring Fish. 48½lb.; 48·5in.; River Tweed; 23 July

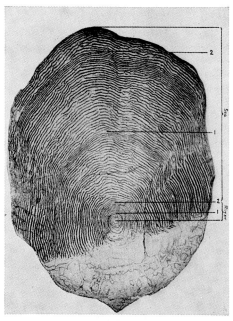

39   Small Summer Fish.
     19¾lb.; 40in.; River Ailart; 27 August

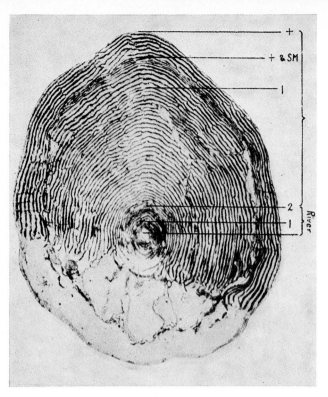

40 Previously Spawne[d]
Fish. $2\frac{1}{2}$lb.; 55·5 cm[.];
River Dee; 1 July

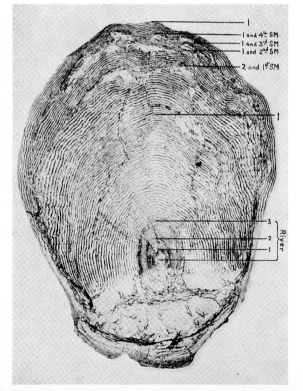

41 Previously    Spawned
Fish.   $29\frac{1}{2}$lb.;   $43\frac{1}{2}$in.;
Loch Maree; 10 May

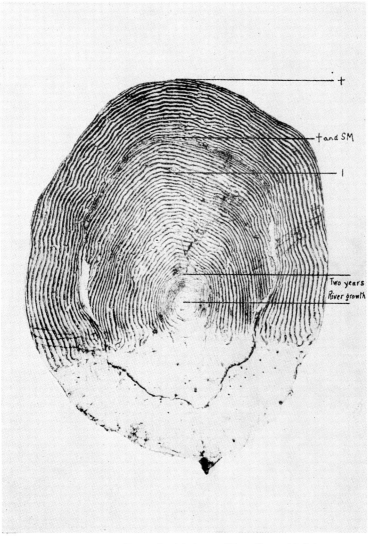

+

† and SM

1

Two years
River growth

42   Previously Spawned Fish. 9lb.; 74·5 cm.; River Spey; 13 July

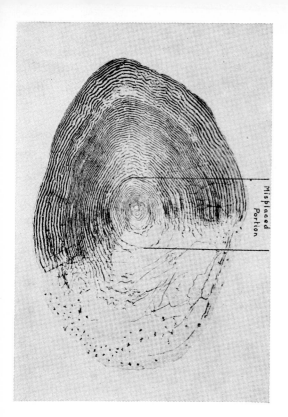

Misplaced Portion

43　Small Spring Fish.
7½lb.; 72·5 cm.; River Dee;
13 April

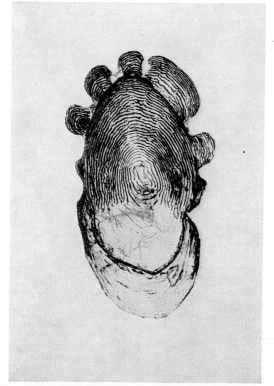

44　An Example of
Malformation.
11½lb.; 82 cm.; Aberdeen
Coast; 25 July

life. So great is the variation that the one can never be confused
with the other. The marine life and the marine scale formation
is a different class of thing altogether, and perhaps a glance at
plate 35, which is a photograph of the scale of a grilse, is more
illuminating than a great deal of descriptive matter. On this
scale is marked the preliminary two years of parr life, and then
the succeeding summer, winter and summer of sea feeding. Under
the higher magnification employed for plate 34 the parr scale
assumed an almost illusory size and importance. When, however,
we have the lower magnification and greater scale area of plate
35 (and later in plate 37 and onwards), it is more easy to recognize
the relationship of the two areas, the river and the sea, in the
growth economy of the fish and the difference in the food supplies
and the growth rates of the two places of residence. Even to one
unaccustomed to view such objects the variation between the
river and sea growth must be quite clear and plain even if the
divisions between the summers and winters may not be so readily
recognized. The river life appears as a central, often darkened,
area with, it almost seems, minute ridges in contrast to the bold
clear growth of the subsequent marine life.

That even the artificial conditions of hatchery life do not by
any means invalidate the scale as an index of age is shown in
plate 36, which is the scale taken from a smolt reared throughout
its life of two years and the portion of a third under control from
the egg onwards. The first year and the second year are both
shown quite clearly and are marked in the photograph. The
growth is perhaps greater in amount and more even in its progress
than is normally the case in northern waters when the little fish
have to fend for themselves but, even if one did not know the
history with exactitude, there would be no hesitation or difficulty
in interpreting the scales. The only departure from the normal
is the addition of the beginning of the rapid growth of the third
year. This would usually not commence until the fish had reached
the sea, and in the case of this specimen was possibly due to the
fact that the fish was retained in the ponds beyond the date when
it was ready to migrate to salt water.

In the Tay experiments smolts were marked by the attachment
of a small piece of silver wire to the forward end of the base
of the dorsal fin. In later years certain of the adult fish captured
in the nets worked for commercial purposes were found to carry

this same wire and their direct connection with the original smolts was by this means established.

In earlier times some writers had considered grilse to be a separate species of fish not connected with either salmon or sea-trout. But in the course of years this school of thought had rather died out and in its place had arisen two other groups of disputants. Both of these latter agreed that grilse were the young salmon, but while one alleged that they were the smolts returned in the year of migration to the sea the other held that rather more than a complete year had elapsed between the two events, and that the grilse had been feeding in the ocean for approximately twelve to fourteen months. The latter group were proved to be correct, for no marked fish were recovered in the year in which the smolts went down to the sea, but a number of marked grilse *were* taken in the following season.

If we examine the scales of a grilse, an early grilse for example, as in plate 35, we find that the known history of something over a year in salt-water is confirmed by the index of age as carried on the scale. In the centre is the parr area and then a broad band of widely spaced ridges indicative of the ample feeding and rapid growth of the months succeeding May when the river was left behind. Following this a much narrower band of less widely spaced ridges denoting the time when feeding fell off and growth declined in rate and amount. Once again rapid feeding is started but is not long continued before the urge to return is felt and the fish leaves the ocean larder and prepares for the fast, but on its way, is captured by the nets and its existence is terminated. Theory and practical proof go hand in hand, and the history of the fish can be demonstrated to entire satisfaction from the scales alone.

During the summer further growth is to be expected and is shown in the much wider band of widely spaced ridges at the outside of the scales of grilse taken later in the season. Plate 37 shows how great the addition may be between the month of April when the fish, whose scales are illustrated in plate 35 was netted and the month of July when the last fish (pl. 37) was caught with rod and line.

And so we can continue with the larger and older fish. Each succeeding summer and winter which are spent in feeding and growth are faithfully recorded and remain indelibly marked so long as the scales exist intact. The majority of salmon are maiden fish which have spent not merely one year but it may be two, three, four or even five years continuously in the sea without returning to fresh-water on any, except the final, occasion. A year later and we have the larger fish in the twenty and thirty pounders and after twelve more months the forty and fifty pounders. Their history is as clearly shown as that of the younger specimens and the full three or four years of the very large spring fish will be found marked in plate 38. Even salmon which have spent four and five years in the sea continue to register the fact right to the end of their growth period; the increase in girth may be greater than the increase in length in later life, and the bands of wide and narrow ridges in consequence may be closer together on the scales but they are formed in just the same manner and are just as reliable as an index of the story.

In addition to the bands of closely spaced ridges formed during the colder months of the year narrower bands of a similar type are often to be seen in the marine growth. These accessory bands, usually known as "checks", are evidently the result of some slowing up in the growth and therefore are presumably a reflection of a considerable change in the feeding conditions. No exact explanation of the cause of the change of food supply has ever been attempted for we do not know enough of the sea life of the salmon even to be able to speculate on such matters. In some of the illustrations which appear with this chapter such a check may be seen in the first sea summer : in plate 37 it appears, and is marked, right at the edge of the scale. The fish from which this last scale was taken was caught on July 16th, but, as the commencement of erosion shows, it had evidently been in fresh-water for a short time. By observation of a very large number of scales we have been able to determine that this check is usually formed somewhere about the end of June or in the first week of July, but beyond this it is not possible to say anything.

It is now a well-known and generally accepted fact that salmon do not feed in fresh-water but from the day the sea is left behind gradually fall off in condition and lose in both weight and appearance. If drought or other conditions keep them in the sea after the desire to enter fresh-water has been engendered, loss of condition will start in salt-water and both weight and colour may be affected while the fish are still outside the river-mouth.

The changes which take place have a reaction in the scale material and, instead of the addition of fresh growth, that which has already been made is gradually reabsorbed into the body tissues. The process is not at all well understood nor has the reason for it been adequately explained. At first it was suggested that during and after the time of spawning mechanical action due to the shrinkage of the body was responsible for the wearing and attrition of the scale edge. This, however, obviously is not the sole, or even the major, cause although possibly it might be considered to be a minor contributing factor. The "erosion" of the scale edge starts long before spawning has commenced or before any shrinkage of the body has become at all evident. In winter fish it may be present in quite the early months of the year, and at least six of seven months before the spawning period. Grilse may show quite appreciable erosion in the months of July and August although they will not spawn until November or December. In the late summer and early autumn months many fish straight from salt-water already have the beginnings of the process evident on their scales.

It has been suggested more recently that the removal of the scale material was due to absorption rather than to erosion, and that it formed part of the general call on the resources of the body for the development of the genitalia. This explanation may, or may not, be correct but as yet the subject has not been investigated by the only person properly equipped to deal with the problem, a trained physiologist, and in default of a better suggestion it has been rather generally accepted.

For the moment, however, we are perhaps not so much concerned with the cause as with the effect since the latter is of immediate moment and of great importance when determining the history of the fish from the scales.

Absorption of the scale material starts just at the corner of the skin pocket where the so-called exposed and undifferentiated portion of the scale joins with the part, more deeply buried in the skin, which bears the ridges and furrows. From this beginning, which is well shown in plate 37, the process gradually extends round the scale in both directions and on each side until finally it joins up at the extremity of both anterior and posterior portions and affects the whole scale edge. At the same time as it extends round the scale it eats deeper into the material so that by the time it has reached the apex it has at the sides also made considerable inroads towards the centre. The circumference round the exposed portion being shorter than that of the anterior portion is more quickly covered and the attack here naturally proceeds farther inwards.

Once absorption has properly started the scale edge has the appearance of having been "nibbled" (pl. 39), as by some small rodent. In the scales of male fish it both proceeds more rapidly and to a much greater degree than in those of females. In the former sex it also produces a characteristically pointed apex to the exposed portion, while it very often removes almost the whole of the anterior part. It affects the dentine layer before, or to a greater extent than, the fibrous layer and may even remove patches of dentine without ultimately also taking the underlying fibrous material.

Absorption certainly progresses until the fish has spawned and may even continue thereafter although we have no direct evidence on this latter point. Its final effect, as visible when the kelt is descending to the sea and immediately before it recommences feeding, is very variable. As is natural the extent depends largely on the time which has elapsed since each particular fish ceased feeding and, as I have stated above, also upon the sex. All early spring fish which have been perhaps a year or more in the river show very considerable absorption and, in the very few male kelts of this class which survive, the scale area left is a very small fraction of that which existed when the fish was clean run. In the females the loss is not so great, but, even in their case, the register of an entire winter, or more, may be completely obliterated. Scales showing evidence of absorption are therefore quite unreliable as an index of age if a portion has been lost all round the periphery.

It is rather important for statistical purposes to know, and to record, the degree of absorption which has been reached in the scales of each fish, and I therefore evolved a notation for the purpose. The periphery of the anterior, the ridge bearing, portion of the scale is divided into six equal sections along each side and the section into which the absorption has penetrated is noted. For instance, the numeral 6 indicates that absorption extends all round while 4 (as in pl. 39) indicates that it appears for more than half the distance along each side. While useful the figure

arrived at can only be regarded as an approximation since the
degree of absorption is not the same on every scale off the same
fish nor sometimes on both sides of the same scale; it may vary
within limits but not to such a marked degree as may be the case
in the scales of seatrout.

After absorption has occurred the edge of the scale bears quite
a different appearance to the edge of a scale taken from a fish
which is still, or has only just ceased, feeding. In the case of a
feeding fish the ridges flow along and almost parallel to the edge
which presents a smooth, rounded, unbroken contour. After
absorption the edge has, as I stated above, a nibbled appearance
and its even continuity is lost; it is jagged, uneven and rough.
The ridges no longer follow in parallel with the periphery until
they reach the exposed portion but, owing to the loss of a greater
amount of material towards the middle of the sides than at the
apex, they run out and each in its turn as it reaches the absorbed
edge comes to an abrupt stop.

The original scale of the feeding fish grows in an even progress
as is well shown in the photographs which have been considered
in these pages. When feeding and growth of a kelt recommences
the scales have not the smooth edge as a foundation for the new
material which is to be added and before the orderly arrangement can again be taken up the irregularities as left by the
absorption have to be filled up and the original rounded form
regained.

The junction of the new and the old growth has two distinguishing features. Firstly, as the irregularities are smoothed
out, a very apparent join or scar is left which when viewed by
transmitted light shows up as an irregular white line. Secondly,
the new ridges, as they appear, are not in continuity with those
which are already on the scale, nor are they even parallel with
them, round the part of the scale where absorption occurred.
They follow round in conformity with the new growth and run
at an angle across the line of direction of the older ridges. When,
therefore, these distinguishing features are observed on a scale
as in plate 40 (this fish incidentally weighed only two and a half
pounds), it is a direct indication of a visit to fresh-water and a
spawning period, and is always described as a "spawning mark".

In some cases if the fish originally entered the river as an
autumn fish and the scale absorption in consequence was not

great the subsequent spawning mark may not be very clearly shown. In other cases, as of a spring fish or of a male summer fish for instance, it is very clear and obvious. In very few cases indeed is there any doubt as to its presence, for even if the scar be very slight and extend for only a very short distance the new ridges which run at an angle to the others at this part of the scale give more than a clue to the correct interpretation.

As succeeding winters are registered in the case of maiden salmon so are succeeding spawning marks recorded on the scales of mature fish. The scale growth made after the first spawning mark is subject to absorption in the same manner, and with the same result, as the original scale growth and two, three or four (pl. 41) spawning marks may be recorded, should the fish survive sufficiently long, with the same facility and correctness as one. The extreme absorption of male scales might just conceivably remove all traces of a former spawning mark when the fish was on a subsequent journey, but such happenings must be extremely rare and in any doubtful specimens which I have seen it has nearly always been possible to trace the evidence of the former journey on some, if not on all, of the scales.

Like the subsequent spawning journey the exact history of the fish when feeding and growing after the kelt stage is faithfully and accurately recorded on the scale. Summers and winters are shown in the normal manner and if the fish be clean run without further scale absorption, it is always possible to determine whether it has been of the "short absence" habit, as in plate 42, of the "long absence" habit or whether it belonged to that very limited number which remain in the sea for over a year before returning to the river for the second time. These last incidentally are almost always males.

Fish scales are of use for a second purpose beyond that of age determination. For age assessment no fine gradations may be said to be necessary and the result in general is expressed no closer than in terms of years. With experience one may acquire a somewhat exact knowledge of the approximate time when the fish left the sea, no fine degree of accuracy is demanded or is required. For the second purpose, however, if the results obtained are to be of real use and value for the scientist, a very considerable degree of accuracy is absolutely essential.

Scale examination will not have proceeded for very long before the beginner will recognize certain abnormalities and departures, slight or considerable, from the usual form. The most common is for the central part to be without ridges. Its appearance is as if the nucleus were very much larger than usual or as if the undifferentiated exposed portion had spread to the whole of the scale up to a certain point when normal growth had at last been started. The explanation is that the original scale was lost but that the abrasion which caused the loss was not sufficient to destroy entirely the skin and the scale pocket. After the original scale had disappeared, a new scale was regenerated, but growth was made as rapidly as possible and no lines indicative of the gradual expansion of the body were laid down until the existing scale pocket was completely filled and growth in the normal manner could be resumed.

Apparently smolts during their descent to the sea lose many of their scales for the majority of atypical areas on adult scales cover the parr-portion of the life (pl. 44). To one who has handled smolts and observed how easily the scales are shed the happening is easily understandable. Such loss, however, is not entirely confined to this period of life but may occur at any time from shortly after the scales are formed until several years have been spent in the sea.

Another malformation due to a similar, but less violent, cause results, not in the entire loss of a scale, but in its misplacement in the skin pocket. After such an injury the growth is not hindered, nor is development other than normal, except that the ridges formed before and after the injury do not register the one with the other and do not follow parallel courses. In some respects the effect produced (pl. 43) simulates at a later stage of spawning mark, but may be distinguished owing to the fact that although the later ridges cross the ends of the earlier ridges at an angle there is no distinct scar at the junction and the line where the ridges at a different angle meet is too smooth to represent the absorption of a kelt scale.

Other somewhat curious abnormalities are occasionally met with. A scale may have what appears to be a bare patch on which are a few ridges in the form of a spiral or there may be an actual hole right through the scale as if it had been made by some boring animal. This last type of round hole, however, must not be confused with the oval and more complicated aperture found in scales taken off the lateral line and which forms the termination of the lateral line canal.

Bizarre malformations of the scale are occasionally met with for which no reasonable explanation is evident. One of the most curious that I have ever seen is shown in plate 44.

R

CHAPTER SEVENTEEN

# LITERATURE

*Salmon Fishing*

AS an appendix to this chapter will be found a bibliography of salmon fishing books. The majority of the early volumes are nowadays of little but historic interest, although one or two such as William Scrope's *Days and Nights of Salmon-fishing in the Tweed* (1843) and A. H. Chaytor's *Letters to a Salmon-fisher's Sons* (1919) are delightful reading in their own right. But in the 1930s, the style of salmon fishing literature changed and a new school of writers appeared whose techniques had been influenced by those greased-line tactics of which the famous A. H. E. Wood was the initiator. Amongst them can be found such well-known names as Jock Scott, G. P. R. Balfour-Kinnear, Anthony Bridges and Anthony Crossley.

Of these Jock Scott wrote *Greased-Line Fishing for Salmon* (1935), an explanation of the Wood methods and compiled after his death from the latter's fishing papers. It is written strictly in accord with Wood's views and tactics and can be regarded as the standard work on Wood.

Jock Scott followed this with *Spinning Up To Date* (1937)— a complete guide to spinning for salmon, trout and pike. And in *Fine and Far Off* (1952) he explained his own fishing techniques which are a development of the Wood methods and based upon the teachings of Alexander Grant and Percy Laming. In this book, too, is the first mention of the oiled—as opposed to the greased-line technique.

At the same time as *Greased-Line Fishing for Salmon* a book of a totally different sort appeared, this was Henry Williamson's *Salar the Salmon* which barely needs introduction to the readers of this book. Although strictly out of context among the instructional books already described, *Salar the Salmon* is a book of such charm that it cannot in fairness be deleted from a list of modern salmon fishing literature.

A proponent of the Wood methods is Anthony Crossley whose *The Floating Line for Salmon and Seatrout* (1939) was a useful milestone in the development of low-water fishing techniques.

J. Hughes-Parry (*Fishing Fantasy* (1949)) is a writer with the Welsh Dee as a background. He uses all methods of fishing, and gives sound, practical advice. This is a book which should undoubtedly be read.

Alexander Wanless has written a series of books on threadline-fishing with fly, minnow and prawn. He advocates very fine lines, and this at the time was cause for much controversy. He also mechanized fly-fishing and declared that a fly could, and should, be cast from a fixed-spool reel. He used a "controller" for this purpose, and so eliminated drag while the fly was in the water. This method, however, does not appear to have maintained its popularity.

G. P. R. Balfour-Kinnear has produced four volumes, for the most part with a Tweedside background and respectively entitled, *Flying Salmon* (1937), *Spinning Salmon* (1938), *Catching Salmon and Seatrout* (1958) and *More About Trout and Salmon* (1963). All are interesting, unconventional and show the mark of an enterprising and enquiring brain.

*My Way with Salmon* (1957) by Ian Wood is another very sound piece of work. Ian Wood is essentially the practical angler who does not believe in ultra-fine casts for salmon and who does not advance intricate theories. This, undoubtedly, is a book to read, mark and inwardly digest.

Across the Atlantic, Lee Wulff's *The Atlantic Salmon* (1958) is an interesting treatise. He has much to say which will be new to anglers in Great Britain, and some of his theories are obviously only applicable to salmon fishing in Canada. It is none the less a most rewarding book, representing as it does the latest trans-Atlantic developments in wet and dry-fly fishing for salmon. Any angler who is interested in Canadian fishing should certainly read this book, and preferably more than once for there is a lot of "meat" in it. But the more one digests it the clearer becomes the wide difference between Canadian methods and our own.

Perhaps the most revolutionary books on salmon fishing appeared after the war from the pen of Richard Waddington. These were *Salmon Fishing: A New Philosophy* (1947), *Fly-Fishing for Salmon* (1951) and, more recently, *Salmon-Fishing*

*Philosophy and Practice* (1959). Waddington is a fly-fisherman only and does not use a spinning-rod. He strongly believes in the treble-hook and on the strength of his experience and research invented the well-known Waddington (Elverine) range of triangle salmon-flies. He was also one of the first to introduce a scientific explanation for the behaviour of salmon and in his books develops the view that the oxygen content of water was a major factor controlling salmon angling success or failure.

This is a theme developed in an interesting book by R. V. Righyni *Salmon Taking Times* (1965). The author puts forward the theory that there is a critical amount of available oxygen which stimulates the fish into physical energy and the taking of a fly; too little or too much and the fish lose interest and become dour. The author concedes, with mild reservations, the old theory on which I was brought up, that eleven a.m., and four p.m. are good taking times. But he supports his views with charts showing when a salmon can be expected to take at different times of the year. His chapters on the reading of water currents and his own views on fly types and selection are of equal interest. Another theory was put forward by the biologist Fontaine who suggested in 1951 that variations in the activity of the thyroid gland might cause salmon to come "on" or go down. The reader is left to make his choice.

## A Bibliography of Salmon Fishing Books

| | | |
|---|---|---|
| The Book of St Albans (The Treatyse on Fysshynge) | | 1496 |
| A Booke of Fishing | Leonard Mascall | 1590 |
| The Seconde Booke of the English Husbandman | G.M. | 1614 |
| The Pleasures of Princes | Gervase Markham | 1614 |
| Countrey Contentments | Gervase Markham | 1631 |
| Compleat Angler | Izaak Walton | 1653 |
| Barker's Delight | Thomas Barker | 1657 |
| The Experienc'd Angler | Robert Venables | 1676 |
| The Angler's Vade Mecum | James Chetham | 1681 |
| The Compleat Troller | Robert Nobbes | 1682 |
| The Gentleman's Recreation | Nicholas Cox | 1686 |
| Northern Memoirs | Richard Franck | 1694 |
| The Angler's Sure Guide | R(obert) H(owlett) | 1706 |
| The Country Gentleman's Vade Mecum | Giles Jacob | 1717 |

| | | |
|---|---|---|
| The Compleat Fisherman | James Saunders | 1724 |
| The Art of Angling | Richard and Charles Bowlker | (?) 1746 |
| The Gentleman Angler | James Smith | 1754 |
| The Art of Angling | Richard Brookes | 1766 |
| A concise Treatise on the Art of Angling | Thomas Best | 1787 |
| Angling in all its Branches | Samuel Taylor | 1800 |
| The Driffield Angler | Alexander Mackintosh | 1808 |
| The Angler's Guide | Thomas Salter | 1808 |
| The Fly Fisher's Guide | George Bainbridge | 1816 |
| *Salmonia* | Sir Humphry Davy | 1828 |
| Trout and Salmon Fishing in Wales | George Hansard | 1834 |
| The Angler in Ireland | —Belton | 1834 |
| The Art of Angling in Scotland | Thomas Stoddart | 1835 |
| The Northern Angler | John Kirkbride | 1837 |
| The Angler's Desideratum | —Clarke | 1839 |
| River Angling for Salmon and Trout | John Younger | 1840 |
| The Moor and the Loch | John Colquhoun | 1840 |
| The Fly-Fisher's Text-Book | Edward Chitty, *alias* Theophilus South | 1841 |
| The Art of Angling, &c. | William Blacker | 1842 |
| Days and Nights of Salmon-fishing in the Tweed | William Scrope | 1843 |
| The Practice of Fishing | O'Gorman | 1845 |
| The Angler's Companion | Thomas Stoddart | 1847 |
| Jones' Guide to Norway | Frederic Tolfrey | 1848 |
| The Book of the Salmon | *Ephemera* (Edward Fitzgibbon) | 1850 |
| The Green Bank List of Irish Flies | Thomas Ettingsall | 1850 |
| The Erne, Its Legends and Fly-Fishing | Henry Newland | 1851 |
| Angler's Guide to the Rivers and Lochs of the North of Scotland | Andrew Young | 1857 |
| A Book on Angling | Francis Francis | 1867 |
| The Modern Practical Angler | H. Cholmondeley-Pennell | 1870 |
| Autumns on the Spey | A. E. Knox | 1872 |
| My Life as an Angler | William Henderson | 1879 |
| The Angler and the Loop-Rod | David Webster | 1885 |
| The Badminton Library: Salmon and Trout | J. P. Traherne and Cholmondeley-Pennell | 1887 |
| How to tie Salmon-Flies | J. H. Hale | 1892 |
| The Salmon Fly | G. M. Kelson | 1895 |
| Salmon and Seatrout | Sir Herbert Maxwell | 1898 |
| Haddon Hall Library: Fly Fishing | Sir Edward Grey (Viscount Grey) | 1899 |
| Tips | G. M. Kelson | 1901 |

| | | |
|---|---|---|
| Salmon Rivers of Scotland | Alexander Grimble | 1902 |
| Salmon Rivers of Ireland | Alexander Grimble | 1903 |
| Salmon and Seatrout Rivers of England and Wales | Alexander Grimble | 1904 |
| How and Where to Fish in Ireland | Hi-Regan (J. Dunne) | 1904 |
| Salmon Fishing | Earl Hodgson | 1906 |
| Salmon Fishing | J. J. Hardy | 1907 |
| Salmon Rivers and Lochs of Scotland | W. L. Calderwood | 1909 |
| How to dress Salmon-Flies | T. E. Pryce-Tannatt | 1914 |
| Letters to a Salmon-fisher's Sons | A. H. Chaytor | 1919 |
| Rod Fishing for Salmon in the Wye | J. A. Hutton | 1920 |
| Salmon and Trout in Moorland Streams | Kenneth Dawson | 1928 |
| Fishing for Salmon | C. D. Marson | 1929 |
| Fly and Minnow | W. F. R. Reynolds | 1929 |
| Spinning for Salmon and Trout | Arthur Wanless | 1930 |
| Loch Lomond | H. Lamond | 1931 |
| Where the Spring Salmon Run | P. Chalmers | 1931 |
| Silver, the Life Story of a Salmon | R. L. Haig-Brown | 1931 |
| The Art of Salmon Fishing | Jock Scott | 1933 |
| Salmon Tactics | Percy E. Nobbs | 1934 |
| Greased Line Fishing for Salmon | Jock Scott | 1935 |
| Salar the Salmon | H. Williamson | 1935 |
| Flying Salmon | G. P. R. Balfour-Kinnear | 1937 |
| Spinning Up To Date | Jock Scott | 1937 |
| Salmon Fishing in Little Rivers | Ian Chalmers | 1938 |
| Spinning Salmon | G. P. R. Balfour-Kinnear | 1938 |
| Angling at Lochboisdale | Major R. Chrystal | 1939 |
| Modern Salmon Fishing | Anthony Bridges | 1939 |
| The Floating Line for Salmon and Sea Trout | Anthony Crossley | 1939 |
| Thrifty Salmon Fishing | N. K. Robertson | c. 1945 |
| Further Thrifty Fishing | N. K. Robertson | N.D. |
| Salmon Fishing: A New Philosophy | Richard Waddington | 1947 |
| Modern Salmon and Sea Trout Fishing | Major K. Dawson | c. 1948 |
| Wade the River, Drift the Loch | compiled R. Macdonald Robertson | 1948 |
| Floating the Line to a Salmon | Major R. C. Simpson | 1948 |
| Casts for a Salmon Reel | Major K. Dawson | N.D. |
| Wye Salmon and Other Fish | J. Arthur Hutton | 1949 |
| Fishing Fantasy | J. Hughes-Parry | 1949 |
| Successful Fishing for Salmon and Sea Trout | Major K. Dawson | 1951 |
| Fly-Fishing for Salmon | Richard Waddington | 1951 |
| With Rod Well Bent | R. N. Lochhead | 1951 |

| | | |
|---|---|---|
| Fine and Far Off | Jock Scott | 1952 |
| The Running of the Salmon | E. Taverner & | |
| | W. Barrington Browne | 1954 |
| Salmon and Sea Trout Fishing | W. E. Davies | 1957 |
| My Way with Salmon | Ian Wood | 1957 |
| Catching Salmon and Seatrout | G. P. R. Balfour-Kinnear | 1958 |
| Salmon Fishing: Philosophy & Practice | Richard Waddington | 1959 |
| The Salmon | J. W. Jones | 1959 |
| A Man May Fish | T. Kingsmill Moore | 1960 |
| Six Salmon Rivers & Another—Canada | George F. Clarke | 1960 |
| More about Trout and Salmon | G. P. R. Balfour-Kinnear | 1963 |
| Salmon Taking Times | R. V. Righyni | 1965 |
| Fishing with a purpose | Stephen Johnson | 1969 |
| Salmon | Arthur Oglesby | 1971 |

### In Canada and the United States of America

| | | |
|---|---|---|
| Salmon Fishing in Canada | Sir James Alexander | 1860 |
| Fly Rods and Fly Tackle | H. P. Wells | — |
| The American Salmon Fisherman | H. P. Wells | 1886 |
| Fishing on the Grand Cascapedia | E. W. Davis | 1904 |
| Salmon and the Dry Fly | G. M. L. La Branche | 1924 |
| Secrets of the Salmon | E. R. Hewitt | 1922 |
| Observations on a Salmon River | Gray Griswold | — |
| Fish, Facts and Fancies | Gray Griswold | 1926 |
| Big and Little Fishes | Gray Griswold | — |
| Salmo Salar | Gray Griswold | — |
| A Salmon River | Gray Griswold | 1928 |
| Life-History of the Canadian Salmon | Gray Griswold | 1930 |
| The Atlantic Salmon | Lee Wulff | 1958 |
| Bibliographie du Saumon de l'Atlantique | Julien Bergeron | 1962 |
| The Atlantic Salmon—A Vanishing Species | Anthony Netboy | 1968 |

## CHAPTER EIGHTEEN

# THE LAW AND SALMON FISHING

BY DR R. R. TAYLOR, Q.C.

THE law of England, on which the law of Ireland also is based, is quite different from the law of Scotland. Since so much of the salmon fishing in Britain is in Scotland, it is necessary to consider both Scots and English law. The law of England does not make a distinction between the right of fishing for different species of fish in the way in which Scots law does: there runs from top to bottom of Scots law on the subject a radical difference between salmon fishing, which is treated as a much more valuable right, and the right to fish for trout and other freshwater fish. This may be a reflection of the attitude of the majority of Scotsmen to fish. They do not regard any fresh water fish except salmon and trout as being really edible: certainly not pike or perch! Also English law has many more controls on fishing than Scots law.

In England, the person who wishes to fish for salmon or trout, in addition to having the right to fish, must have a licence from the appropriate River Authority, and pay the appropriate licence duty. In some River Authority areas in England a licence is also necessary to fish for coarse fish. There are no such provisions in Scotland, Scotland has District Boards, one for each river and its tributaries, which are concerned only with salmon. The members of the Boards are elected by the proprietors of the salmon fishings. The Boards may appoint water bailiffs, and their duties are to enforce the laws against poaching salmon, and to acquire by agreement for demolition dams and cruives for the protection and improvement of the fisheries within the district. They do not however issue licences, and they obtain their funds from an assessment on the proprietors of salmon fishing in their area.

In both England and Scotland there is no absolute property

in living fish in their natural habitat, because they are wild animals, and at common law a trespasser who catches and kills fish is not stealing. But in England it is a statutory criminal offence for a trespasser to take fish.

In England everyone who unlawfully takes any fish in water which is private property is liable to a fine of up to £50 on a first conviction; if the offender did this by angling in the daytime the fine does not exceed £20. In addition the Court may forfeit anything which the offender had with him for use for taking fish.

A suspected offender may be arrested without warrant by the police, or anyone else, and the implements seized, provided there was reasonable cause for the suspicion.

In Scotland it is not a criminal offence for a trespasser to catch trout—or any other fish except salmon—by rod and line in the daytime. The only remedy which the owner of trout fishing in Scotland has for the protection of his fishing is a civil action of interdict against the poacher. In order to serve an action on the poacher, the proprietor has first of all to find out the poacher's name and address, which the poacher is under no obligation to give; secondly the proprietor must show that there is a likelihood of the offence being repeated by this individual. If an interdict is obtained, and the poacher disobeys it, he can be imprisoned for contempt of court. This remedy may be helpful against the known local poacher, but it is useless against the day-tripper. Hence the misconception in some quarters that trout fishing, and all other fishing except salmon, in Scotland is "free". This is a misconception in law, but a law-breaker can often get away with his misdeed.

Regarding salmon:

### ENGLAND AND WALES

In England one can distinguish between tidal and non-tidal waters. There is a presumption of English law that the soil between high- and low-water mark belongs to the Crown, and the right of fishery thereover is common to all subjects of the realm. This presumption can be rebutted by a person proving that he has a private fishery in the tidal waters. Private fisheries in tidal waters owe their origin to some act of the Crown before Magna Charta whereby the public right of fishing was excluded, and the

S

fishery was made exclusive either for the Crown or some subject. Fisheries of this type can now be created only by Act of Parliament.

In non-tidal waters the right of fishery was an incident of the ownership of the soil. There is a presumption of law that the owner of land abutting on a non-tidal river is entitled to the soil of the river up to the middle line of the river, and a further presumption that the owner of the soil of a river is the owner of the fishery thereover. The right of fishery may in the past have been separated from the soil, and may be separated now. The owner of a fishery may of course lease it. When the owner of the fishery is also riparian owner, a lease by him of the riparian land presumptively carries with it the right of fishing in the river opposite the land up to the middle line of the river, and to defeat this presumption, the lessor has to reserve the right of fishing in the lease. The opposite presumption applies in Scotland.

The public can not acquire a right of fishing over another man's property by exercising such supposed right for any length of time, nor can the owner abandon his right by non-use.

Salmon may be lawfully caught, provided there is no by-law to the contrary, by rod and line, fishing weirs and fishing mill dams and fixed engines which were lawfully in use in 1861, fixed engines erected by a river board, certain moveable nets, with the permission of a river board by a light, gaff, etc., or stones or other missiles if done to preserve a private fishery, or by fish roe if done for that purpose or a scientific purpose or for propagating fish. Rods must not be baited with roe or with any other lure or bait forbidden by by-law. Fishing weirs which extend more than half way across the river may not be used for taking salmon unless they have a free gap or opening at the deepest part of the stream with a width equal to one-tenth of the width of the stream. There are also statutory provisions about the other fixed methods of fishing, in order to ensure that fish can migrate.

The weekly close time in England is that fixed by by-law, or if there is no by-law, from 6 a.m. on Saturday to 6 a.m. on Monday. During this time fishing is prohibited except by rod and line or putts and putchers. The angler has no weekly close time.

The annual close time for rods is that fixed by by-law, and if there is none, from 31st October to 1st February; the close time

for putts and putchers is 31st August to 1st May; and the close
time for other methods of fishing is that fixed by by-law or alternatively 31st August to 1st February. No person may use in any
waters frequented by salmon any eel traps or device to catch or
obstruct fish descending the river between 1st January and 24th
June. Baited eel baskets less than ten inches in diameter are however permitted where they are not used at an artificial obstruction.

By-laws are made by the River Authority of which there are
twenty-seven in England and Wales.

## SCOTLAND

The right of fishing in the rivers of Scotland, and in the territorial waters around Scotland's coasts, belongs to the Crown. Any
subject who owns salmon fishing in Scotland does so because he
has succeeded to, or received a conveyance from, a person who
has received such a grant in the past. Where the Crown has
retained the ownership of salmon fishing, it may lease the right
of fishing, as is common in the sea around the coasts.

There is a popular belief in Scotland that no one can prevent
a member of the public fishing for salmon and seatrout in the
tidal estuary of a river. This is a complete fallacy. The right of
fishing there is either vested in some subject, or, if not, it belongs
to the Crown. Not only does the public have no right to fish for
salmon in tidal waters, it is a criminal offence under The Salmon
and Freshwater Fisheries (Protection) (Scotland) Act 1951 to fish
for salmon without legal right, or without written permission
from a person having such a right, in any waters, including the
sea within one mile of low-water mark. This fallacy perhaps
arises from the rule that the public are entitled to fish for white
fish and trout in any public river, that is one which is both tidal
and navigable, and from the different law in England.

The right of fishing for salmon in Scotland is a separate estate,
and the person who owns the bank or bed of a river does not
thereby have the right of salmon fishing. He will only own
the salmon fishing if he has a Crown grant, or derives his
right, by succession or purchase, from one who had such a
grant.

A proprietor, even of both banks of a river, can not acquire
the right of salmon fishing by use for the prescriptive period

of twenty years. Nor can the public acquire the right of salmon fishing by use.

Where the proprietor of the salmon fishing does not own any of the bank, he has an implied right of access to the water through lands belonging to other proprietors.

The right of trout fishing is different in nature. It belongs to the riparian proprietor.

The right of salmon fishing includes the lesser right of fishing for sea-trout and trout, but where the owner of the salmon fishing does not also own the banks, the owner of a bank will also have the right of fishing for trout opposite his property.

The owner of salmon fishing is entitled to lease it, but because of the separate nature of the right of salmon fishing, a lease of the banks and bed of a river, without mention of the right of salmon fishing, does not carry the salmon fishing. The opposite result occurs in England.

The legal methods of fishing for salmon in Scotland are by rod and line, and by net and coble, with a saving for some existing methods of fishing which were still lawful at the passing of the 1951 Act. In fishing by net and coble the net must not leave the hand of the fisherman, and must be kept in motion during the operation of the fishing. Unlike the position as regards trout, there are ample provisions for the prosecution of salmon poachers. It is an offence without legal right or without written permission from a person having such right, to fish for salmon. It is a special criminal offence to use explosives, poison, or electrical devices to take salmon. A person can also be charged with being in unlawful possession of salmon, or any instrument, explosives, or poison which could be used in the taking of salmon, in circumstances which afford a reasonable ground for suspecting that he had obtained possession as a result of, or for the purpose of committing, one of the offences mentioned above. Although two witnesses are always required in Scotland in order to convict, exceptionally it has been provided that for these offences one witness is enough. A water bailiff in his district, and in the adjoining one, and police constables, may search boats, nets, baskets, and pockets, and take possession of salmon, and may seize a boat or vehicle. The penalties which may be imposed by the Court include not only fines and imprisonment, but the forfeiture of tackle, fish, boats and vehicles.

There is a weekly close time for rods in Scotland, namely Sunday—from Saturday midnight to Sunday midnight.

Nets must be off for slightly longer—from 12 noon on Saturday to 6 a.m. on Monday. The annual close time varies for each district of a river board, and enquiry should be made about this locally. Here again the close time is slightly longer for the nets than for rod fishing.

## SCOTLAND AND ENGLAND

The Scottish statutes apply to the whole of the Tweed, and the English statutes to the whole of the Esk, notwithstanding that part of each of these rivers is in the other country. There are special statutes applicable solely to the Tweed, one of the provisions of which is that a cleek, or any other instrument than a net, may not be used when rod fishing between 15th September and 1st May. It is customary on the Tweed throughout the year to use a net, and not a gaff.

In England, when sending salmon and trout by carrier, the package must be conspicuously marked as salmon or trout. In Scotland the package must in addition bear the name and address of the sender, and seatrout must be marked as such. Power is given to police and fishery officers to open suspected packages.

It is an offence in England to buy or sell fresh salmon between 1st September and 31st January. This does not apply, among other circumstances, to clean salmon caught within Great Britain or Ireland if it was lawful at the time and place of capture to catch them by means other than rod and line. But be careful if you catch a quantity of salmon by rod in Scotland at the end of the season there. If the net fishing is closed in that part of Scotland and the date is after 1st September, you could lawfully send your fish to a friend in England, but could not send them there for sale. Let us hope that after reading this book, your success will be such that you will be worried by such problems as disposal!

In both England and Scotland the common law provides ample protection to the proprietors of fishings against pollution, interference with the flow of the stream, or abstraction of water, which may affect the salmon fishing. An action of interdict (injunction) can be brought to prevent repetition, and damages can be obtained for the injury to the fishing which has already occurred.

If the action is successful, the other party must pay the fishing proprietor's legal costs. Those not wishing to take the risk of losing and having to pay costs, can join bodies like the Anglers Co-operative Association, which pays for the legal costs of members fighting such cases.

## APPENDIX

# SALMON-FISHING WATERS
# OF THE WORLD

It is outside the scope of this book to advise or describe where to fish for salmon. But to assist anglers, below is a list of authorities and agencies who can produce up-to-date information about salmon fishing in their respective countries. However, the publication *Where to Fish* which is produced annually by *The Field* of 8 Stratton Street, London, W1, is the authority on salmon fishing in the British Isles and Ireland as well as being a mine of information about fishing, not salmon fishing alone, world wide.

*Canada*

    The Canadian Government Travel Bureau
    19 Cockspur Street
    London SW1

*Denmark*

    Danish Tourist Board
    Sceptre House
    169–173 Regent Street
    London W1

*Finland*

    Finnish Travel Information Centre
    Finland House
    56 Haymarket
    London SW1

*France*

    French Tourist Office
    178 Piccadilly
    London W1

*Iceland*

Iceland Tourist Information Bureau
161 Piccadilly
London W1

*Norway*

Norwegian National Tourist Office
20 Pall Mall
London SW1

*Portugal*

Portuguese State Tourist Office
Lower Regent Street
London SW1

*Spain*

Spanish National Tourist Office
70 Jermyn Street
London SW1

*Sweden*

Swedish National Travel Association
52–3 Conduit Street
London W1

*United States*

The American Embassy
Grosvenor Square
London W1

# INDEX

Abumatic reel, 187, 190, 191
Aerial reel, 187
*Aeromonas salmonicida*, 28
age, determining, 244–55
alevin, 23, 239
Almond, River, 24
Ambassadeur reel, 187, 188, 189
Anglers Co-operative Association, 270
Annan, River, 20
Ashley-Dodd, G. L., 167
Association of Fishing Tackle Makers, 48–9; their numbering system, 49
*Atlantic Salmon, The* (Wulff), 259
Avon, River (Hants), 25

backing, 50–1; attaching to fly line, 69–70
baggot, 22
bait: artificial, 195–7; how to release from river bed, 114–17; how to sink, 193–5; how to throw, 199, 200; natural, 197–9; prawn as, 204–12; shrimp as, 212–18; worm as, 218–21
bait-casting reel, *see* multiplying reel
Balding, D. L., 22
Balfour-Kinnear, G. P. R., 258, 259
Baudelot, E., 244
Blackwater, River (Cork), 93
bleak, as bait, 197
Blood Bight Knot, 67
Blood Knot: Double, 63; Half, 66, 191
blowline fishing, 171–2
Blue Charm fly, 139, 144, 180, 182
Bran, River, 27
Bridges, Anthony, 258
brogues, 58–60

Cairnton, 131, 132, 175
Cairnton Jamb, 64–5, 66
Canada, salmon-fishing in, 165, 166, 259, 263
Canadian Wildlife Service, 27
Canary fly, 182
Carron, River, 182
carrying a fish home, 54–5

cast, 51; choice of, 97; for dry-fly fishing, 166; how to make a loop at head of, 67
casting, 73–90; double or false, 138–43, 164; double-handed overhead, 73–81; double Spey, 80, 88–90; how to learn, 73; overhead, 37, 83, 200; single-handed overhead, 81–2; single Spey, 85–8; Spey, 38, 78, 85–90; steeple, 78; switch, 37, 38, 39, 40, 78, 83–5, 86
*Catching Salmon and Seatrout* (Balfour-Kinnear), 259
Chaytor, A. H., 127, 258
Chaytor's Reef-Knot Jamb, 66
Cholmondeley-Pennell tackle, 217, 218
close time, 266–7, 269
Clyde, River, 31
colly, as bait, 197
Conn, Lough, 171
Connemara loughs, 171
Conon, River, 32
Conway, River, 200
Corrib, 171, 172
Crosfield, Ernest, 133, 179
Crossley, Anthony, 93, 258, 259
Currane, Lough, 172
current, learning the, 96–7
Curtis, Gerald, 162, 167

dace, as bait, 173, 197
daddy-long-legs, as bait, 172
Dart, River, 210
*Days and Nights of Salmon Fishing in the Tweed* (Scrope), 91, 258
DDT, its effect on salmon, 31
Dee, River (Aberdeen), 28, 29, 94, 99, 131, 134, 155, 162, 167, 175
Dee disease, 29
Dee, River (Chester), 181
Dee, River (Wales), 105, 180, 182, 200, 259
Devon minnow, 194, 195
Dinas, Llyn, 171
diseases of salmon, 28–30
double-handed overhead cast, 73–81
Double Taper line, 38, 47–8, 81, 85, 126
drag, 156, 157, 259

drift netting, 32
dropper-fly, 63–4
drought, location of salmon during, 99–100
dry-fly fishing, 66, 162–9, 259; suitability for British conditions, 167–9

Eden, River, 181
eel, 244; as bait, 197
Egglishaw, H. J., 23, 24
Elson, K. R., 30
Elson, P. F., 25
Elverine flies, 72, 260
Esk, River, 269
Esmond Drury flies, 72
etiquette in fishing, 91–2
*Eubothrium crassum*, 28
Exaggeration Theory, 180–1

feather-drag, 129–30
*Fifty Years with the Rod* (Stirling), 171
Figure-of-eight Knot, 62, 70
Findhorn, River, 20
*Fine and Far Off* (Scott), 133, 258
Fisheries Research Board of Canada, 27
Fisherman's Knot, Double, 62, 64
*Fishing Fantasy* (Hughes-Parry), 259
fixed-spool reel, 187, 190–1, 192, 259
Flashing Illusion flies, 182
flies, 175–85; changing, 182–3; Flashing Illusion, 182; for dry-fly fishing, 166; for harling, 173; for loch fishing, 171; hanging, 127–8; how to fasten to nylon, 65; how to recover from tree, 111–14; how to tie to the cast, 64; Normal Image, 182; pattern of, 144, 180–2, and see under individual names; presentation of, 145–7; reasons for salmon taking, 175–8, 184; selection of, 178–82; Silhouette, 182; size of, 127, 143–4, 180–2; Translucent Illusion, 182
floating line, 47, 48, 126; with a sinking tip, 47, 48, 126; semi-floating, 165
floating-line fishing, 41, 48, 80, 131–61, 258; in dead water, 152–4; when to use this method, 150–2
*Floating Line for Salmon, The* (Crossley), 93, 259
flood, location of salmon during, 96, 100–3
fly-boxes, 61

*Fly-Fishing for Salmon* (Waddington), 259
*Flying Salmon* (Balfour-Kinnear), 259
Fold-over Lead, 193, 194
Fontaine, M., 20, 260
Forward Taper line, 38, 47, 81, 83
Franck, Richard, 175
Fraser, Major J. R., 167
fry, 23, 244
furunculosis, 28–9

gaffing, 53, 233, 234–6, 237; types of gaff, 52–3
Garry, River (Inverness), 20
gill maggot, 23, 27–8
Grant, Alexander, 131, 132, 133, 158–61, 184, 258
grasshopper, as bait, 172
greased-line fishing, *see* floating-line fishing.
*Greased-Line Fishing for Salmon* (Scott), 258
greasing the line, 136
'greenbacks', 20
Green Highlander fly, 182
Greenland salmon fishery, 33
grey seal as predator, 27
grilse, 19, 20, 21, 22, 166, 170, 171, 237–8, 249, 250
Grimersta chain of lochans, 170
gudgeon, as bait, 197

Hairy Mary fly, 182
hanging a fly, 127–8
harling, 41, 172–4
Hasler, A. D., and Wisby, 20
Hayes, F. R., 20
Hewitt, E. R., 175
Hillman lead, 193 194, 195, 205
homing instinct of salmon, 20
hook, 71–2; double, 71–2, 126, 132, 133; for prawn-fishing, 205–8; for shrimp-fishing, 214; for worm-fishing, 217, 218; pulling in, 129, 147; single, 71, 132; treble, 129, 260
hooking a salmon, 71–2, 146–50, 222–3
Hughes-Parry, J. 259
Hunter Committee, 33
hydro-electric development, 31–2, 172

Interceptor lead, 193, 194

Jardine lead, 193, 194
Johnston, Henry W., 244
Jones, J. W., 25

Kelson, G. M., 180
kelt, 19, 22, 26, 28, 29, 30, 31, 177, 237, 253, 254, 256
killing a salmon, 54
knots, 62–70
Koch, H. J. A., Bergström, E., and Evans, J. C., 22

La Branche, G. M. L., 162, 163, 165, 175
Lady Caroline fly, 180
Laming, Percy, 131–2, 133, 157, 258
landing a salmon, 52–3, 233–4, 237–8
law, the, and salmon fishing, 264–70; in England and Wales, 265–7; in Scotland, 267–9; in Scotland and England, 269–70; in Ireland, 264, 269
lead, 193–4
leaping of salmon, 21
leather bait, 195
leeches, 28
*Lepeophtheirus salmonis*, 27
*Letters to a Salmon-Fisher's Sons* (Chaytor), 258
Level line, 38, 47
licence, fishing, 264
Limerick hook, 71
lines, 47–9; care of, 49–50; Double Taper, 38, 47–8, 81, 85, 126; floating, 47, 48, 126; floating, with a sinking tip, 47, 48, 126; for spinning, 191–2; Forward Taper, 38, 47, 81, 83; Level, 38, 47; multi-taper, 165; nylon mono-filament, 190, 191; plaited nylon, 192; running, 50–1; semi-floating, 165; silk, 192; Single Taper, 38, 40, 47, 83, 85, 126; sinking, 47, 48, 126; Terylene, 192; Weight Forward, 47, 48
loach, as bait, 197
loch-fishing, 170–2
lodge, salmon, 95–6
log, fishing, 110–11, 236
Lomond, Loch, 170, 171
Loop Finish, 69
low-water fishing, 103–4
Lubnaig, Loch, 171

Mallard and Olive fly, 171
March Brown fly, 144, 171
Maree, Loch, 170
Margaree, River, 27
Mar Lodge fly, 183
Mayfly, as bait, 171–2
merganser, as predator, 27

microelectrophoresis, 22
Mills, D. H., 24
minnow: as bait, 197, 198, 259; Devon, 194, 195, 199–200, 201; wooden, 195
Mitchell reel, 187
*More About Trout and Salmon* (Balfour-Kinnear), 259
multiplying reel, 187–9, 190, 191, 192
multi-taper line, 165
*My Way with Salmon* (Wood), 259

Nail Knot, 48, 69–70
Namsen, River (Norway), 172–3, 197
Needle Knot, 69–70
Ness, River, 161
netting a salmon, 53, 237
Normal Image flies, 182
Norway, 191, 197; harling in, 172–4
Nottingham reel, 187, 190, 191, 192
nylon monofilament line, 190, 191

oiled-line technique, 158–61, 258
overhead casting, 37, 38, 73–81, 82, 200
oxygen, supply of in water, 94–5, 99, 260

packing salmon for transit, 55–7, 269
parasites, 27–8
parr, 23, 24, 25, 247, 248, 249, 250, 256; as bait, 197; how to distinguish from trout, 23–5
peat-stained water, 93, 102, 167
pfleuger reel, 187
pike, as predator, 27
*Piscicola geometra*, 28
plaited nylon line, 192
playing a salmon, 225–33; applying side-strain, 230–3
plug bait, 197
poaching, 264, 265
pollution of rivers, 31, 94
prawn, as bait, 204–12, 259; pre-serving, 208–9; sink and draw method, 207, 209, 211; spinning, 105–7, 209; tackle, 205–8
predators, 27
pricking, 224–5
'priest', 54
putchers, 266, 267
putts, 266, 267
Pyefinch, K. A., and Mills, D. H., 32

races of salmon, determining, 22
rawner, 22

redds, 19, 23
Reef-Knot Jamb, Chaytor's, 66
reel, 44–6; care of, 46–7; for dry-fly fishing, 166; for spinning, 186, 187–91
resting-place of salmon, 95–6
Righyni, R. V., 94–5, 175, 182, 260
rings, putting on, 70
River Authorities, 31, 264
River Purification Boards, 31
Rivers (Prevention of Pollution) Acts, 31
Roberts, R. J., 30
rod: actions of, 37–8; care of, 43–4; choice of, 42–3; construction of, 39; fast, 38; for harling, 173; for spinning, 186–7; functions of, 36–7; glass-fibre, 38, 186; green-heart, 38, 39, 186; holding, 127; length of, 41–2; materials made from, 38; rings, 39–40; slow, 38; split-cane, 38, 39, 186; steel, 38, 186
Round Bend hook, 71

*Salar the Salmon* (Williamson), 258
*Salmincola salmonea*, 28
salmon: how to distinguish from seatrout, 25; sea food of, 26, 176–7
Salmon and Freshwater Fisheries (Protection) (Scotland) Act, The, 267
*Salmon Fishing: A New Philosophy* (Waddington), 259
*Salmon-Fishing Philosophy and Practice* (Waddington), 259–60
*Salmon Fly, The* (Kelson), 180
Salmon Research Trust of Ireland, 21
*Salmon Taking Times* (Righyni), 94, 260
sand-eel: as bait, 197, 198; tube, 195
scales, salmon, 239–57
*Scales of Some Teleostean Fish, The* (Paget), 239
Scott, Jock, 258
Scrope, William, 91, 95, 176, 258
sea life of salmon, 26–7, 176–7
sea louse, 27, 236
seatrout, 171, 237–8, 250
semi-floating line, 165
Shannon, River, 172
shooting line, 79
shrimp as bait, 212–18; sink and draw method, 213; spinning, 213, 214–15; tackle, 214
side strain, 230–3

Silex reel, 186, 187, 188
Silhouette flies, 182
silk line, 192
Silver Blue fly, 144
Silver Doctor fly, 182
Silver Grey fly, 176, 180, 182, 183
Simplex lead, 193, 194
single-handed overhead cast, 81–2
Single Taper line, 38, 40, 47, 83, 85, 126
sinking line, 47, 48, 126
smolt, 22, 24, 25, 31, 247, 248, 249, 256; migration, 25–6
Sneck hook, 71
spawning, 19, 22
Spey, River, 20, 31, 108, 125, 131, 134, 166, 181, 200–1
Spey cast, 38, 78, 85–90
spinning, 186–203; tactics of, 199–203
*Spinning Salmon* (Balfour-Kinnear), 259
*Spinning Up To Date* (Scott), 258
spoon, 195, 196–7, 201; Colorado, 196; hog-backed, 196; kidney, 196; Namsen, 173; Norwegian, 196
sprat, as bait, 173, 197, 198
spring fish, 21, 22
Sproad hook, 71
steeple cast, 78
Stewart tackle, 217, 218
Stirling, John, 171
Stuart, T. A., 21
sunk-fly fishing, 42, 118–30; fishing the sink-tip line, 126–7; hanging the fly, 127–8; holding the rod, 127; in spring, 125–6; pulling in the hook, 129–30
switch cast, 37, 38, 39, 40, 78, 83–5, 86

tailer, 53, 238
tailing a salmon, 53, 237–8
taking-area, 95, 96; indications of, 97–9, 104–7
tapeworm, 28
Taw, River, 20, 181
Tay, River, 20, 41, 172, 200, 248, 249
Teal and Olive fly, 171
Tees, River, 31
temperature, changes in, 93–5, 179
Terylene line, 192
Test, River, 167
Thames, River, 31
Thomson, Stuart, 244
threadline-fishing, 259
Thumb Knot, 62

Thunder and Lightning fly, 180, 182
Torridge, River, 20
Torrish fly, 180
traces, 192–3
Translucent Illusion flies, 182
Trent, River, 107
trout, as predator, 27
tube flies, 72, 180
Turle Knot, 64; Two-circle, 65
Tweed, River, 20, 28, 30, 31, 41, 259, 269

ulcerative dermal necrosis, 28, 29–30

Venables, Robert, 175
Vibration Rod, Grant, 158
*Vibrio anguillarum*, 29
Vibriosis, 28, 29

Waddington, Richard, 175, 259–60
waders: care of, 57; choice of, 57; how to wear, 58

wading, 107–10; staff, 60
wagtail, 195
Wanless, Alexander, 259
Weight Forward line, 47, 48
weights, 193–5
Wharfe, River, 107
Whip Finish, 67–8
White Wulff fly, 166
Wilkins, N. P., 22
Williamson, Henry, 258
wobbler, 195
Wood, A. H. E., 175, 179, 182; his floating-line technique, 131–4, 156, 258
Wood, Ian, 259
worm, as bait, 218–21; tackle, 217, 218–19
Wulff, Lee, 162, 165–6, 167, 259
Wye, River, 162, 200
Wye lead, 193, 194